Transcaucasian boundaries

Transcaucasian boundaries

Edited by
John F. R. Wright
Suzanne Goldenberg
Richard Schofield

Geopolitics and International Boundaries Research Centre
School of Oriental and African Studies
University of London

St. Martin's Press
New York

For information, address:
St. Martin's Press, Scholarly and Reference Division
175 Fifth Avenue, New York NY 10010.

Printed in Great Britain
First published in 1996 by UCL Press.
The name of University College London (UCL) is a registered
trade mark used by UCL Press with the consent of the owner.

ISBN: 0-312-12912-2

Library of Congress Cataloging in Publication Data
Transcaucasian boundaries / edited by John F. R. Wright, Suzanne
Goldenberg, Richard Schofield. — 1st ed.
    p.   cm.
Includes bibliographical references and index.
ISBN 0-312-12912-2
1. Transcaucasia—Boundaries.   2. Transcaucasia—Foreign
relations.   3. Transcaucasia—Ethnic relations.   I. Wright, John F.
R.   II. Goldenberg, Suzanne, 1962–   .   III. Schofield, Richard N.
947' .9—dc20
                                                    95-33150
                                                    CIP

First Edition 1996

Contents

Acknowledgements

The editors gratefully acknowledge the efforts of the following individuals in preparing this text for publication. The late Patricia Toye initiated the process with her customary flair and diligence; her special qualities are sorely missed and the memory of her remains a constant source of inspiration. Roger Jones of UCL Press completed the editing of the text. Sebastian Ballard was responsible for the cartography.

Contributors

Sulejman Alijarly teaches history in the Azerbaijan Academy of Sciences at Baku.

Nicholas Awde is a consultant and specialist on Caucasian affairs, with a particular interest in the northern Caucasus and the issues of Islam and ethnic strife.

Julian Birch teaches politics at the University of Sheffield. He is a specialist on Russian politics and Ossetian affairs.

Suzanne Goldenberg was, until 1995, *The Guardian* correspondent for the Caucasus.

William Hale teaches politics at the School of Oriental and African Studies (SOAS), University of London.

Fred Halliday teaches international relations at the London School of Economics and Political Science.

George Hewitt teaches Caucasian languages at the SOAS.

George Joffé is co-director of the Geopolitics and International Boundaries Research Centre, SOAS, and a respected commentator on contemporary Middle Eastern and North African affairs.

Margot Light teaches international relations at the London School of Economics and Political Science.

Richard Schofield is deputy director of the Geopolitics and International Boundaries Research Centre, SOAS.

Christopher Walker is a specialist on Transcaucasian affairs, with a particular interest in the history and contemporary politics of Armenia.

John Wright is a consultant and specialist on Caucasian affairs, with a particular interest in Georgia, where he is currently based.

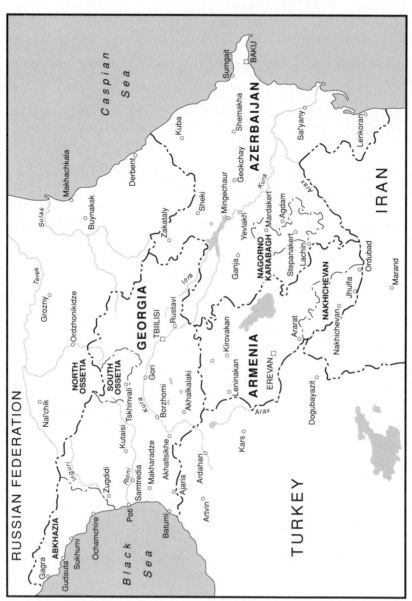

Contemporary Transcaucasia

Introduction
NICHOLAS AWDE

The Caucasus is perhaps best described as a mosaic of peoples ancient and modern intertwined across a complex, often inaccessible geography that has made it a crossroads linking not only east and west but equally north and south. Part of the Silk Route, the region has long been the object of imperialistic ambition, and there are few empires of Europe and Asia that have not included a slice of the Caucasus within their marches. The Caucasian map of today owes as much to the upheavals and invasions of Byzantium and the Ottoman Empire as it does to eighty years of Soviet rule and the pipeline lobby. The fact that the area today is considered internationally to hold a significance far greater than its size and population at first glance would merit, is therefore unsurprising.

Even from its first inklings, the idea of a conference to examine the geopolitical and territorial problems of the Caucasus was going to have a natural bias towards looking at the historical record. At the very least, such an examination promised to provide useful initial principles for understanding the present and future situation in a vastly complex field, rarely subjected to effective exploration. A conviction of the importance of such a historical process for an understanding of the whole Caucasian question – whose importance might have been intuited, but whose manifestations are still sometimes uncertainly grasped – was therefore intrinsic to the original planning for the conference on Transcaucasian boundaries. At the same time, it is always worth bearing in mind that "history may be of limited relevance to explaining the contemporary post-Soviet situation", as Fred Halliday points out in his chapter.

For many in the West, the Caucasus long conjured up images that reflected Russia's own nostalgic view of the area – their "Jewel in the Crown". But gone now is the land that inspired Tolstoy, Pushkin and Mayakovsky, and which provided idyllic holidays by the Black Sea for millions of Russians; now the associations are rather of mafia "hotbeds", ethnic strife, ethnic cleansing, border clashes, the war in Chechnya. The Caucasus of today, as Margot Light in her chapter wryly observes, is said to be "the most militarized area in the world". Central to continuing instability in the region is the proliferation of ethnic nationalism. In a patchwork of more than 50 peoples – indigenous or otherwise – numbering from under 300 to

1

over 3.5 million, there are today over 30 conflict issues in the north Caucasus alone that are, or could become, violent. Naturally, in view of the region's bewildering variety of religion, ethnicity, language, terrain, politics and demographics, the expression of ethnic nationalism has adopted many guises and is frequently multi-layered to a degree that baffles even the most informed of external observers, yet is readily grasped by the Caucasian "man in the street" and, more pertinently, by the local politician.

Ethnic nationalism in the Caucasus, although ingrained, is hardly a static movement, as each fresh claimant comes armed with a battery of often abused historical "fact" to back their struggle. Of course the key to resolving these issues is in understanding the factors that created conflict but, as stated above, history cannot provide solutions, only clues to future solutions. As the invasion of Chechnya has shown, the different parts of the Caucasus, sovereign or not, have a wider role to play on the world stage and not just for Russia, as the chapters in this volume will prove, if only for the recurrent question of the disruptive factor of Caucasian instability. This continuing instability derives, paradoxically, from the diverse efforts in the region for national stability, a process muddied by the fact that, contrary to opinions both inside and out of the area, such stability is something the area has rarely seen.

The majority of the chapters in this volume were originally presented as papers at the July 1992 School of Oriental and African Studies Conference on Transcaucasian Boundaries, convened by John Wright, the principal editor of this volume. These chapters have subsequently been revised and updated by their authors, and further coverage has been provided with the addition of two pieces by co-editor Suzanne Goldenberg and Sulejman Alijarly. Brief biographical sketches of all contributors precede this introduction. The following introductory remarks make no premature attempt at any grand meta-discourse on Transcaucasian geopolitics, but confine themselves to acting as a minimal guide to some of the most salient points of substance and of detail that are raised by the ten richly heterogeneous chapters here presented.

Every effort has been made to ensure harmonization of terminology and names throughout this volume, but it should be noted that in certain chapters established variants will be encountered. The term Transcaucasus refers to the area covered by the modern republics of Armenia, Azerbaijan and Georgia, although the reader will find a certain degree of interchangeability with Caucasus, i.e. the territories of Transcaucasus and northern Caucasus combined.

In her introductory background note, "Reflections on Chechnya", a timely commentary on the Russian invasion, Suzanne Goldenberg demonstrates the price exacted for any effort for national stability and the attentions it can attract from external forces. In concentrating on the recent developments that led to the Russian invasion of Chechnya – Russian territory yet indelibly Caucasian – she makes the sober warning that "Chechnya has shared the fate of the other countries of the Caucasus – war and economic collapse, but the devastation it has undergone since the fall of the Soviet Union is a clearer illustration of Russia's intent to secure its interests in the region."

Goldenberg makes a clear parallel with the way internal dissent has been dealt with in the neighbouring republics of Georgia and Azerbaijan. The immediate post-Soviet period saw many upheavals in each of the sovereign nations in the area, claimed by chauvinistic popular regimes that were antagonistic towards the claims of the minorities within their borders, such as Gamsakhurdia of Georgia and Elchibey of Azerbaijan. The actions of both caused alarm in Moscow, ever concerned that instability within Russia itself could arise from conflict in the Caucasus. There is strong evidence that Moscow intervened in both their subsequent removal and the installation of their successors – Shevardnadze and Aliyev respectively. The latter came to power because of their Moscow connections and not, initially at least, because of any local support base. If these were crucial examples of indirect intervention by the Republic of Russia, it was the war in Chechnya, as Goldenberg observes, which "marked the first time that Russian forces had intervened directly to defeat a demand for independence", thus confirming Moscow's longstanding strategic interest in the region.

It is clear that even after more than two centuries of direct involvement with the Caucasus, the Russians badly misjudged the aspirations of the Chechens, an error that can only reinforce the inherent problems in understanding the complexity of the whole region. In his chapter "Nationalities and borders in Transcaucasia and the northern Caucasus", George Joffé offers an informative guide through this complexity. Examining the history of the status of each region and the crises that arose in post-Soviet times as a result of this legacy, he sets the theoretical backdrop for conflicts – actual or potential – within the Caucasus.

Joffé usefully defines the complexities from ethnic, administrative and political points of view, and identifies four main influences at play: nationalism and tribalism, territorial claims, Islam and anti-Russian sentiment. Some of these are unifying in their effect, while others can be seen to be working against stable political structures. In fact, there are many obstacles slowing the process of political reconstruction, and Joffé observes that while the governments of the Transcaucasian states – Russia too – are recognized at international level, they are not always regarded as legitimate by substantial, "sub-national" minorities of their populations.

In applying the concept of sovereignty and the importance of cultural homogeneity to the region as they shape modern nationalism and ethnic boundaries, Joffé acknowledges the difficulty in creating nation-states directly as a result of those Soviet definitions of territories and administration that deliberately ignored population location in order to reduce any prospect of regional unity. Changing demographics throughout the Caucasus have further complicated the situation – one need look no further than the consequence of the deportation of the entire Chechen nation in February 1944. In-migration and out-migration are still a major factor, creating the interesting situation that while minorities are tending to become minorities in their eponymous areas, the republics are becoming more homogeneous with regard to overall population. In the case of Georgia and Azerbaijan, for example, this has largely occurred by default as a result of out-migration. While admitting there are alternatives to the nation-state, Joffé notes that even the Islamist state offers little hope for minorities, although for the disparate peoples of the North Caucasus a federal system may hold some answers.

As a crossroads of continents, the Caucasus naturally presents a special challenge to the triangle of powers – Russia, Turkey and Iran – that surrounds it. In "Russia and Transcaucasia", the first of three chapters that take a close look at the background and justifications of the vested interests and claims of each of these powers, Margot Light examines the Russian view of the Transcaucasus through recent history up to the present day and how it reflects Russia's perception of its own identity. With the break-up of the USSR, for example, most non-Russians "celebrated the simultaneous destruction of two empires: the Soviet and the Russian", while the Russians themselves felt a sense of loss not only to their territory but also to their central status.

Current Russian foreign policy toward the Transcaucasus takes much of its thrust from the period between 1985 and 1991, when nationalism grew in importance and "became the most important, and perhaps least expected obstacle to *perestroika* and in the end to the survival of the USSR". The problem was of the Russians' own making; Soviet division of the Caucasus had done more to foster nationalism than Russian imperialism, and created a sense of nation where once there was simple clan identity. Many of the conflicts that have erupted since *perestroika* derive directly from this division, as well as the mass deportations, presenting serious consequences for the Russians. Indeed, Light points to the conflict over Nagorno–Karabakh as being a "watershed in Soviet politics" and the start of the unravelling of the USSR.

Light argues that there has never been a true Russian nation-state, the Russians finding their identity of statehood instead in the concept of their empire, thereby explaining why many Russians find it difficult to accept or even understand the break up of the USSR and the loss of the "near abroad". Their attitude was further compounded by the twin influences of the myth of "friendship of peoples" and Soviet historiography, which maintained that incorporation of the Caucasus into the Russian Empire was a good thing all round. The events of 1992 showed the Russians that the greatest danger lay not in the outside world but in the near abroad, and their fears have grown over a perceived danger that conflicts in the Transcaucasus could spill over into Russia. At the very least, these conflicts have adversely affected Russia's economic relations with nations such as Iran.

Light sees Russian policy in the area as officially bent towards bringing violence to an end through the processes of mediation and increasing its economic presence through the rouble zone, supplying oil and other fuel on credit, and so on. But such policy is severely offset by the presence of the Russian military throughout the entire Caucasus, and over which Russia does not seem to have complete control, so mirroring its own internal political situation. This military presence, through the covert sale of arms or even active participation in conflict, actively contributes to violence in the Caucasus.

This image of Russia in the dual role of peacemaker and troublemaker in the Caucasus has, unsurprisingly, generated conflicting responses in its erstwhile neighbours Iran and Turkey. In "Turkey, the Black Sea and Transcaucasia" William Hale shows precisely how complex an issue the Caucasus is for the modern state of Turkey, particularly in light of Turkey's downward shift in status within NATO since the break up of the USSR. Turkey is nevertheless anxious to maintain its position within the Western alliances; it therefore finds that it cannot be as flexible with the Caucasus as it is able, and perhaps would wish, and has instead to work within the constraints of accepted Western foreign policy.

Because of its position, geographically and culturally, Turkey has other avenues of dealing with the Caucasus, perhaps best exemplified in the key role it has created for itself in working towards greater economic cooperation between the Black Sea nations. Despite the potential for conflict created by the addition of nations such as Armenia and Azerbaijan, Turkey sees "an advantageous position in such a scheme" for itself politically and economically.

A major plus for Turkey is its natural kinship with Turkic Azerbaijan, and it has carefully cultivated economic and cultural ties with the new Republic. This relationship, however, has been strained by differences over questions such as Turkey's commitment to a pipeline from Azerbaijan. Hale details the particular difficulties facing the Turkish government in maintaining its policy of non-intervention, despite growing domestic pressure, during the escalating conflict between Azerbaijan and Armenia over Karabakh, Armenian threats to Nakhichevan, which borders directly onto Turkey, and the Georgian/Abkhaz conflict. Karabakh also significantly affected the patchy relationship between Turkey and Iran, the issue bringing together the longstanding rivals against Armenian expansionism and its perceived Russian support.

Turkey's dilemma of status and non-intervention as a result of events in the Caucasus reveals many parallels to the situation facing Iran. In "Condemned to react, unable to influence: Iran and Transcaucasus" Fred

Halliday points to the decline and collapse of Soviet power in the Transcaucasus as "one of the major challenges facing Iran", which spent the greater part of this century secure in the knowledge that its northern borders were secure and clearly defined, in sharp contrast to the turbulence on its other borders. The collapse of the Soviet frontier re-established a link for the Transcaucasus with the rest of the Middle East that had until 1921 been "very alive". This helps explain the impact of the ethnic conflicts in the Transcaucasus on the Middle East, reflecting as they do conflicts involving similar ethnic groups or religions over the border, particularly in Iran. Iran's concern has also been that the Transcaucasus has lost its function both strategically and economically, and could be used against Iran by hostile external powers.

Halliday examines the historical record of ethnic minorities within Iran, many of which are mirrored across the border in the new Republics, and concentrates on the position of its substantial Azerbaijani and Armenian communities – 15 million and 120,000 respectively. Despite a display of open hostility to Soviet communism, Iran did not encourage the break up of the USSR, and, in fact, actively distanced itself from charges of encouraging secession, if only for the simple reason that it had no wish to encourage any such demands among its own ethnicities. An independent Azerbaijan in particular caused nervousness in Iran because of its potential impact on its own Azeris on the border in northwest Iran and because of its deepening links with Turkey. Meanwhile, there were repercussions from the Karabakh crisis created by the flow of refugees and a drying up of trade. Nevertheless, Halliday concludes that Iran still finds itself limited in its ability to exert any influence over the area.

Until the war in Chechnya, Karabakh (or Nagorno–Karabakh) was the most quoted conflict in the region, particularly, as stated above, since it was the first serious territorial flashpoint on the contemporary map of the post-Soviet Caucasus. The following two chapters examine the history of claims on the disputed area from two very different perspectives.

In "The Armenian presence in mountainous Karabakh" Christopher Walker sets the scene for the historical and ethnic background of Armenians in Karabakh – ancient Artsakh – and its place in the development of historical Armenia. The presence of Armenians in Karabakh is easily traced through records of the dynasties of local rulers who flourished under their many overlords through history: Seljuks, Mongols, Timurids and so on, through to the establishment of "melikdoms", and thence to the Safavids and the Persian Empire, finally succumbing to the Russian conquests of the early nineteenth century.

Walker stresses that from 1840 to 1991, however, "the people of mountainous Karabakh, despite being Armenian, have always been administratively united with Turco–Islamic peoples, and have had to struggle for recognition of their Armenian identity". Here the roots of the Azerbaijani/

Armenian hostility have been so easily and so violently exploited by external forces throughout this period, sealed by the first decisions of the Soviet leadership that were finally to create Karabakh as an administrative unit within Azerbaijan, strategically separated from Armenia by the "Lachin corridor". An "apartheid" system was established in Karabakh, which resulted in the movement of significant numbers of Armenians out of the territory and to its repopulation by Azerbaijanis.

The impact of these actions was severe for the Armenian population of Karabakh, but they found their voice in the movements of protest that slowly gathered force over the ensuing decades. Although the Armenian motherland was the only resource of help for the Karabakh Armenians, the authorities there were slow to respond, even with the arrival of *perestroika*. But popular demonstrations in Erevan, as Walker pointedly observes, showed that "the issue of Karabakh tapped a sense of deep national justice", and that it "was the catalyst for change within Armenia, but nothing changed for the people of Karabakh themselves". Karabakh's declaration of independence in January 1992 forced the hand of the Armenian Republic's leadership, and their subsequent combined military actions led to the present annexation of the territory of Nagorno–Karabakh as well as the adjoining Lachin corridor and other Azerbaijani territories. Any lasting peace and resolution of the impasse must now come, Walker argues, from an acceptance on all sides that the area is a truly disputed one, and that today "the wishes of the great majority should be the deciding factor".

The argument for Azerbaijan casts the evidence in a different light, as Sulejman Alijarly proposes in his chapter, translated from Russian and entitled "The republic of Azerbaijan: notes on the state borders in the past and the present". While concurring that the wishes of the majority should decide, Alijarly's contention is that Karabakh is in no way disputed, based on the evidence of records of the diverse territories that have made up the territory that is today the republic of Azerbaijan. While acknowledging problems in amassing the necessary demographic data for the past 1600 years, Alijarly has pieced together a picture of the movements of peoples in the area, stating – perhaps contentiously – that for the past millennium the "geographical co-ordinates" of Azerbaijan "underwent insignificant change".

Alijarly makes especial use of Arab and Persian sources to chart the status of Karabakh and the varying provinces that historically constituted Armenia, focusing on the problems posed of ethnic overlapping, a process that has occurred throughout the Caucasus with terrible consequences. The traditional arguments for Armenian statehood are challenged in historical terms, and thus Alijarly changes the modern argument for Karabakh in Transcaucasian terms. By presenting data on the administrative processes by which incorporation into modern Azerbaijan allegedly took place through the crucial years of the Tsarist and Soviet periods, Alijarly attempts to bolster his argument that Karabakh was never an Armenian homeland and legitimately belongs to the Azerbaijani whole, since it has for 1600 years formed a part of Azerbaijani state formations or provinces.

The perceived threat of Armenian expansionism also casts its shadow over Nakhichevan, a modern creation and source of conflict since it is an exclave of Azerbaijan separated geographically by Armenia. Such territorial disputes, however, should not be resolved by violence, but by recognizing the inviolability of existing state borders and the constitutional rights of those who live within them. This is a view shared by the final three chapters in this volume, which address the unique geopolitics of Georgia and two of the disputed regions within its borders, South Ossetia and Abkhazia.

In "The geopolitics of Georgia" John Wright warns of the dangers in regarding geopolitics as something static, fixed by the fact of geography, to the extent that we may misunderstand the geopolitics of Georgia and the wider Caucasus if we exclude nations who do not have a state. The evolution of borders has been decided "not through local mutual agreement by neighbouring state entities, but instead by external imperial powers" – in this case the USSR. Present Georgian perceptions of its own geopolitical and geostrategic position are best exemplified through the policies of Head of State Eduard Shevardnadze and the manner in which he argues their foundation.

Wright asserts that the contemporary Georgian geopolitics are qualitatively different to those pertaining in earlier times, especially the first two decades of this century. Historical arguments are employed routinely by Georgians to perpetuate the widespread contemporary belief that initially local disputes tend to draw in other powers and destroy the essential and international role of the Caucasus as an international "bridging point". This is not the case: Georgia is no longer a strategic buffer zone, rather its problems are internal, a situation "which in turn produces a different set of challenges for local political leaders".

Wright emphasizes the most fundamental territorial fact of the post-Soviet Caucasus. For the first time in almost 200 years Russia no longer borders Iran and Turkey. This has led to the creation of a "vacuum in Transcaucasia, where for the first time it should be up to local groups to determine and codify their fate". Such a position is completely new to the region and is exacerbated by the legacy of the communality of areas of conflict, namely areas that were autonomous regions of varying degrees created on the basis of ethnicity or religion. Georgia's main problems in dealing with this state of affairs, particularly internal territorial dissent, are linked to the fact that it is a weak state. As a result, subsequent Georgian attempts to create a lasting nation-state, combined with strong nationalist pressures, have led to an overstrict defining of borders and the resulting dilemmas for those local movements cut off within them.

8

The Abkhaz question presents a clear example of this process in action, involving as it does the workings of the uneasy Georgian triumvirate of Shevardnadze–Kitovani–Ioseliani, the complex position Russia has played in the decision-making of both sides, and the role of the Confederation of Mountain Peoples. The peace-making attempts since 1994 for Abkhazia, Wright observes, will make little progress if the different sides concentrate purely on political solutions. Only a geopolitical solution that fully takes into account economic necessity will present some degree of reduction of threat, beneficial to all sides concerned – both internal and external.

Using another Georgian territorial problem – that of South Ossetia – Julian Birch, in "The Georgian / South Ossetian territorial and boundary dispute" seeks answers to the dispute by referring to such problem areas "in terms of the titular nationality of the area", and asking how far such an eponymous group really is or was the cause of the problem and how far the problem was created by outside forces. A look at the historical geography reveals much of the sources of the "Ossetian dilemma", identifying such crucial factors as patterns of settlement, demographics, status of Ossetians within their own area, ethnic identification, and sources of external pressures to press for self-assertion, pressures stoutly resisted by the Georgians.

In parallel to the relationship of South Ossetia with Georgia, Birch details the development of North Ossetia within the RSFSR, sowing in this century the seeds of the two Ossetias, neither with the unilateral right of secession. The motivations of this twin creation are still uncertain, but the consequences are clearer, resulting in the violent clash of interests within South Ossetia. Demographic statistics, however, indicate that the combined population of the autonomous area is too small to create a situation of any serious threat to the general stability of the Caucasus, but only if the danger is avoided of involving on an international scale the two "overlords" of Georgia and the Russian Republic as they point the fingers of blame at each other. The present conflict started with bloody clashes in 1989, aggravated by Georgian insensitivity to Ossetian needs for self-determination and Soviet collusion with the Ossetians. Birch admits the difficulty here of separating USSR involvement from that of the Russian Republic, but one clear difference is that the Ossetians have lost the protection formerly offered them by the USSR.

While South Ossetia is one of the few ethnic disputes affording some degree of solution, Abkhazia presents quite a different problem. In "Abkhazia: a problem of identity and ownership", George Hewitt puts the Abkhazian question firmly into context by demonstrating how the ethnic affiliations of the peoples concerned contributed to the development of the disputed boundaries between Abkhazia and the rest of the Republic of Georgia. To ease understanding of the complex ethnic issues at play, Hewitt opposes "Georgian" – purely a geographical term – with "Kartvelian" –

9

ethnic Georgians and the related Mingrelian, Svan and Laz peoples. The intricately interwoven territorial issues here, therefore, are not between Abkhaz and Georgians but between Abkhaz and Kartvelians, reflecting as they do the difficulties characterizing Abkhaz–Kartvelian inter-ethnic relations in general.

The position appears simple enough: the Republic of Georgia stands by its declaration that any territory within its present borders is indisputably Georgian, referring to Abkhazia as either "an indivisible part of Georgia" or as "Georgian territory from earliest times", while the Abkhazians resent Kartvelian encroachment on their land, indicating that their territorial independence has to be re-established with Russia along similar lines as under the USSR. Underpinning these arguments are the significant movements of populations in the nineteenth century that saw forced mass migration of Abkhazians from Abkhazia as a result of Tsarist movements, and the subsequent influx – also often forced – of non-Abkhazians.

Of particular importance are the Mingrelians, a Kartvelian people related to the Georgians who have their own language and customs, yet were denied by Stalin the right to their own territory. Their territory borders onto Abkhazia and a historic intermingling with the Abkhazians has found them very much caught up in Georgian claims on Abkhazia whereby ethnic Abkhazians have been reclassified as "Mingrelian" and therefore Kartvelian. Leading Abkhazians sent the "Abkhazian letter" in 1988 to Gorbachev, in an attempt to defend their non-Kartvelian status, thus provoking a war of words, in which Georgia made the accusations that "[t]he Abkhazians stand accused of being an ungrateful and hugely privileged minority", resulting in the bloody warfare of 1992.

The Abkhazians, as Hewitt observes, see the struggle as one for survival of their ethnic identity while the Kartvelian concern is not to lose valuable territory. The dilemma now facing Abkhazia – should the future be within or without Georgia – is the same in principle for all nations of the Caucasus. Transition is inevitable but it is only external influences that can help ward off violence and ease its passage. The pressing question is what will the response of these external influences now be towards the Caucasus and towards each other? It is certainly in the interests of these forces to work for a speedy solution to the upheavals if only to expedite movement of trade, as Wright suggests. Stability in the Caucasus would bring not only an end to conflict but also the promise of exploiting its own not inconsiderable natural resources.

Certainly, the West is committed to an active role in the Caucasus, anxious as it is to open up a direct gateway to the nascent economic boom in Central Asia. The stake of Russia, however, is equally as clear, desperate that nothing falls outside its sphere of influence, to the point of keeping troops stationed throughout the region. It is this ambiguity in Russia's position that makes it an uneasy partner in any solution for the territorial conflicts that have placed a stranglehold on democratic and economic movement and closed off almost every major trade route in and out of the region. Indeed, how are we to reconcile the fact that a sovereign state such as Georgia is seen on today's map to share a common border with Turkey, yet in reality is separated by a corridor of territory barely 20m wide that is forever Russia?

The recent challenge raised by the crisis in Chechnya has demonstrated that the territorial framework of Stalin's legacy in the Caucasus poses a continuing danger in its present form and cannot last. Efforts must now be intensified to find speedy, peaceful resolutions for breaking the cyclical nature of the disputes and establishing a new framework acceptable to all nations, be they internal or external, large or small, nation-state or sub-nationalist.

Background note: reflections on Chechnya
SUZANNE GOLDENBERG

Three years after independence, the conflicts that have defined the countries of the Transcaucasus have receded against the devastation that has been visited upon Chechnya. By spring 1995, Russian military forces had claimed to have captured the last centres of the Chechen resistance at Shali and Gudermes, and gained control of 80 per cent of the secessionist republic. Four months of war had left more than 20,000 people dead and, according to some estimates, some 250,000 refugees. The Chechen capital, Grozny, was in ruins following weeks of Russian aerial bombardment and house-to-house fighting.

"Active combat actions on the Chechen republic are over", Oleg Soskovants, Russia's deputy prime minister, declared on 31 March 1995.[1] He announced that the process of rebuilding (for which the Kremlin had allocated a reported US$1 billion) could now begin and that the Russian-appointed administration headed by the former Soviet petrochemicals minister, Solombek Khadjiev, would prepare for the drafting of a new constitution and the holding of fresh elections. Similar claims had been made before in the four months since the Russian assault against Chechnya's president, General Dzhokhar Dudayev, was launched on 11 December 1994, notably after the capture of Grozny in January 1995. The Russians were proved wrong on those occasions. But following the capture of Shali, military analysts in Moscow were sceptical that resistance based in the southern mountains of Chechnya could continue for long against Russian air power.[2]

Chechnya has shared the fate of the other countries of the Caucasus –

---

1. Reuter, March 31, 1995.

war and economic collapse, but the devastation it has undergone since the fall of the Soviet Union is a clearer illustration of Russia's intent to secure its interests in the region.

As in Georgia and Azerbaijan during the late 1980s, in Chechnya the debate that emerged about democratic and economic reform became subsumed by nationalist demands. Georgia and Armenia were among the earliest of the non-Russian republics to seek to secede from the Soviet Union. Their struggles for independence set off a corresponding campaign within Russia itself. By 1992, Chechens and Tatars were seeking to renegotiate the status of their territories within the Russian federation.

Chechnya's president General Dzhokhar Dudayev properly belongs to this first stage of post-Soviet society: the era during which Russian official policy towards the former Soviet Union was ill-defined, and militant nationalists were in the ascendancy in the Caucasus. Some analysts have said Boris Yeltsin and his supporters in Moscow welcomed the emergence of these overtly nationalist leaders as part of their struggle against Mikhail Gorbachev and the communist bureaucracy.[3]

When General Dudayev was elected president of Chechnya in October 1991, the former dissident Zviad Gamsakhurdia was president of Georgia. Though resoundingly popular among ethnic Georgians at the time of his election in May 1991, he was openly chauvinistic and antagonized the country's Abkhazian and Ossetian minorities, who in turn looked towards Russia for support. Months later, the leader of Azerbaijan, Ayaz Mutalibov, was overthrown during a series of upheavals that was to end in the election of the pan-Turkic intellectual Abulfaz Elchibey as president in June 1992.

Dudayev, though reduced to a fugitive outlaw by the Russian military victory, managed to survive longer than either leader. In January 1992, he offered a refuge to Gamsakhurdia, who was overthrown during a civil war embarked on by his own National Guard. In the summer of 1993, a mutiny in the Azeri armed forces forced Elchibey to flee Baku.

The presidencies of both Gamsakhurdia and Elchibey marked a consolidation in Russian policy. Moscow began to view with greater concern the growing closeness between Azerbaijan and Turkey under Elchibey, and more importantly the potential for instability within Russia itself arising from conflict in the Caucasus region.

Both Gamsakhurdia and Elchibey were seen as inimical to Moscow's interests. There were indications that their removal was accomplished with Russian covert support. Certainly there was a widespread belief in Georgia

---

2. "Russians seize their last city as rebels flee", *New York Times*, 1 April, 1995. Steven Erlanger notes a Russian strategy of leaving relatively unscathed those villages that demonstrated little resistance to the invasion, while comprehensively destroying areas that had sheltered Chechen militias, including the town of Argun.

3. Shireen T. Hunter, *Post-Soviet transition in the Transcaucasus* [sic]: *regional and international implications*. Paper 61, Centre for European Policy Studies, Brussels (1994: 112).

that events had been engineered so that the former Soviet foreign minister, Eduard Shevardnadze, could return to his native country as president in the spring of 1992.[4] Similar suspicions were voiced in Azerbaijan after the former republic communist party chief Heydar Aliyev came to power.

Because of their previous associations, both men have tried hard to re-establish their nationalist credentials. Solombek Khadjiev also owes his return to the political centre stage to his connections in Moscow rather than a local support base. He has been trying to convince his fellow Chechens that he is not a pawn of Moscow. "I want sovereignty too, but there are different types. We will win ours peacefully." he told the *Economist* recently. He also pledged to hold a referendum on independence "something like Tatarstan".[5]

The war in Chechnya marked the first time that Russian forces had intervened directly to defeat a demand for independence. The savagery with which its reintegration into the Russian federation was effected put into sharp relief Moscow's re-assertion of its abiding strategic interest in the region.

With a population of 1.2 million at the time of the 1989 census, the Chechen-Ingush republic was one of the largest autonomous republics within the former Soviet Union. Like other territories in the region, its population was not exclusive to one ethnic group. The breakdown was 55 per cent Chechen, 12 per cent Ingush and 22 per cent Russian. Though it produced its own oil, Chechnya was important mainly as a refining centre.

In August 1991, the people of the republic distinguished themselves by their popular opposition to the putsch against Gorbachev despite the ambivalence of the republic's leader, Doku Zavgayev. Dudayev, who led the opposition to the putsch, took advantage of his new prominence to press for independence and elections by launching a general strike. The strike lasted 10 weeks.

Although Yeltsin had sent a telegram to Dudayev thanking him for his opposition to the coup, his subsequent actions caused alarm in Moscow. By 2 November, when General Dudayev declared Chechen independence, Yeltsin had begun to ally himself with Russian conservatives such as the then parliamentary Speaker Ruslan Khasbulatov and then vice-president Alexander Rutskoi, who had been demanding firm action against the secessionists.[6]

Almost immediately after the declaration of independence, Yeltsin announced a state of emergency in Chechnya and ordered Dudayev's arrest.

---

4. Suzanne Goldenberg, *Pride of small nations: the Caucasus and post-Soviet disorder*, 92–4 (London: Zed Books, 1994).
5. "Chechnya's puppet or saviour", *The Economist*, 1 April, 1995.
6. Marie Bennigsen Broxup (ed.), *The North Caucasus barrier: the Russian advance towards the Muslim world*, 220 (London: Hurst, 1992).

He despatched troops to the republic on November 10. But two days later, Yeltsin was forced to retreat when the Russian parliament refused to sanction the measures.

Though the troops were withdrawn, Russia's relations with Chechnya continued to deteriorate. The soldiers retreated only as far as North Ossetia where their presence remained as an irritant to Dudayev. An economic blockade was imposed; salaries and pensions were frozen. Dudayev interpreted the forced withdrawal of Russian troops as a victory, but in the event it signalled only a change of tactics. At no point over the next three years was there any concerted effort on either side to seek a negotiated compromise. Instead, events unfolded in a way to increase Russian anxiety about its security.

The next phase of the dispute was characterized by a perceived breakdown of law and order – both in Chechnya and the entire region. Within the republic, Dudayev's hold soon became tenuous and his inexperienced government increasingly unpopular. In March 1992, his forces intercepted several truckloads of weapons in the home district of Doku Zavgayev, aborting what his officials claimed as a coup planned in Moscow. In April 1993 there was an impeachment motion against Dudayev and a series of protests so unsettling that he imposed a curfew in Grozny, and dissolved parliament. Life in the republic was characterized by frequent eruptions of small weapons fire by the militiamen who patrolled the streets. Concern was raised for the safety of ethnic Russians, especially those who had been settled in regions expropriated from Chechens during the second world war deportations.

Beyond the republic's borders, ethnic Chechens figured in several hijackings of air passengers for ransom, and there were a series of explosions along oil pipelines. The incidents served to complete the demonization of the Chechens. Within the popular Russian imagination, Chechnya became synonymous with mafia, and the gangs terrorizing Moscow and St Petersburg. By the time of the intervention on 11 December, few Russians harboured much sympathy for the Chechens. The protests that have marked the campaign have focused as much on Russian casualties – officially 1400 troops – among the demoralized conscripts rather than the huge civilian losses.

If events in Chechnya are to conform to the pattern established in Georgia and Azerbaijan, the months following the reported defeat of the resistance will be crucial. Gamsakhurdia retained pockets of support nearly two years after his ouster, endangering Shevardnadze's control on the western part of Georgia. In Azerbaijan, Aliyev has faced unrest from within his armed forces. But both men were able to legitimize their positions through elections, and more importantly by bringing a measure of stability. The success of Moscow's efforts to subdue the Chechens now rests with its ambitious reconstruction plan.

CHAPTER ONE

Nationalities and borders in Transcaucasia and the northern Caucasus

GEORGE JOFFÉ

Transcaucasia and the northern Caucasus – the region of the former Soviet Union bounded by the Black Sea and the Azov Sea to the west, the Caspian Sea to the east, international borders with Turkey and Iran to the south, and roughly delimited by a horizontal line drawn between the Don and the Volga rivers to the north – is a region of staggering ethnic and national complexity. There are at least 30 major ethnic groups within it, one of which, the Avars of Daghestan, can be subcategorized further into 12 different groupings. Nor do these 30 odd communities in the Caucasus live in discrete, compact geographic units; in some instances the degree of intermixing is profound.

Some groups, however, such as the Azerbaijanis, the Armenians and the Georgians, have managed to avoid such territorial discontinuity to a marked extent, a factor that has considerable political implications today. They are organized into three of the 15 former Union republics that made up the USSR and which have now become independent states. Nonetheless, all of them had large concentrations of other ethnic groups on their soils, which had received administrative attention in the past, in that they enjoyed special territorial status as autonomous republics or as autonomous provinces within the three republics.[1] This was true of the Abkhazian Autonomous Republic and the South Ossetian Autonomous Province in Georgia and of the Nakhichevan Autonomous Republic in Azerbaijan, from which it was separated by a strip of Armenian territory.[2]

The other region that had this status was the Nagorno–Karabakh Autonomous Province in Azerbaijan, with its majority Armenian population (75.9 per cent of the total – 123,076 persons – in 1979 and 76.9 per cent of the total in 1989 – 145,450 persons – compared with 94.4 per cent in 1921

---

1. S. Akiner, *Islamic peoples of the Soviet Union*, 2nd edn, 17 (London: Kegan Paul International, 1986).
2. Ibid., 42.

when its status was first declared).[3] Nagorno–Karabakh saw its administrative status altered on 12 January 1989, when the Supreme Soviet decreed that it should in future be directly administered from Moscow, in an attempt to divert the growing clash over its future between Armenia and Azerbaijan. However, by 1992 it had been reoccupied by force by Armenia, and the "Lachin Strip" which separates it from Armenia was also occupied, thus effectively integrating it into Armenian territory. Despite a consequent political crisis in Baku, accompanied by a change in government there, Azerbaijan has found it extremely difficult to reverse this Armenian *fait accompli*, and the issue has threatened to widen into a generalized ideological and cultural confrontation between the two republics, the one Christian and the other Muslim.

The Nagorno–Karabakh crisis is not the only confrontation that has developed inside the Caucasus and Transcaucasia region since *perestroika* and the dissolution of the USSR in late 1991. This has been particularly the case in the Republic of Georgia, where, in addition to a struggle for control of the republic itself, there has also been an intensifying crisis in Abkhazia and in South Ossetia, the old South Ossetian Autonomous Province which, in terms of sovereign control, was originally part of Georgia. Independence was declared in September 1990, as part of a process designed to lead to union with North Ossetia, which is part of the Russian Federation. This was rejected by the Georgian Supreme Soviet in December 1990. This, in turn, caused an intervention from Moscow in early 1991 to force out Georgian armed units and irregulars. Conflict continued until the ousting of the former Georgian president, Zviad Gamsakhurdia, in January 1992, when fighting died down.[4] Fighting erupted once again in mid-1992, as Georgian irregulars bombarded the capital, Tskhinvali, despite attempts by the new Georgian government and its president, Eduard Shevardnadze (the former Soviet Foreign Minister) to prevent further conflict.[5] Eventually, Russia and Georgia were able to impose a peace-keeping force on the region, as an interim solution designed to lead to the emergence of Ossetia as a separate political entity. Since then, a far more serious crisis has exploded in Abkhazia, with open fighting between Abkhazian nationalists, backed by a federation of minorities in the northern Caucasus, and the Georgian Government.

The remaining minorities in the northern Caucasus are all within the Russian Federation, which now shares a common border with Azerbaijan and Georgia. However, the ethnic complexity of this region long ago per-

---

3. C. J. Walker (ed.), *Armenia and Karabakh: the struggle for unity*, 109, 116 (London: Minority Rights Group, 1991); P. B. Henze, "The demography of the Caucasus according to the 1989 Soviet census data", *Central Asian Survey* 10, 155, 1991.

4. *Eastern European Newsletter* VI(10), 3, 1992.

5. *Financial Times* 1992, 9 June, 1.

suaded the Soviet authorities that a degree of delegation of administrative responsibility would be necessary. As a result, a series of seven autonomous republics and provinces was created in the northern Caucasus: the Kalmyk, the Chechen–Ingush, the Kabardino–Balkar, the North Ossetian and the Daghestan autonomous republics, and the Adyghei and Karachai–Cherkess autonomous provinces. In virtually all of them, secessionist and independence movements have now appeared, often accompanied by violence. Even though the northern Caucasian federation of minority groups was formed in November 1991, it was quite unable to influence these potential conflicts in the short term, although its longer-term prospects might well be more encouraging.[6]

Against this complex ethnic, administrative and political background, the issue of identifying those factors that would facilitate a pacific redefinition of the future political structures for the region seems impossibly difficult. As one commentator has pointed out, there are four main influences at play: nationalism and tribalism, territorial claims, Islam and anti-Russian sentiment.[7] Two of these factors – Islam and anti-Russian sentiment – could have a partially unifying effect. However, the other two will continue to be profoundly divisive and will tax negotiators in trying to formulate some underlying set of principles around which stable political structures could be created. Amongst the independent republics, indeed, new alignments have already begun to develop, with Muslim Azerbaijan turning against Moscow and towards Turkey and Iran, whereas Christian Armenia now sees the Russian Federation as its major foreign protector, as does Georgia, in an interesting realignment of pre-Soviet cultural identities, with new alliance patterns developing along the lines of religious identity.

This process of political reconstruction will be rendered far more difficult by the fact of economic interdependence between all parts of the former USSR. This will continue into the foreseeable future, whatever political arrangements are made. Detailed statistics are available only for the new republics, but there can be little doubt that the situation for autonomous republics and provinces would demonstrate an even greater dependence on the federation, despite the generalized sentiment of hostility towards Moscow that is evident in public opinion and popular attitudes in virtually all of them. All the new republics depend on Russia for more than 50 per cent of their trade and on the other former Union republics for more than 80 per cent. Indeed, factors such as growth of national debt and consumer price inflation in all three republics have tracked similar growth patterns in Russia, even if domestic credit growth has been more restrained in Georgia and Armenia, largely because of this trade

---

6. *Eastern European Newsletter* VI(10), 4, 1992.

7. Ibid., 5.

dependence. All have economies that are still heavily dependent on agriculture and in which the industrial sector is still underdeveloped. Only Armenia has an economic structure similar to that of the Russian Federation and even that is still, by Western standards, profoundly distorted towards agriculture. All of the new republics, too, have living standards significantly below that of the Russian Federation.

The simple fact is that the Russian Federation is and will continue to be dominant in the external economies of all the entities involved, whatever their final form. Also, there are, of course, potential future links with surrounding states, such as Turkey and Iran. Indeed, in early February 1992, Turkey proposed the formation of a Black Sea Council, designed to foster a free trade zone among states around the Black Sea littoral, which would include all three of the Caucasian republics, as well as the Russian Federation, Ukraine, Moldova, Romania and Bulgaria, with the eventual objective of bringing in Greece and some, at least, of the former Yugoslav republics as well. The more immediate purpose of the proposal was to lower barriers to trade and to foster joint projects in the fields of transport, tourism and the environment, with Turkey being in a position to take the leading role and thus becoming a new regional power. Ankara has also proposed the creation of a development bank, to be capitalized at $10 million, as part of the joint venture proposals. However, Turkey's ambitions range further afield as well and, in mid-1992, Ankara proposed aid worth $1.2 billion to Central Asia, aid that would also benefit Azerbaijan, if the plans come to fruition.[8] However, Turkish political leaders are cautiously realistic about the very limited potential for rapid economic change in the region and clearly look to more immediate diplomatic and political, rather than economic, benefits from this proposal.

At about the same time as Turkey was proposing a Black Sea Council, Iran proposed a plan for the integration of the six new Muslim republics of Central Asia and the Caucasus into the virtually defunct Economic Cooperation Organization (ECO) it shared with Turkey and Pakistan.[9] The ultimate objective was to create a customs union or free trade zone within the ECO, as an apparent counterweight to Turkey's Black Sea Council proposal. Indeed, Iran, despite its own serious economic plight, was the prime mover in this new plan, offering to construct infrastructure links between Central Asia and the Gulf, in the form of a new railway, in order to speed economic integration. It remains to be seen to what extent such promises will be honoured, given the parlous state of the Iranian economy. In any case, such initiatives take time to evolve and, furthermore, none of the three original member states has the economic resources or capacity that would make any or all of them a genuine alternative market or supplier to

---

8. *Eastern European Newsletter*, vol. VI(12), 8, 1992.
9. *Eastern European Newsletter*, vol. VI(7), 8, 1992.

the Russian Federation. This fact alone is bound to have a profound influence on the political debate over new political structures that will eventually develop.

Nationalism and the state

The problem is that, quite apart from these practical difficulties, there are very few appropriate theoretical guidelines available to suggest how these structures should evolve. The usual political paradigm is the nation-state, the archetypal independent political structure that developed in Europe and that has since become the preferred model for the international political system. However, the nation-state concept seems quite inappropriate for a region such as the Caucasus, yet the paradox is that the populations and ethnic groups articulate their demands as if no other viable political framework is available, and in this they may well be correct, even though it is most unlikely to provide the political stability they seek.

Even the traditional view of the state is replete with problems as far as the Caucasus is concerned, whether it is defined in Weberian, Hegelian or legal terms. In international law, the state is the primordial legal personality: an entity with a defined territory, a permanent population, under the control of a government and with the capacity to engage in formal relations with other entities.[10] Over its territory, a state exercises territorial sovereignty – "the exclusive right to display the activities of a state".[11]

Implicit in these definitions are certain basic factors relating to the legal nature of the state. First, the international legal definition of the state is concerned with the legitimate exercise of power and thus approximates to the Weberian definition of the state as an entity that monopolizes the use of legitimate violence throughout the territory concerned.[12] Secondly, the territory in question has precise limits: internationally accepted boundaries, in other words. Thus, for example, the governments of Azerbaijan, Armenia and Georgia, as successor governments to those of the Union republics that preceded them, legitimately exercise their authority within the administrative bounds established by the former government of the USSR. They acquired their state title and their defined territorial extent through the principle of *uti possidetis*,[13] whereby successor states acquire innate legitimate title to the territories administered by their predecessors.

That these states legitimately exercise their power is also implicit in the

---

10. R. M. Wallace, *International law*, 53 (London: Sweet & Maxwell, 1986).
11. Island of Las Palma case, vol. II, 829, 839 (London: RIAA, 1928).
12. R. Scruton (ed.), *Dictionary of political thought*, 446–7 (New Haven: Yale University Press, 1982).
13. T. S. Murty, *Frontiers, a changing concept*, 169 (Delhi: Palit & Palit, 1978).

fact that their governments have been recognized, *de jure* or *de facto*, as the governments of independent states by most other governments world-wide.[14] They have also been able to join international organizations, such as the Conference on Co-operation and Security in Europe (CSCE), now the Organisation on Co-operation and Security in Europe (OCSE), and the United Nations, and they have begun to enter into international agreements with other states, such as Iran and Turkey. However, there is a difficulty in that governmental power in the new republics – except, perhaps, for Armenia – is *not* recognized as legitimate by substantial minorities of their populations. This is not a problem as far as recognition in international law is concerned, since there is a general presumption against supporting secessionist movements against accepted governments. Furthermore, there is also a general predisposition, under the Stimpson Doctrine, to reject forcible attempts to alter the existing boundaries of a state, particularly if this is done at the behest of another state, as is the case in Nagorno–Karabakh. In any case, many governments, such as the British government, accept the Estrada Doctrine and claim to recognize states, rather than governments, so the question of popular acceptance of government is irrelevant, provided it remains in control.[15]

To the political scientist, however, these legal niceties are not particularly helpful. Governments facing widespread popular opposition, for whatever reason, lack political legitimacy and cannot ensure stability. In some cases this is simply a consequence of the fact that the governments themselves do not correspond to the popular vision of what they should represent and they lack the commitment to be able to impose themselves or to amass sufficient popular support to legitimize themselves. They and the states they control are then inherently *defective* and will survive only through repression, as is the case throughout the Middle East and North Africa.[16]

However, political legitimacy is usually a far more profound factor, related in large measure to the sovereign exercise of power in which sovereignty is construed to be far wider than the conventional post-Westphalian view of territorial sovereignty.[17] The most extreme expression of this view is contained in current views of popular sovereignty, whereby sovereignty is no longer the property of a state but of a people, in the sense in which the term is used in the United Nations Charter. Governments, then,

---

14. M. Akehurst, *A modern introduction to international law*, 57–67 (London: Unwin Hyman, 1987).

15. Ibid., 62.

16. E. G. H. Joffé, "A view from the south: terrorism and fundamentalism in the Middle East". In *Conflict and consensus in North/South security*, C. Thomas & P. Saravanamuttu, 165 (Cambridge: Cambridge University Press, 1989).

17. J. Mayall, *Nationalism and international society*, 18–19 (Cambridge: Cambridge University Press, 1990).

only have sovereign power if they are legitimized through popular support, not, as required by international law, because of their independence or their legislative and administrative competence. Sovereignty, in effect, becomes an extension of democratic consent.[18]

However, this is a very recent view. Nonetheless, the problem of government legitimacy within the state has long been a concern of politicians and political scientists alike. Indeed, within western Europe, the view formed that the legitimizing factor for a government was the fact that the population over which it ruled and from which it was derived was culturally homogenous. This population, therefore, formed a defined and autonomous group and, as such a group, was internally egalitarian and externally unique, for it was different from any other such group in another state. It was a nation, in short, around which the ethnic and territorial boundaries coincided.

This nation (the national society, as it were) then legitimized government through a form of contractual dependence, whereby government was intended to express the collective objectives of the society over which it ruled, which, in turn, would thereby support it. Concepts such as these were developed by Rousseau, among others, in his concept of the general will and the social contract. They reached their apogée in Article 3 of the *Declaration of the rights of Man*, proclaimed in the early days of the French revolution, which states that, "The nation is essentially the source of all sovereignty".[19] Legitimate government, therefore, has to do with popular consent and is, in effect, similar to the "actuality of the ethical idea" – the vision of the state propounded by Hegel.[20] The crucial importance of cultural homogeneity in this process is highlighted by the major theoreticians of modern nationalism, Ernest Gellner:

> In brief, nationalism is a theory of political legitimacy, which requires that ethnic boundaries should not cut across political ones, and, in particular, that ethnic boundaries within a given state – a contingency already formally excluded by the principle in its general formulation – should not separate the power-holders from the rest.[21]

This is, in effect, the concept of the nation-state, developed and perfected in western Europe, that has become the paradigm worldwide during the twentieth century. It is now enshrined within the United Nations Charter, in that the "peoples" to which the Charter refers and who have

---

18. M. W. Reisman, "Sovereignty and human rights in international law", *The American Journal of International Law* **84**, 871, 1990.

19. T. Paine, *The rights of man*, 132 (Harmondsworth: Penguin, 1969).

20. Scruton (1982: 447–8).

21. E. Gellner, *Nations and nationalism*, 1 (Oxford: Basil Blackwell, 1983).

the fundamental right of self–determination are equivalent to the concept of independent nations.

It may reasonably be objected, of course, that few of the historic nations from which nation-states have been formed are, in reality, the spontaneous product of cultural cohesion. Indeed, many of them – not least in western Europe – have been forged over centuries by the repressive and centraliz-ing forces of despotic government creating, or rather enforcing, thereby, cultural homogeneity and political conformity amongst populations which had often been culturally heterogeneous and sociopolitically diverse. The result has therefore been the creation of the *staat-nation* rather than the *nation-staat*. This may well be true, as, indeed, it has been in large parts of the Third World, where the major domestic political process has been one of nation building – often through considerable repression and with less than successful results. In Africa and the Middle East, for example, where the principle of the intangibility of colonial borders has been explicitly or implicitly accepted as a basic rule of international relations,[22] the process of nation building has been an inevitable consequence, as well as a conscious objective, since otherwise the states concerned would have remained permanently defective.[23]

In any case, in reality, the historical record is only of marginal impor-tance in establishing government legitimacy if such a national consensus eventually develops. It is not so much the accuracy of the historical myth that nations create to justify their claim to autonomous political existence that matters. It is rather that the myth should be cohesive and integrated into the generalized culture to which the national society as a whole sub-scribes. In this respect, therefore, all nationalist history is mythical, whether it accurately reflects the historical record or not, for its sole pur-pose is, in effect, to justify and reinforce the nationalist consensus. Yet, in any case, such a nationalist consensus perceives itself to be synchronous, not diachronic and, furthermore, defines itself as both timeless and eter-nal, in which case an historical record of whatever kind is an irrelevance.

Of course, if this consensus breaks down, then the legitimacy of govern-ment is also called into question, a process that has occurred with increas-ing frequency in western Europe in recent decades. The usual form is through the development of "subnationalisms" that seek either secession or decentralization. It has been cogently argued that this phenomenon cor-responds to a greater popular perception of the need for democratic polit-ical structures[24] and of the inability of such structures in what were *staat-*

22. Viz. the Organization of African Unity Cairo Resolution of 1964. I. Brownlie, *African boundaries, a legal and diplomatic encyclopaedia*, 11 (London: Hurst and Royal Institute of International Affairs, 1979).
23. Joffé (1989: 165). See Thomas & Saravanamuttu (1989).
24. A. D. Smith, *Nationalism in the twentieth century*, 150–65 (Oxford: Martin Robertson, 1979).

nationen to respond to such demands. In other words, subnationalist demands for recognition are really a protest against centralist and unaccountable bureaucratic administration, rather than the articulation of cultural distinction, however real such distinctions may be. This is a somewhat dangerous assumption, for nationalism, whether at state level or at some sublevel, is really a statement about exclusion and exclusiveness. Legitimacy in that context is really more a statement about the articulation of the collective cultural identity than about democratic accountability. Democracy and nationalism, in short, are not automatic and inevitable bedfellows.

Yet, even if this is the case, it does not undermine the basic principle governing the constitution of the nation-state, namely that of governmental legitimacy through collective consent by a culturally homogeneous group that sees itself as a distinct and unique cultural entity. Of course, in the name of an overriding and greater national ideal, existing states resist pressures for secession, even if they respond grudgingly to demands for decentralization – as the recent examples of Britain and Spain show. However, the interesting aspect of this response is that it is based on assumptions very similar to those of the "subnationalists" themselves. Governments of states that claim to be national entities thereby use the same source for their legitimacy as that employed by subnationalists when demanding secession or autonomous administration.

Indeed, the typical response to such demands has been the creation of federal states – in a system that, in effect, is designed to accommodate the demands of both levels of political organization simultaneously. Over half the world's population live, apparently, under one form or another of federalism,[25] in which a central government handles external affairs alone, whereas responsibility for internal affairs is divided between central government and the governments of the states making up the federation. The problem with this arrangement is that the member states of a federation do not have autonomous political status within the international system and are thus not construed to be states under international law, for they cannot engage in independent relations with other states. For many nationalists, therefore, the federal solution is inherently unacceptable, for it negates recognition of the absolute and unique nature of the national community, even if it provides an opportunity for national and subnational expression. Furthermore, there is often a competition for the allegiance of the population between the national (federal) and subnational (state) level, which undermines the ultimate cohesion of the state, as the experience of the USSR, Yugoslavia and Czechoslovakia have demonstrated so effectively.

A further problem arises when subnationalist entities within the nation-state are not geographically located within it as discrete demographic agglomerations, but are, instead, intermixed with other subnationalist

---

25. Akehurst (1987: 54–5).

groups or are present as agglomerations that are too small to exercise administrative functions themselves. The problem of minority representation within such states has never been satisfactorily resolved, despite attempts to create appropriate legal structures for it in international law since the end of the First World War. The most usual assumption is that the interests of such groups will be best preserved by democratic government, although, as minorities within a wider nationalist majority, such assumptions seem inherently unrealistic. More recently, there have been proposals based on the concept of active citizenship, which are supposed to counter these deficiencies, although it is difficult to see how this will be achieved.

In any case, there is a basic ideological conflict within the idealized view of the nation-state between the concepts of the state as subservient to individual will and the state as expression of collective consensus, which reflects this dilemma. On the one hand, it is an instrument for the collective authentication and legitimacy of governmental monopoly of violence to preserve the structure of the state. On the other hand, it is designed to integrate popular support for such legitimacy through membership of the unique national group; it provides a vehicle for individual participation in collective action and individual identity within the collectivity. However, it does not do so on the basis of individual decision but on the basis of adherence to a collective cultural identity. In fact, the nation-state concept cannot be an inherently democratic vision, for it is not concerned with expression of individual views and their balance within the wider society; rather, it represents a collective statement of political intent on the part of society as a whole.

Nonetheless, in western Europe and the USA, if not elsewhere, it has become a staging post along the road towards the idea of government legitimacy by democratic consent. The UN Charter and the Declaration of the Rights of Man – which articulate the role of the nation in legitimizing the state – have now been conjoined to the American constitution and the Universal Declaration of Human Rights in justifying the claim that the legitimacy of governments is not merely a matter of national consent but of democratic consent as well. The danger is that many nationalists assume that this more recent extension of the original concept is inherent in the concept itself and that nationalist cohesion is, thereby, an automatic guarantor of democratic governance. Unfortunately, this is not the case, nor, indeed, does it follow from the basic precepts of nationalism itself.

Nationalism and the Caucasus

As far as the northern Caucasus and Transcaucasia are concerned, this vision is virtually irrelevant as a political prescription, in any case. Although identifiable majority national communities exist in the three independent republics, this is clearly not the case in many of the autonomous republics and provinces within them, or in that part of northern Caucasus within the Russian Federation. This is not merely or even mainly a consequence of a policy of Russification: it follows on from the dual factors of the massive territorial discontinuity of population location, magnified by deliberate policies of Russification and administrative control through territorial definition that ignored population location by the Soviet government. At the same time, whereas for a variety of factors, homogenization of the populations of the three republics has intensified in recent years, this has not been the case in the northern Caucasus, nor in minority areas within the republics themselves.

The situation in the republics

Only in Nagorno–Karabakh and Nakhichevan, among the autonomous enclaves within the republics, has a process of population homogenization been so explicitly carried out. In Nakhichevan, for example, pro-Armenia commentators have claimed that the Armenian population in the autonomous republic was 40 per cent of the total in 1917 but had dropped to 5 per cent by the 1970s and is today around 2 per cent of the total.[26] In fact, according to the 1989 census, the Armenian population there was halved from 3,406 in 1979 to 1,858 in 1989 – just 0.6 per cent of the total – whereas the Azerbaijani population has risen to 95.5 per cent of the total.[27] Current events are likely to force the remaining 0.6 per cent of Armenians out of the enclave in the very near future.

Similar accusations of "Turkification" have been made in the case of Nagorno–Karabakh – although recent events have profoundly altered the picture. From a high of 94.4 per cent of the total population of the enclave in 1921, the Armenian proportion of the population has steadily declined in favour of the Azerbaijani population – to 89.1 per cent in 1926, 88.1 per cent in 1939, 84.4 per cent in 1959, 80.6 per cent in 1970 and to 75.9 per cent in 1979, when the population was measured as 160,000.[28] However, in 1989 the Armenian proportion of the population had risen slightly to 76.9 per cent of the total, equivalent to a total of 145,450 persons out of a total population of 189,029, of which Azerbaijanis totalled only 40,632 persons.[29] This trend has certainly been intensified by the Armenian victory in the war in the region during May 1992, although continuing hostilities and Azerbaijani nationalist anger at what has happened in Azerbaijan itself make any prediction of the final outcome highly uncertain.

In the two enclaves in Georgia – South Ossetia and Abkhazia – the sit-

26. Walker (1991: 64).
27. Henze (1991: 154).
28. Walker (1991: 116).
29. Henze (1991: 155).

uation seems very different. In Abkhazia, for example, Abkhazians are a small minority within their own republic, with 15.1 per cent of the total population in 1959, 17.1 per cent of the total in 1979 and 17.3 per cent of the total in 1989. The Russian minority population is larger but declining, at 21.4 per cent of the total in 1959, only 16.4 per cent of the population in 1979 and 14.2 per cent of the total in 1989.[30] The balance is made up of Georgians (43.9 per cent in 1979 and 46.2 per cent in 1989), Armenians (15.1 per cent in 1979 and 14.6 per cent in 1989) and Ukrainians (2.1 per cent in 1979 and 2.2 per cent in 1989). It should be borne in mind that this situation is a direct consequence of in-migration, mainly by Georgians, Armenians and Russians between 1926 and 1959, which saw the proportion of the population that was Abkhazian reduced from 30 per cent to 15 per cent.[31] It had originally been reduced from a majority of the total after Russia's victory in the Caucasian War of 1878, when many Abkhazians, together with large numbers of other north Caucasian ethnic groups, migrated southwards into the Ottoman-controlled Middle East, where they form today's Circassian community.[32] It should also be noted that the definition of the term "Georgian" is ambiguous, since it subsumes a variety of different nationalities – some of them permanent residents of Abkhazia – under the same ethnic rubric.[33]

The same factor of in-migration also applied in Ossetia, where the policy of Russification was even more marked. The Ossetian proportion of the population remained almost constant between 1926 and 1959 in South Ossetia, but was cut by half, from 84.3 per cent to 47.8 per cent, in North Ossetia during the same period. In South Ossetia, the Ossetian proportion of the population has been virtually static since 1959, when it formed 65.8 per cent of the total. This rose to 66.5 per cent in 1970 and to 66.4 per cent in 1979. The Russian population has remained static at between 2.5 per cent (1959) and 2.1 per cent in 1979.[34] There was virtually no change in these population ratios during the decade between 1979 and 1989, when the proportion of Ossetians fell to 66.2 per cent and that of Russians rose to 2.2 per cent.[35] Ossetians, therefore, form a majority of the population, but there is a considerable minority, around one third of the total, of Georgians. Incidentally, the situation in North Ossetia, which is part of the Russian Federation and now seeks unity with South Ossetia, is even more heterogeneous, for Ossetians form a bare majority of the population there, ranging from 47.8 per cent of the total in 1959 to 50.5 per cent of the total

30. Akiner (1986: 42); Henze (1991: 153).
31. Akiner (1986: 220).
32. R. Tapper (ed.), *Some minorities in the Middle East*, Occasional Paper IX, 78–9 (London: CNMES/SOAS, 1992).
33. See G. Hewitt, ch. 9.
34. Akiner (1986: 42).
35. Henze (1991: 154).

in 1979 and 52.9 per cent in 1989. Here the dominant minority is Russian, which has declined from 39.6 per cent in 1959 to 33.9 per cent in 1979,[36] and has declined further since then to 29.9 per cent in 1989,[37] but is still a powerful factor in local affairs, as General Dudayev in neighbouring Chechenia has found to his cost.[38]

In the republics themselves, the reverse tendency has been demonstrated by the majority populations. In addition to general tendencies towards population homogenization over the past two decades, events since *perestroika* have intensified this trend. This has been particularly the case in Armenia and Azerbaijan. Since the conflict over Nagorno–Karabakh broke out, it is estimated that the 160,841-strong Azerbaijani minority population in Armenia, according to the 1979 census, had been reduced by almost half to 84,860 in 1989 – a 48.2 per cent fall – out of a total population of 3.3 million and has fallen even further since then. The Armenian population in Azerbaijan, set at 475,486 in 1989, out of a total population of 7 million, has been also cut in half after 230,000 fled Baku after the massacres there in 1990.[39]

The Armenian population in Georgia has decreased slowly in absolute terms and in relative terms in recent years, from 443,000 (11 per cent of the total population of 2.6 million) in 1959 to 448,000 (9 per cent of the total) in 1979 and to 436,615 (8 per cent of the total 5.396 million population) in 1989. The Russian population of Georgia, incidentally, has also shown a steady decrease in recent years, from 408,000 (10.1 per cent of the total) in 1959 to 397,000 (7.4 per cent of the total) in 1979 and has declined further since then to 336,645 in 1989.[40] Indeed, as in the case of Azerbaijan but for different reasons and at a much slower speed, the growing homogenization of the population in Georgia, as a *Georgian* national population is also largely due to out-migration.

In short, although the majority of the three republics can certainly claim sufficient cultural and ethnic homogeneity to create nation-states, they are still left with serious problems of minority representation in the form of subnationalities. In the case of Armenia, there is no pre-existing administrative entity that can articulate this factor. Given the fact that Armenians form over 95 per cent of the population (96.1 per cent in 1979 and 95.1 per cent in 1989)[41] and have a very long tradition of national identity, there is little likelihood that subnational protests will endanger the legitimacy or the operation of an Armenian government.

---

36. Akiner (1986: 185).
37. Henze (1991: 164).
38. *Eastern European Newsletter* VI(10), 2, 1992.
39. Walker (1991: 67–8); Henze (1991: 150).
40. Henze (1991: 151).
41. Ibid.: 149.

However, this is not the case elsewhere. In Azerbaijan, the twin problems of Nagorno–Karabakh, as a compact alien geographical and administrative unit within the Azerbaijani state and of Nakhichevan as an Azerbaijani entity outside it, present major problems for government. These do not in themselves threaten the national legitimacy of the Azerbaijani state or its government, but they do render the government inherently unstable until the irredentist Armenian claims on both regions are somehow resolved. In this connection, the Iranian attempt to mediate a solution has some very interesting implications, particularly since an outright Armenian annexation of Nagorno–Karabakh, at least, will set a very dangerous precedent for the region and will seriously threaten the principle of *uti possidetis* (see p. 6) as a viable instrument of state succession in the Caucasus.

Yet, even though both these autonomous regions are discrete, geographically compact and culturally/ethnically homogeneous, they are hardly viable as separate state entities – with populations of 162,000 in 1979 and 189,000 in 1989 (Nagorno–Karabakh), and 240,000 in 1979, 262,000 in 1984 and 294,000 in 1989 (Nakhichevan).[42] The same is true of the two enclaves in Georgia: South Ossetia had a total population of only 97,988 in 1979 and of 98,527 in 1989,[43] whereas Abkhazia had a total population of 486,082 and 524,161 in the same years respectively.[44] If North Ossetia – really part of the Russian Federation –is amalgamated with that of South Ossetia, Ossetia's population in 1979 would have risen by 592,002 to 689,990 and by 632,428 to 730,955 in 1989.[45] Such populations are hardly viable for separate states, particularly given the problems of infrastructural dependence on surrounding states and, in the cases of Nakhichevan, Ossetia and Nagorno–Karabakh, of landlockedness. In any case, as far as two of these entities are concerned, there is insufficient ethnic homogeneity for them to survive as effective state units based on the assumptions of the nation-state.

The Russian Federation

These problems of ethnic or cultural homogeneity are even more marked in the cases of the potentially secessionist entities in southern Russia. In Chechenia, for example, the Chechen population is only just a majority, at 52.9 per cent of the total in 1979 and 57.8 per cent of the total in 1989, although it had been rising throughout the previous two decades from a low of 34.3 per cent in 1959, whereas the Russian population had declined from 49 per cent to 21 per cent of the total during the same period.[46] The

---

42. Akiner (1986: 111), Henze (1991: 154–5).
43. Akiner (1986: 186), Henze (1991: 154).
44. Akiner (1986: 221), Henze (1991: 153).
45. Henze (1991: 164).

major reasons for this were the influx of Russians after the Second World War, which increased the Russian population 35 times to 348,343 (or 49 per cent of the total) in 1959[47] and the deportation of between 400,000 and 450,000 Chechens and 100,000 to 150,000 Ingush immediately after the Second World War, on the grounds that they had collaborated with the Nazis. The Karachai and Balkars suffered a similar fate in the late 1940s, with 85,000 Karachai and 45,000 Balkars[48] – losses of 30 per cent and 26.5 per cent of their total populations respectively between 1939 and 1959.[49]

In Karachai–Cherkessk, the Russian population is the dominant element, at 45.1 per cent of the 1979 total of 367,364 and 44.1 per cent of the 1989 total of 414,970.[50] Karachais were only 29.7 per cent of the total in 1979 and 31.0 per cent of the total in 1989, compared with 81.3 per cent of the total in 1926. No other ethnic group constituted more than 9 per cent of the total population. In the Kabardino–Balkar autonomous republic, Kabardians and Balkars, it is true, formed 55 per cent of the 667,000-strong population in 1979 and 59 per cent of the 754,000-strong population in 1989, but this is far too small for a viable state – a problem, indeed, that also faces Karachai–Cherkessk, in addition to the implications of its dominant Russian minority. Only Chechenia, with a population of 1,155,805 in 1979 and 1,270,429 in 1989,[51] has a viable population base for independence. However, even if this is achieved, there is no ethnic homogeneity to legitimize a nationalist government generally throughout the region.

The most depressing case of all, however, is Daghestan, with 31 different ethnic groups, of which only the so-called Daghestinians – themselves a combination of 13 smaller groups – represented a significant group at 25.7 per cent of the total population of 1.7 million in 1979[52] and 27.5 per cent of the total population of 1.8 million in 1989.[53] Quite apart from the difficulties of infrastructure (the Daghestan region is very mountainous and has always been very difficult to subdue and administer), this bewilderingly complex population pattern and ethnic composition renders irrelevant any idea of an independent state based on the concepts of the nation-state. As a result, there is a danger that public order there could degenerate into a welter of clan feuds over land issues and administrative control.[54]

46. Akiner (1986: 42–3).
47. Ibid.: 176.
48. A. Bennigsen & M. Broxup, *The Islamic threat to the Soviet state*, 32–3 (London: Croom Helm, 1983).
49. Akiner (1986: 204, 228).
50. Henze (1991: 165).
51. Ibid.: 160.
52. Akiner (1986: 126–7).
53. Henze (1991: 161).
54. *Eastern European Newsletter* VI(10), 4, 1992.

The future

The administrative and ethnic complexity of Transcaucasia and the northern Caucasus is largely a result of the pattern of administrative organization foisted on these regions by the central government of the USSR. As has been said of Central Asia, but is equally true of the Caucasus, "Stalin drew the map of Soviet Central Asia not with an eye to consolidating natural regions, but rather for the purpose of reducing the prospects for regional unity".[55] Of course, Stalin saw himself as the great Marxist theoretician of nationalism, as a result of his work at Lenin's behest on *Marxism and the national question* in 1913. Despite a degree of apparent tolerance for nationalist movements – he recognized territorially based, culturally defined national communities – Stalin basically considered them a potential threat to the interests of the proletariat, as they would cut across class lines.[56] Although Lenin originally approved Stalin's ideas, he eventually opposed their application in practice. He particularly objected to Stalin's reaction to the Caucasian Social Democrats' attempt to persuade him that national cultural autonomy would not threaten proletarian interests and over the way in which Stalin, as Commissar for Nationalities, permitted Ordzhonikidze to force Georgia into the Transcaucasian Federation with Armenia and Azerbaijan.[57]

Lenin's premature death enabled Stalin to enforce centralizing policies on the Caucasus that destroyed all vestiges of nationalist expression, except at the most formalistic level. This policy was rammed home during the purges, in which the governments of 30 republics were eliminated for the crime of "nationalist deviation", and by the Greater Russian nationalism that accompanied the Soviet recovery during the Second World War and led to the mass expulsions of several Caucasian peoples, led by the Chechens during and after the conflict.[58] Stalin's successors effectively maintained his centralizing policies, replacing coercion by other techniques (such as economic development) in the struggle to counter local nationalisms. Nonetheless, these sentiments have persisted and have become the dominant mode of political expression in the post-Soviet era.

At the same time, nationalist sympathies have become enmeshed with other tendencies, including ethnic confrontation and tribalism, territorial disputes and Islam. This complex series of responses to the collapse of the centralizing power of the old USSR – which Russia is unable and, appar-

---

55. M. B. Olcott, "Central Asia's post-empire politics", *Orbis*, 256, 1992.
56. J. V. Stalin, "Marxism and the national question." *Works* vol II, 300–381. (Moscow: Foreign Languages Publishing House, 1953),
57. R. Munck, *The difficult dialogue: Marxism and nationalism*, 76–85 (London: Zed Press, 1986).
58. Munck (1986: 126–7).

ently, unwilling to take over – further vitiates the concept of a nation-state as the solution to the problem of creating new political structures that are stable, legitimate and, it is to be hoped, democratic. Indeed, the problem of population size and ethnic dispersion and interpenetration add to these more immediate problems. Nonetheless, perhaps some general principles can be proposed here.

It is clear that, in Transcaucasia, state structures already exist that are legitimized by nations that inhabit them. Once the interstate conflicts between Armenia and Azerbaijan are resolved – and this may take a very long time – there is certainly the possibility that such embryonic nation-states will evolve into stable democratic structures, despite the manifold economic and environmental problems they face. There is also the threat of demands for border revision from Moscow, although it is still unclear how significant a threat this really is. The nation-state, incidentally, is not the only model available to these new states, particularly in the case of Azerbaijan. In this case there is, in theory, the Islamist alternative as a model for state organization – although, unlike Tajikistan, Islamist parties in Azerbaijan are still weak. Nonetheless, Islam survived the Soviet experience, particularly through the subterranean manifestations of Sufi orders, such as the Naqshbandi and the Qadiriya orders.[59] It now has the examples of Iran and Afghanistan to spur it into political action, should other political prescriptions fail.

However, all three states face major problems of integrating minority groups into the structure of the nation-state, if that is the model they choose, as seems likely. Minorities are a major problem for such institutions, for their very presence is a contradiction of the innate idea of the nation-state itself. No provision is made for ethnic minority rights and interests in the UN charter – although unsuccessful attempts had been made to deal with the problem in its precursor, the Covenant of the League of Nations. Nor are there any principles in international law that can provide an effective guide as to how their rights can be protected.[60] Indeed, the minority issue is, after all, still a major problem for the supposedly stable states of western Europe, where attempts are being made currently to create a legal framework to protect minority rights. Even the Islamic state offers little hope for minorities, outside the old Ottoman concept of the *millet* and the older Islamic concept of the *dhimmi*.

The only possibility of effectively dealing with this problem in the independent republics will be through some version of internal autonomy and a federal-type relationship between the autonomous administration pro-

---

59. A. Bennigsen & S. Enders Wimbush, *Mystics and commissars: Sufism in the Soviet Union*, 70–5 (London: Hurst, 1985).
60. P. Thornberry, "Self-determination, minorities and human rights: a review of international instruments", *International and Comparative Law Quarterly* 38, 874–7, 1989.

vided for such minorities and central government. However, for that to work successfully, stability at the nation-state level is essential and a democratic system of government should be a desirable guarantor of minority rights. Yet, even then, secessionist problems could arise, particularly over Abkhazia, South Ossetia and Nagorno–Karabakh. Georgia is most reluctant to allow secession in the cases of Abkhazia and South Ossetia. Their problems, therefore, are likely to be solved through population transfer and violence. Abkhazia might well be prepared to join a north Caucasian federation, once it gets off the ground. South Ossetia, which rejects the federal ideal whereas Georgia objects to its continued autonomous existence, may only solve its problems by transfer of its population to North Ossetia under Russian protection. An effective solution to these problems, however, may be long delayed, particularly if hostilities and annexations by force of arms continue in situations such as Nagorno–Karabakh or South Ossetia.

The real problem for the future lies in the northern Caucasus. The ethnic complexity and discontinuity of the region, allied to the disastrous consequences of Russification and centralization over the past 70 years, together with the persistence of patron–client systems based both on the old Communist Party structures and informal social structures, makes any type of traditional nationalist solution impossible. On top of this, the demographic and geographical size of the units concerned, and their economic dependence on the Russian Federation, guarantees that any attempt in the direction of national independence will ultimately fail.

The only viable political structure for the future must be based on some federal model, whether in geographic or demographic terms. In effect, the old Soviet system of granting everyone citizenship in the USSR and a Union republic, while also according them a nationality,[61] will have to be transferred to the new collectivity, whatever it may be, and its legal significance will have to be inverted. In a geographically based federation, citizenship will become primarily the prerogative of the substate entity – which will probably have to be based on the administrative divisions that already exist – while each such entity will have to associate itself within a federal system inside the northern Caucasus. In a demographically based system, substate entities would not exist as separate geographical administrative units; instead, members of different ethnicities would operate as separate political entities, each of equal constitutional weight within the federation, whatever their numerical size, in a system of "active citizenship". This is, in effect, a variant of the nationalist theories first put forward by Otto Bauer and the Austro-Marxists, in which a culturally defined nationalist community – a *gemeinschaft* – would be defined as a politically autonomous administrative unit – thus becoming a *gesellschaft* – within the state,

61. Akiner (1986: 18–19).

despite the community's lack of territorial continuity.[62] It remains to be seen whether the proposed Federation of Mountain Peoples of the Caucasus provides the basis for a permanent arrangement on one or other of the variants outlined here.

Given the lack of ethnic homogeneity throughout the region, nationality will have to be discarded in favour of such citizenship and the rights and duties it offers. However, within such geographical administrative entities there will be major issues to be addressed of minority/majority interests and democratic control. This would not apply, of course, to a demographically defined federal system. In any case, the federation will still have to address the crucial issue of what its political and economic relationship with the Russian Federation will be. Indeed, in the end, despite the profound antagonisms that still exist towards Russia, the Russian Federation may still offer the only realistic framework for economic development.

Yet the tangled web of ethnicity is so complex that it is difficult to see how this mass of nations, subnations and ethnic groups could cut through the Gordian knot created by demography, geography and ethnicity to clear a path to a viable political future. Perhaps the Russian embrace cannot and should not be avoided. However, there are other alternatives, particularly for Daghestan and Chechenia, where *sufism* has had a long tradition and played a part in anti-Soviet resistance as late as the 1921–5 Daghestan–Chechenian revolt.[63] Indeed, Islam might provide a better basis for federation than any other ideological mobilizer in those regions of the Transcaucasus and north Caucasia in which it predominates – although, of course, it would heighten tensions with the majority populations of non-Muslims elsewhere in the region. However, as frustration grows at the lack of any viable solution, Islam may still come to be seen as an attractive alternative – and that will present Moscow with an old problem in a new guise.

62. O. Bauer, *Die Nationalitaetenfrage und die Sozialdemokratie*, 2nd edn (Vienna: Volksbuch-handlung, 1924)
63. Bennigsen & Wimbush (1985: 25).

CHAPTER TWO

Russia and Transcaucasia

MARGOT LIGHT

When the USSR disintegrated in December 1991, many Russians rejoiced. They celebrated the end of a Soviet empire which had, they believed, exploited Russia rather more than it had ill used other parts of the country and in which Russians had suffered disproportionately under Stalinism. Few Russians identified themselves with the pre-revolutionary Tsarist empire and none saw Russia as the exploiter of the other peoples within that empire. On the contrary, many of them nurtured the belief that Russian imperialism had been a civilizing force that had enriched the peoples who had been incorporated into the Russian empire.

Few of the other nationalities within the USSR shared their perceptions. Most non-Russians celebrated the simultaneous destruction of two empires: the Soviet and the Russian. It was not only that they had been colonized by Russia well before the revolution in October 1917, nor that the brief independence that some of them had enjoyed after the revolution ended when the Union of Soviet Socialist Republics was established in 1922.[1] It was also that they did not believe that the Soviet system had treated Russians worse than other nationalities. In the minds of non-Russians, Russia had become associated with Soviet power and with their own lack of freedom. The predominance of Russians in the government of the USSR and in the apparatus of the Communist Party of the Soviet Union (CPSU), the privileged status and relative affluence of Russians living in other republics, as well as the fact that mastery of the Russian language was obligatory for anyone with ambition seemed to them irrefutable evidence that Soviet power was essentially Russian.[2] For many non-Russians, therefore, the declarations of sovereignty and independence before and

---

1. In the case of the Baltic states and Moldova independence lasted until the Molotov–Ribbentrop pact was concluded in 1939.

2. A few non-Russians did, of course, reach positions of authority in the Soviet state. Of the Transcaucasians who achieved prominence, the most notorious were Joseph Stalin and Lavrenti Beria, both Georgians. Anastas Mikoyan, an Armenian, was president of the Soviet Union during the Khrushchev period and Geidar Aliev, currently President of Azerbaijan, was a member of the Politburo during Brezhnev's later years. But they were exceptions; Russians and other Slavs heavily outweighed other nationalities in the upper echelons of both state and party.

after the abortive coup in August 1991 represented liberation both from the USSR and from Russia.

Underlying Russian attitudes to the other successor states of the Soviet Union there is, therefore, a set of perceptions vastly different from the views of the majority of the people who live in those states. Although this does not entirely explain Russian relations with "the near abroad"[3] in general, and with Transcaucasia in particular, it is an essential ingredient to understanding them.

An equally important factor affecting Russian policy towards Transcaucasia is the impact events there have on Russian security. To some extent, security fears are also a question of perception, since they may arise from the memory of past threats. But there is little doubt that the most serious *external* threat facing Russia at present is the danger that conflict on its periphery will spill over into, and threaten the fragile integrity of, the Russian Federation (RF), or that Russia will be drawn into a wider war because of those conflicts.

Since both the perceptions and the security fears underlying Russian policy towards Transcaucasia are rooted in history, it is as well to begin an account of Russian–Transcaucasian relations by briefly highlighting relevant aspects of their past relations. Therefore, the first section of this chapter offers an historical overview of Russian and Soviet policy in Transcaucasia up to the period between 1985 and 1991, when nationalism became the most important, and perhaps least expected, obstacle to *perestroika* and, in the end, to the survival of the USSR. The second and third sections of the chapter explore in more detail, first, the origins of Russian perceptions of Transcaucasia and, secondly, the perceived threats to Russian security that emanate from Transcaucasia. The concluding section outlines the main thrust of Russian policy towards Transcaucasia since all four states became independent.

Historical overview

Russian penetration of Transcaucasia in the eighteenth century occurred as much by invitation as by conquest. In the 16th and 17th centuries Transcaucasia had been divided and passed backwards and forwards between the Persian and Ottoman empires. Since Russia was seen as the protector of eastern Christians against the Muslim empires, it was relatively simple to extend Russian influence into the Christian areas of Georgia and Armenia. Although the first major expedition into Transcaucasia in 1723 was for the purposes of conquest, King Erek'le of Georgia voluntarily placed his

---

3. The term coined by Russian politicians and political scientists to distinguish the former republics of the USSR from other foreign countries.

kingdom under Russian protection in 1783 to save it from Turkish conquest. His successor decided that Georgia would be safer if it was incorporated in the Russian empire, and in 1801 Alexander I annexed the country.[4]

In the first half of the nineteenth century, Russia gradually acquired control of northern Azerbaijan and eastern Armenia, whereas southern Azerbaijan remained in the Persian and western Armenia in the Ottoman empires. However, the protection Russia promised Transcaucasia was difficult to exercise, since Russia "had yet to overcome the non-Christian mountaineers of the Caucasus proper",[5] who were extremely hostile. Many of the mountain peoples were finally subdued during the early decades of the nineteenth century, in a process so violent that in the north Caucasus Russia won bitter enemies rather than reliable subjects.[6] However, Russian troops could not conquer Circassia or Daghestan even though land was confiscated and given to Russian Cossack settlers. In the 1830s and 1840s, fighting spread from Daghestan into Chechnya, and resistance continued under the legendary leadership of Shamil until 1864, when the entire north Caucasus finally came under firm Russian control. In 1878 Turkey ceded Batumi to Russia and the Russian empire in Transcaucasia was complete.[7]

Some of the "non-Christian mountaineers" of the north Caucasus are now located in the Russian Federation, whereas others live in Georgia. Many of them are involved in local conflicts and this complicates Russian policy in Transcaucasia. But the fact that Russia's first incursions into Transcaucasia were to defend the Christian peoples of the area contributes to the perception that many Russians have of the essentially benevolent nature of Russian imperialism and of Russia's civilizing influence on non-Christians. Similarly, Russian influence in Transcaucasia led to continual wars against Turkey and Persia, and the interest presently shown in the area by Turkey and Iran revives historical memories of those conflicts, just as the problems in the north Caucasus recall memories of the difficulties Russia had in pacifying the area in earlier times.

Although there were intermittent efforts to Russify the empire during the nineteenth century, it was only in the 1890s that it became official pol-

---

4. M. B. Broxup (ed.), *The north Caucasus barrier: the Russian advance towards the Muslim world* (London: Hurst, 1992).
5. V. O. Kluchevsky, *A history of Russia*, vol. V, 259. Translated by C. J. Hogarth (London: Dent, 1931).
6. H. Seton-Watson, *The Russian empire, 1801–1917*, 183 (Oxford: Oxford University Press, 1967).
7. According to Seton-Watson the Caucasus represented to Russia what the Indian frontier was to the British army in the nineteenth century. In the Russian case, the Caucasus inspired some of the greatest nineteenth-century literature. Broxup points out that the effect of the Caucasian wars on Russian culture and folklore has been more profound than that of the Napoleonic wars. See Seton-Watson (1967: 293) and Broxup (1992: 14).

icy in the Caucasus. However, Russian cultural imperialism had remarkably little effect. The Armenian or Georgian churches were not incorporated into Russian orthodoxy, for example, nor were the Muslims of Azerbaijan and the north Caucasus converted to Christianity. What is relevant to the present conflicts in the former Soviet Union, however, is the fact that the Russian authorities, using divide and rule tactics, encouraged Azerbaijanis to attack Armenians in towns where both lived.[8] Nonetheless, there was remarkably little resentment of Russian imperialism in Armenia. In fact, whereas young Armenians wanted autonomy for Armenia, the older generation were far more worried about the fate of the Armenians in the Ottoman empire than they were about Russia, and with good reason, since the mass killings of Armenians by Turks, which had begun in the 1890s, reached genocidal proportions in 1915.[9]

Although there was little national separatism in Transcaucasia, there was considerable sympathy for revolutionary ideas.[10] The Russian Social Democratic Party enjoyed great support in Georgia in 1905,[11] for example, and an All-Russian Muslim League was created that year. Georgian nationalism increased as a result of the repression of the 1905 revolution, but the ethnic frontiers between Georgians, Armenians and Azerbaijanis were ill defined. In fact, there were more Armenians than Georgians in Tbilisi, the capital of Georgia, and more Armenians in Azerbaijan and Georgia than in Armenia itself.[12] As a result, national animosities were more frequently directed against rival national groups than against Russians. With the exception of the Bolsheviks, the revolutionary parties did not give high priority to the problems of non-Russian nationalities. Bolshevik policy, designed by Stalin under Lenin's instruction, was to support the right of self-determination for all nations. However, once the Bolshevik Party attained political power it modified this policy, reluctant, like its Tsarist predecessor, to give up any land that belonged to the empire.[13]

Independent states of Georgia (under a Menshevik government), Armenia and Azerbaijan were established after the 1917 revolution. However, by the end of 1920 there had been a successful communist uprising

8. Seton-Watson (1967: 500–1).
9. J. Aves, *Post-Soviet Transcaucasia* [Post-Soviet Business Forum 5] (London: Royal Institute of International Affairs, 1993).
10. Seton Watson (1967: 417).
11. Most of the 18 Social Democrats elected to the first *Duma* in 1906 came from Georgia. They belonged to the Menshevik wing of the party. Seton-Watson (1967: 620).
12. E. H. Carr, *The Bolshevik revolution, 1917–23*, vol. I, 344 (Harmondsworth: Penguin, 1966).
13. R. Pipes, *Russia under the old regime*, 79 (Harmondsworth: Penguin, 1977). Pipes maintains that a "patrimonial system of government", in which sovereignty is confused with ownership, has been a distinctive feature of Russia since the fifteenth century (pp. 22–4). He believes that this explains "the tenacity with which Russian governments, whatever their professed ideology, have held on to every square inch of land that has ever belonged to any of them" (p. 79).

in Azerbaijan, and Armenia had been saved by Soviet Russia from being taken over by Turkey, but at the expense of conceding territory to Turkey and having an autonomous Azerbaijani enclave, Nakhichevan, geographically within Armenia but under the jurisdiction of Azerbaijan. Nagorno–Karabakh was initially an autonomous area united to Armenia, but in 1923 it was transferred to Azerbaijan despite the fact that its population was predominantly Armenian. In 1921 the Menshevik government in Georgia was forcibly removed and Georgia, too, fell to the Bolsheviks. Adzharia and Abkhazia became autonomous republics, whereas South Ossetia was turned into an autonomous region within Georgia. The north Caucasus, divided into a variety of autonomous republics and regions, was incorporated into the Russian Soviet Federative Socialist Republic (RSFSR).

There was considerable resentment of the union of the three republics into a Transcaucasian federal republic in 1922. The new federation was immediately incorporated into the Union of Soviet Socialist Republics.[14] The constitution of the USSR was, in substance, an enlarged version of the constitution that had been operating in Russia since 1918. But the Council of Nationalities, in which nations (irrespective of size or self-consciousness of national identity) were represented rather than constituent states, was established as a second chamber. Paradoxically, this, and other aspects of the policy of *korenizatsiya* – the division of the country into administrative areas based on nationality, the training of national cadres for local government, and the encouragement of national cultures – did more to foster nationalism than previous centuries of Russian imperialism had done. Indeed, it can be argued that, although Soviet rule did little to satisfy the aspirations of established nations, it "created" nations in cases where there had previously been little more than a sense of clan identity. As one Western specialist puts it:

Whatever the intentions and predictions of self-styled Marxist internationalist officials and theorists, the actual history of most of the major Soviet peoples has been one of greater consolidation of ethnic nations, heightened national consciousness, and increased capacity to act in defense of their perceived national interests.[15]

The repercussions in the post-Soviet period are demands by a number

---

14. The undue force used by the Bolsheviks in Georgia made Lenin comprehend Stalin's faults. He regretted Bolshevik behaviour in Georgia until the end of his life, and objected to the imposition of the Transcaucasian federal republic. See Carr (1966: 400). Under the 1936 constitution, the Transcaucasian federal republic was dissolved, and Armenia, Azerbaijan and Georgia became separate republics within the USSR.

15. R. Suny, "State, civil society and ethnic cultural consolidation in the USSR: roots of the national question". In *The Soviet system in crisis: a reader of Western and Soviet views*, A. Dallin & G. W. Lapidus (eds), 414–29 (Boulder, Colorado: Westview, 1991).

of fictitiously autonomous republics for full sovereignty and independence from the state in which they are located. But even within the three large nations in Transcaucasia, national identity was strengthened under Soviet rule with the encouragement of cultural development, the introduction of mass education and media in the local languages, and the establishment of governments and legislatures in the three capitals.[16]

In one of the more sinister chapters of Soviet history, Stalin decided during the Second World War that various national groups had co-operated with the German occupation forces. He retaliated by deporting whole peoples to Central Asia. At the end of 1943 the Karachai autonomous area disappeared from the map when the Karachai were deported from the north Caucasus. In early 1944 the Chechens and Ingushi were removed and their autonomous republic was abolished, while the Kabardino–Balkar autonomous republic became the Kabardin autonomous republic when the Balkars were deported. In November 1944, the Meskhetians were removed from Georgia. Khrushchev condemned the deportations in his secret speech at the 20th Party Congress in 1956 and began to rehabilitate the deported peoples. Most of the autonomous areas were re-established but there were some changes. The Karachai, for example, were now united with the Cherkess in an autonomous republic and, although Chechen–Ingushetia was re-established, some of its former territory remained in Ossetia. Although many deportees returned home (only to find that in their absence, people from other parts of the Soviet Union had been settled there), the Meskhetians remained in Uzbekistan.[17] Many of the national conflicts that have erupted since *perestroika* began are the result of these deportations and the territorial changes that followed them.

Given this contradictory history of fostering nationalism and of repression, reformist Soviet officials should, perhaps, have been less surprised when the introduction of *perestroika* in 1985 unleashed wave after wave of nationalism. In fact, by legitimizing criticism, permitting freedom of expression and, above all, exposing previously suppressed aspects of Soviet history, *glasnost* made it almost inevitable that national grievances would be aired. Democratization and the emergence of a more pluralist, less centralized political system enabled the establishment of nationalist movements that soon challenged local communist authorities. The expression of nationalist sentiments soon became *de rigueur* for any political group or leader wishing to achieve popular legitimacy. However, it was the conflict over Nagorno–Karabakh that began to unravel the USSR. It was a watershed in Soviet politics.

---

16. Aves (1993: 2–9).
17. The Crimean Tartars and Volga Germans, also deported during the war, like the Meskhetian Turks, did not receive the right to return home or to recover their confiscated property until much later.

In the USSR, central control of the republics had always been assured not only by the threat of coercion and the centralized, hierarchical structure of the CPSU but also through the co-optation of local elites. Although this system led to the creation of local fiefdoms and, as *glasnost* revealed, enormous corruption, it ensured that local leaders obediently adhered to policies formulated in Moscow and, therefore, did not come into conflict with one another.[18] However, with regard to the future of Nagorno–Karabakh the Armenian political leadership advocated its transfer to Armenia in 1988, whereas the Azerbaijani leadership supported its retention within Azerbaijan. This was the first time that the CPSU had divided along national lines.[19]

At the same time, nationalist movements in the Baltic republics began demanding more autonomy, and cultural demands were voiced in Moldavia and Byelorussia. A year later, when conflict began between Georgia and Abkhazia, Georgians began to call for independence from the USSR. The economic failures of *perestroika* aggravated national discontent. In some republics, economic grievances turned into communal violence; in most the conviction grew that independence from the Soviet Union would improve economic wellbeing. Mikhail Gorbachev tried to renegotiate relations between the centre and the republics and in 1990 and 1991 he struggled to find an acceptable decentralized federal formula. In July 1991 it looked as if he had succeeded. However, his reactionary opponents were appalled by his plans and timed their coup to prevent the signing of the new treaty. By the time they had been defeated most of the 15 republics had declared their sovereignty and independence.

It was not only the non-Russian republics that demanded independence, however. In their struggle against Gorbachev and the central Soviet authorities in 1991, Boris Yeltsin and his followers claimed the sovereignty of the RSFSR. Moreover, they made common cause with the nationalists in other republics, and supported their moves towards independence. In January 1991, for example, immediately after Soviet troops had used force against Lithuanian separatists, Yeltsin recognized the right of the Baltic republics to independence. He also supported the Georgians when they rejected Gorbachev's new federal treaty in March 1991.

For all their dislike of the central Soviet government and their sympathy for the national aspirations of the Balts and the Georgians, however, most Russians found it difficult to conceive of Russia without an empire. Russian nationalism had become quite widespread and Yeltsin found it

---

18. S. White, A. Pravda, Z. Gitelman (eds), *Developments in Soviet and post-Soviet politics*, 2nd edn, 137 (London: Macmillan, 1992).
19. G. Lapidus, "Gorbachev's nationalities problem". In *The Soviet system in crisis: a reader of Western and Soviet views*, A. Dallin & G. W. Lapidus (eds), 435 (Boulder, Colorado: Westview, 1991).

convenient to adopt some of the positions of the Russian nationalist cause. In part an attempt to attract the nationalist vote in the presidential elections, it was also a useful weapon against Gorbachev. For example, when Yeltsin declared that Russia would never give up Kaliningrad or the Kurile Islands, he seemed to imply that Gorbachev might barter them away.[20] But this raised the question of whether Russia would part with other territories that had previously been part of the Russian empire.

The separation of Russia and Ukraine, for example, seemed particularly inconceivable to Russians. In the wake of the coup in August 1991, the Ukrainian government declared Ukraine's sovereignty and independence. Yeltsin's response was to threaten that Russia would, if necessary, readjust its borders with republics that withdrew from the Union. This statement immediately fuelled fears in the non-Russian republics of a resurgent Russian imperialism. Russians, on the other hand, seemed unaware of these fears or of the significance of Yeltsin's celebration of the rebirth of "Mother Russia".[21] They found it difficult to understand why non-Russians associated Russia with Soviet power, they were convinced that Russian economic wellbeing had been sacrificed to subsidize the other less well developed republics and they rejected the idea that modern Russians could be held responsible for the imperial behaviour of the Russian Tsars.

This is the historical background to Russia's relations with Transcaucasia. Let us turn now to its impact on the perceptions that influence Russian policy.

Russian perceptions of Transcaucasia

Two major influences on Russian perceptions of Transcaucasia and the other former Soviet republics will be considered here: the problem of the identity of Russia, and the effect of Soviet historiography about the Russian empire. Although the former is a subject frequently discussed by the Russian intelligentsia, few Russians would admit to being influenced by Soviet historiography. Yet the distinctions drawn by Russians, between the negative effects of colonialism elsewhere and the beneficial consequences of Russian imperialism, indicate that certain myths fostered by Soviet historians have been internalized. Most Russians believe, for example, that

---

20. Kaliningrad and the Kurile islands were both gained by the Soviet Union at the end of the Second World War. Although Kaliningrad was not a disputed territory, the argument over the Kuriles had long prevented Russo–Japanese rapprochement. Yeltsin defended Russian possession of the Kurile islands on the eve of Gorbachev's departure for Tokyo, when it was strongly rumoured that the islands would be returned to Japan in return for economic assistance.
21. For reports of Yeltsin's announcements and their effects, see *The Guardian*, 29 August 1991.

the peoples of the Russian empire coexisted in friendship and mutual respect, that most annexations took place with consent, that there was general acceptance of Russia's leadership, and that non-Russians benefited from their association with Russians.[22]

As far as Russia's identity problem is concerned, its source lies in the historical origins of the Russian state. It is not only that the history of Russia began not in Muscovy, but in Kiev Rus' (which makes the independence of Ukraine particularly painful). It is also that, unlike other empires, the Russian empire and the Russian state developed simultaneously. The great Russian historian, V. O. Kluchevsky, maintained that:

> Russia's history, throughout, is the history of a country undergoing colonization, and having the area of that colonization and the extension of its state keep pace with one another . . . Thus, in migration, in colonization, we see our history's fundamental factor. With it every other factor in that history has been more or less bound up.[23]

This means that the identity of Russia, that is, of Russian statehood, has always been closely associated with the idea and the fact of empire. There has never been a Russian nation-state, and nor is there one now, of course, since the Russian Federation (RF) is a multinational state invented in 1922, some argue, to legitimize the continuation of the Russian empire within the newly formed USSR.[24] The Tsarist statesman, Sergei Witte, pointed out that "ever since the time of Peter the Great and Catherine the Great there has been no such thing as Russia; only a Russian empire".[25] Witte, however, considered "Little Russians" (Ukrainians) and "White Russians" (Belorussians) to be part of Russia, and not separate members of the empire.

Given this association of statehood with empire, it is not surprising that many Russians find it difficult to accept that some areas are no longer part of Russia. A new identity and a new role has to be forged for Russia and there is uncertainty and disagreement about what this should be. As Aleksandr Tsipko, a liberal political philosopher, put it, "without today's

22. One political scientist, for example, maintains that the purpose of building and strengthening the Russian empire "was not to effect economic expansion not to plunder the peoples of the territories incorporated into Russia, as was the case with British, French, Spanish and Portuguese colonisation, but to meet an incontestable necessity . . . [which] lay in unifying the state, organising it and ensuring its security". E. Pozdnyakov, "Russia is a great power", *International Affairs* (January), 3–13, at p. 7, 1993.

23. Kluchevsky (1931: 209).

24. V. Tolz & E. Teague, "Russian intellectuals adjust to loss of empire", *Radio Free Europe/ Radio Liberty Research Report*, 21 February 1992, 4–8. After the break of the USSR, the name of the RSFSR was changed to the Russian Federation.

25. Cited in Maksudov & Taubman (1991: 26).

Ukraine, there can be no Russia in the old, real sense of the word".[26] Although the same sense of inseparability might not pertain to Transcaucasia, the Caucasus is an integral and important component of Russian culture and literature, apart from being the area in which millions of Russians have always spent their holidays. Its loss has contributed to the perception that "the old real sense" of Russia no longer exists.

The problem of forging a new post-imperial identity is not just a question of finding out what it now means to be Russian, however, or of defining a new relationship between Russia and the other successor states. There is also a dilemma about Russia's role in the world. As far as international status is concerned, Russia is smaller now than it has been for many centuries, except, perhaps, for a brief period during the Civil War from 1918–20. It is still a vast country, of course, but without the Soviet Union it is not a superpower. Indeed, economic collapse and political paralysis make it doubtful that it can even be considered a great power at present, although Russian politicians and political commentators of all hues insist that it is.[27] And although it was the Soviet Union and not Russia that was a superpower, the loss of superpower status is experienced by many Russians as a national humiliation.[28] As one Russian writer expressed it, "We are no longer one-sixth of the earth's surface . . . But we continue to carry within ourselves one-sixth of the globe . . . It is a scale we have become accustomed to".[29]

Finally, the loss of empire raises the question whether Russia is part of Europe, or whether it has been turned into an Asian or Eurasian power. Geographically, it is certainly further from Europe now than it has been for 300 years. In other words, the place where the Russian state originated is no longer in Russia, Russia's status in the international system has diminished with the collapse of the empire and, without the empire, it is debatable whether Russia is a European state. Russian perceptions of Transcaucasia are affected by the extent to which the "loss" of the area has contributed to a diminution of Russia's status. However, the question of Russia's identity and boundaries are important not only because they affect Russian perceptions of the near abroad. As we will see, they also matter in terms of how Russia defines its national interests and how it conceives its security.

The second major influence on Russian perceptions of Transcaucasia and the other successor states is the effect of Soviet historiography and the

---

26. Cited in Tolz & Teague (1992: 7).
27. See, for example, Konstantin Pleshakov, "Russia's mission: the third epoch", *International Affairs* (January), 17–26, 1993, or E. Pozdnyakov, "Russia is a great power", *International Affairs* (January), 3–13, 1993.
28. V. Tolz, "The burden of the imperial legacy", RFE/RL *Research Report*, 14 May 1993, 41–6.
29. S. Razgonov, *Moskovskie Novosti* 45, 1991; cited in I. Bremmer & R. Taras, *Nations and politics in the Soviet successor states*, 68 (Cambridge: Cambridge University Press, 1993).

way it depicted Russian imperialism and relations between the nations that constituted the empire.

In the 1920s there were competing views about Russian history, but historians were generally critical of Russian imperialism and its effects on non-Russian peoples. Although a single authorized version of history began to emerge in the 1930s under the impact of Stalinism, strict control over the writing of history could not be maintained during the war. Patriotism was fostered by adopting a more lenient attitude towards religion, encouraging nationalism (previously considered a retrogressive, "bourgeois" phenomenon) and permitting a limited amount of intellectual pluralism. However, there was a pressing need to promote unity between the various nations making up the Soviet Union to ensure a united stand against Germany. The myth of the "friendship of the peoples" was propagated with the aim of buttressing a superordinate Soviet patriotism that would subsume separate nationalisms.[30]

The intellectual clamp-down that occurred in 1947 (the *Zhdanovshchina*) was intended to eliminate the permissiveness of the war years, including the bourgeois nationalism that had been allowed to flourish. But in the atmosphere of the Cold War, unity against the external enemy remained vital, and the friendship myth was retained as a useful instrument in this endeavour. Historians were instructed to extol Great Russian leadership, to emphasize the progressive nature of Russian colonialism and to affirm the cordiality of the relationship between Russians and non-Russians.[31]

Soviet histories of Russia and the Soviet Union accordingly began to emphasize the longstanding friendship between Russians and non-Russians in the Russian empire, and the help given to non-Russians against foreign enemies. Annexation of territory, according to these histories, was almost always voluntary, occurring because local people wanted to join Russia. The colonization of Siberia was interpreted as the peaceful settlement of undeveloped lands by intrepid Russian pioneers, whereas the Caucasus and Central Asia had been saved from incorporation into the Turkish, Persian or British empires. Historians maintained that incorporation into the Russian empire was a progressive phenomenon, bringing political stability, a higher standard of living through industrialization, the provision of railways, increased trade and improvements in agriculture. Moreover, the non-Russian peoples derived great benefit from contact with Russian culture. Many people obtained a written language for the

---

30. As we have seen, however, Stalin deported the nations whose loyalty he doubted.
31. I have drawn heavily in this section on the excellent study on Soviet historiography by Lowell Tillet, *The great friendship: Soviet historians on the non-Russian nationalities* (Chapel Hill: University of North Carolina Press, 1969) who bases his account on the academic and political debates about the function of historians, as well as on the histories published in the Soviet Union up to 1967.

first time and all gained from exposure to the advanced ideas of Russian revolutionaries. As a result of economic development, the class struggle was strengthened and the subject peoples of the empire embarked on the path that led to the socialist revolution.

Throughout these accounts, the acceptance of Russian leadership by non-Russians is assumed. Moreover, the historical conflicts that existed between non-Russian peoples are ignored or explained as class struggles rather than national or religious conflicts. Thus, non-Russians were allied not only with the Russian people but also with one another.[32] Leaving aside the historical inaccuracies, there are also omissions: the phenomenon of Great Russian chauvinism, for example, which persisted well after the revolution and created a problem about which Lenin was deeply concerned, is completely absent from postwar accounts of Russian imperialism.

As part of this general process of rewriting history, the Russian conquest of the Caucasus was reconstructed: annexation to Russia gave the peoples of the Caucasus security, the opportunity for economic development and for contact with advanced Russian culture and revolutionary thought. Great non-Russian national heroes such as Shamil, who had resisted Russian imperialism (and who had been admired in pre-war histories), were now identified as reactionary and nationalistic.

During the thaw after Stalin's death, and particularly after 1956, some of the historical distortions of Stalinism were exposed and corrected and there was less overt interference by the CPSU in the writing of history. Curiously, however, the portrayal of Russian annexation as progressive and voluntary, and the theme of friendship between Russians and non-Russians, were not modified. Moreover, de-Stalinization did not extend to rehabilitating nationalist leaders or groups that had opposed the Bolsheviks.[33] Similarly, the relations between Russians and non-Russians in the Soviet period continued to be defined as mutually beneficial and invariably amicable. The wartime deportations, for example, were explained as regrettable manifestations of the cult of personality, which did not affect the friendship of peoples. Indeed, the deported people were said to have benefited from the friendship of the people in whose republics they spent their exile.[34]

In the *perestroika* period, historians were once again encouraged to rewrite history, this time to fill in the blank spots and reveal what had really happened. However, they tended to concentrate on the Stalin period although by that time many members of the intelligentsia had access to both Soviet dissident and Western sources, and had long since dismissed the official versions of Soviet history. But even the most diehard support-

---

32. Tillet (1969: 14–17).
33. Suny, in Dallin & Lapidus (1991: 421).
34. Tillet (1969: 315–7).

ers of the old official version of history must have had their belief in the friendship myth shaken when seemingly intractable conflicts flared up between non-Russians after 1986, and when independence was pursued in the Baltic republics and Georgia, even at the possible cost of bringing the whole reform programme to an end. However, neither these conflicts, nor the rewriting of the history of the Soviet period, seem to have affected the view that Russian imperialism was, on balance, benevolent and that the non-Russians willingly accepted the Russians as natural leaders. In the case of the Caucasus, the fact that Russia intervened to defend the eastern Christians serves to support the perception of benevolence and of the essentially civilizing nature of Russian imperialism.

A view of Russian superiority is implicit in this version of Russian history and it is reflected in another of the psychological factors that affect Russian perceptions of Transcaucasia. At a popular level an endemic racism has become quite overt in the past few years and, in relation to Transcaucasia, it manifests itself as a dislike of "southerners", who are accused of manipulating the market and establishing the mafia that is responsible for organized crime in Russia. This aggravates the common perception that Russia was the victim of the other republics, and that Russian wealth was expropriated to subsidize them. According to one political scientist, for example, "while Russia as the *metropole*, declined, her outlying districts developed and grew richer. But today many of them, having become independent not without support from the *metropole*, seem to have forgotten this, for they accuse Russia of having exploited them, and this at a time when the economic, social and demographic decline of the centre is recognised as a fact".[35]

The possibility that even if Russian imperialism saved Transcaucasia from the Islamic empires and brought great economic benefit, it might nevertheless have been deeply resented by the colonized peoples, is not frequently discussed in Russia. As a result, Russians find it very difficult to understand why non-Russians are suspicious of Russia's intentions, or why they tend to interpret the actions of Russian leaders in relation to the near abroad as attempts to reconstitute the Russian empire. It seems self-evident to Russians that events in the other republics, and particularly in Transcaucasia, undermine the security of the Russian Federation and require policies designed to defend Russia. What are the perceived threats to Russian security?

---

35. Pozdnyakov (1993: 7–8).

Security factors

Russian politicians and military personnel have found it extremely difficult to define Russia's national interests, identify potential threats and to extrapolate from these a suitable military doctrine and the security requirements to put it into effect. In part, initial concentration on policy towards the West led to neglect of other aspects of foreign policy. There was also a problem in identifying the enemy once the Cold War had ended and the traditional enemy (the West) had become Russia's main hope for aid and support. But perhaps the most serious stumbling block was the reluctance, particularly on the part of the military, to come to terms with the loss of the empire and to jettison the initial expectation that the Commonwealth of Independent States (CIS) would have combined armed forces. However, throughout 1992 it became increasingly evident that the most immediate dangers facing Russia emanated not from some external enemy but from the near abroad. The Russian Ministry of Foreign Affairs declared, for example, that "the crisis phenomena of the post-totalitarian period [taking place in the former republics of the USSR] directly affect the security of Russia and the rate and possibility of overcoming the economic and social crisis in Russia itself".[36]

There are six ways in which events in the former republics of the USSR are perceived to threaten Russian security:

- conflicts on the periphery of Russia might spill over into Russia
- separatist movements in the near abroad, it is feared, will have demonstration effects that endanger the integrity of the Russian Federation
- Russian minorities living in other republics appear to be at risk
- external powers might intervene in the conflicts on Russia's periphery, thereby directly or indirectly threatening Russia's interests
- there is apprehension that regional alliances will be formed that include some of the former republics but exclude, and therefore isolate, Russia
- Russia's precarious economic situation seems likely to be undermined by the refusal of some of the republics to either leave the rouble zone, or adopt similar economic reforms to those which have been introduced in Russia.

The fear that conflicts in Transcaucasia will spill over into the Russian Federation is very realistic. Indeed, two of the present conflicts already directly involve Russia, in that the South Ossetians demand independence from Georgia in order to join the RF (either as a separate autonomous republic or by uniting with North Ossetia), and the Abkhazians have mooted the possibility of joining the RF.[37] However, the danger of spill-

---

36. "Conception of the foreign policy of the Russian federation", *Diplomatichesky vestnik*, special edn, 3 (Moscow: Ministry of Foreign Relations of the Russian Federation, 1993)

over arises particularly because of the involvement of people from the north Caucasus in the conflict in Abkhazia.[38] Since there are already several conflicts within the north Caucasus itself, the Russian government is concerned lest the war spreads to Russian territory.[39] In August 1992, Yeltsin appealed to people in the north Caucasus and south Russia "to keep their emotions in check and not allow themselves to be drawn into dangerous activity" since this would threaten the security of Russia.[40] However, as we shall see in the next section Russian policy itself sometimes threatens Russian security.

Apprehension that permitting a change in the territorial boundaries or administrative status of one area might set off a chain reaction of further demands seems to have been the main reason why the Soviet government did not resolve the issue of Nagorno–Karabakh in favour of Armenia. The Russian government similarly fears that successful separatist movements in the near abroad might inspire secessionist forces in the RF. The fear is well grounded, since several autonomous republics in the RF have claimed sovereignty, regions have demanded similar rights to those enjoyed by autonomous republics, and one republic in the north Caucasus, Chechnya, no longer considers itself part of the RF. In relation to the conflicts in Transcaucasia, therefore, the Russian government has wanted to retain the territorial *status quo*. For example, Yeltsin insists that Russia supports the unity, sovereignty and territorial integrity of Georgia.[41]

The likeliest reason for Russian intervention in the near abroad is to defend Russian minorities perceived to be in danger, either because they are caught up in local conflicts or because they are repressed. The defence of the rights, freedoms, respect and wellbeing of all Russians has been identified as a priority of Russian foreign policy, and Russia wishes to conclude agreements with the other successor states guaranteeing those rights.[42] There is no great danger at present that Russian minorities will be

---

37. C. W. Blandy, "Drivers of instability in the Caucasus", *Brief* 2, 4–5 (Camberley: Soviet Studies Research Centre, Sandhurst, 1993).

38. In 1990 a Confederation of the Mountain Peoples of the north Caucasus (KGNK) was established with the long-term objective of establishing a north Caucasian or mountain republic which, it was envisaged, would include Abkhazia (Blandy 1993: 25–6). In August 1992 the parliament of KGNK instructed its members to send volunteers to Abkhazia, declared that all Georgians in the KGNK were hostages, and ordered the impounding of all goods en route to Georgia (Interfax, 22 August 1992). Although these actions were condemned by the Russian Government, north Caucasian involvement has continued (Interfax, 26 August 1992).

39. Blandy (1993: 7–20) identifies 31 conflict issues in the north Caucasus which are, or could become, violent.

40. "Appeal from the President of Russia to the peoples of the north Caucasus and the whole population of southern Russia", *Krasnaya zvezda*, 28 August 1992.

41. Ibid.

42. *Diplomatichesky vestnik* 1993, 5, 7.

repressed in Transcaucasia, both because there are relatively few Russians in the area (in 1989 Russians formed 1.5 per cent, 5.6 per cent and 7.4 per cent of the populations of Armenia, Azerbaijan and Georgia respectively; since then many Russians have left Transcaucasia), and because other national minorities are in the main line of fire. However, Russians have already been caught up in local conflicts. In August 1992, for example, 5,000 Russians (holiday-makers and families of servicemen) had to be evacuated from Abkhazia.[43] Moreover, there are Russian army units stationed in Transcaucasia and the Russian government constantly repeats that it will do whatever is necessary to protect Russian lives and Russian property.[44]

Russians are also worried that external powers might intervene in the conflicts on Russia's periphery. This, it is perceived, would threaten Russia's interests, with the attendant danger that Russia would be drawn into broader conflicts. The Russian government has expressed its intention "to counteract any attempts of third countries to establish a politico-military presence in the countries bordering Russia".[45] The interest presently shown in Transcaucasia by Turkey and Iran has, inevitably, revived historical memories of previous conflicts between Russia and the Ottoman and Persian empires.

Related to the fear of external intervention is concern that former Soviet republics might join regional alliances that exclude, and therefore, isolate, Russia. When the Warsaw Pact disintegrated, the Soviet Union tried to include in the bilateral treaties that were to replace it a clause preventing the east and central European countries from joining any military alliances. Their response was to request membership of NATO, which led to the formation of the North Atlantic Co-operation Council (NACC). When NATO countries recognized the danger of isolating the former Soviet Union, however, all 15 republics were also invited to join. The idea that the Partnership for Peace agreement reached with east and central European countries at the NATO summit in January 1994 should be a first step toward their inclusion in NATO was condemned in Moscow. The exclusion of Russia from regional defence alliances which included former Soviet states would be perceived as even more threatening, not only because it would isolate Russia but also because it would make it impossible to create the "single military–strategic space" which remains an important aim of Russian foreign policy.

In its attempts to counteract the threats to security perceived to emanate from the near abroad, Russia has been least successful in preventing its economy being undermined by other republics. Interrepublican trade has

---

43. *Reuters* news service 1992, 18 August.
44. See, for example, the statements from the Ministry of Foreign Affairs, 15 and 17 August 1992, carried by Interfax.
45. *Diplomatichesky vestnik* (1993: 8).

been badly disrupted by the disintegration of the USSR and, given the interdependence of the Soviet economy, this has done enormous damage to all the republics. Even where interrepublican trade has revived, Russia has been damaged by the enormous debts owed to it by the other republics.[46] Moreover, it has proved impossible to create a rouble zone in which all the members play to the rules of a central bank. Those republics that have introduced their own currencies refused to return their roubles to Russia, using them instead to buy goods in Russia, which vastly increased the amount of money in circulation in Russia and contributed to Russian inflation. "Old" roubles were, as a result, withdrawn from circulation. As far as Transcaucasia is concerned, the conflicts in which all three states are immersed have damaged their economies enormously. Normal trade and commerce have been interrupted, particularly in the case of Armenia, which has been blockaded by Azerbaijan.

It is thus clear that Russia faces very real threats from events in the near abroad and particularly from Transcaucasia, both because this is where the most intractable conflicts are occurring and because Transcaucasia borders the most restive region of the RF. Accordingly, Russian policy towards Transcaucasia has primarily been directed at containing these threats.

Russian policy towards Transcaucasia

With regard to Russia's economic security, the Russian government has attempted to invigorate Russian–Transcaucasian trade. However, given the war-torn state of the economies of all three countries little progress has been made. In fact, Russia agreed to continue supplying oil and other fuel to Armenia on credit, despite the unlikelihood of speedy repayment. The conflicts in Transcaucasia also affect Russia's economic relations with Iran, since communications are constantly interrupted. With regard to the rouble zone, one alleged aim of the "rouble coup" (that is, the sudden withdrawal of all pre-1993 rouble notes within two weeks, with restrictions on the amount that could be exchanged for new banknotes) in July 1993 was to force republics that wish to remain in the rouble zone to co-ordinate their monetary policies with Russia and to render the roubles of those who have left it worthless.[47] The terms Russia imposed on republics wishing to join the economic union negotiated by the CIS in September 1993 were similarly designed to ensure that members subordinated themselves to Russian economic policy.[48]

---

46. There are frequent reports in the press of the curtailment of oil and gas supplies from Russia to the other republics in an effort to extract payment of debts.
47. *The Guardian*, 27 July 1993.
48. *The Economist*, 18 September 1993.

Since the conflicts in Transcaucasia represent a pressing and very real danger to Russia and affect all other relations, the main thrust of Russian policy in the area has been directed at bringing the violence to an end. From mid-1992 onwards Russian mediators, working on their own or with CSCE negotiators, have been trying to broker agreements between Georgia and South Ossetia, between Georgia and Abkhazia, and between Armenia and Azerbaijan. Russians see themselves as disinterested agents. One prominent political scientist maintains, for example, that "[h]aving seceded from Russia, the people that have done so, particularly small ones, may either disappear or be absorbed by stronger neighbours. And where they live – as in the Caucasus – dozens of tribes rent by mutual hostility, it is only an impartial and strong arbiter that can prevent bloody strife".[49] The implication is that only Russia can serve as "the impartial and strong arbiter".

Russian policy is rather more contradictory, however, than this view of simple, impartial mediation suggests. Although Armenian, Azerbaijani and Georgian politicians have usually co-operated with Russian mediation and peace-keeping efforts, they have also frequently accused Russia of participating in the conflicts. From October 1992 to June 1993, for example, Shevardnadze constantly maintained that Russian troops were aggravating and participating in the conflict in Abkhazia. Armenia and Azerbaijan have also both accused Russia of assisting the other side. Whether or not there is any truth in all or any of these accusations, as long as regular Russian forces are stationed in other republics, there will always be suspicions that they are not impartial. Furthermore, there was a long delay after the break-up of the Soviet Union before Moscow formulated a policy towards the near abroad, and there has been a continuing and paralyzing power struggle within Russia since that policy was articulated. This has enabled the Russian military to establish its own policy, frequently on the private initiative of local military commanders.[50] As a result, Yeltsin does not always seem to be in command of the armed forces.[51]

The situation is further complicated by the fact that the army does not always seem to be in command of its weapons. Transcaucasia is said to be the most militarized area in the world. Although the Armenian, Azerbaijani and Georgian governments, like all the governments of the successor states, "nationalized" or "privatized" as many of the conventional Soviet weapons located in the republic as they could, there is little doubt that a large proportion of the weapons in the area have either been stolen from, or sold by, the Russian army.[52] It would seem, therefore, that Russian

49. Pozdnyakov (1993: 8).
50. *The Economist*, 28 August 1993, 19.
51. J. Lough, "The place of the 'near abroad' in Russian foreign policy", RFE/RL *Research Report* 1, 21–9, 1989.

troops (with or without Moscow's approval) participate in, and provide the arms for, the violent disputes that official Russian policy is dedicated to resolve.

As far as Russian mediation is concerned, the most successful effort has been in South Ossetia. In June 1992 an agreement was signed by Yeltsin and Shevardnadze, which brought about a ceasefire.[53] In July, peace-keeping forces, consisting of Russian, Georgian and Ossetian battalions, were deployed to monitor a disengagement corridor and to supervise economic reconstruction, the return of refugees and a stage-by-stage resolution of the political dispute between Georgia and South Ossetia.

It proved more difficult to broker a reliable ceasefire in Abkhazia, and Russian policy has been far more ambiguous here. In September 1992 Russian, Georgian and Abkhazian leaders, together with representatives from the north Caucasus, negotiated an agreement (signed by Yeltsin and Shevardnadze) on a ceasefire to be monitored by a joint Georgian–Abkhazian–Russian commission. Foreign troops in the area were to be disarmed and removed, and the strict neutrality of Russian troops located in the area was promised. In return, Georgia would withdraw its forces from Abkhazia, apart from a limited contingent required for specific local purposes. Ground, air and sea communications through the area (vital for the economies of Russia, Georgia and Armenia) would be restored. CSCE and UN assistance was requested to implement the agreement.[54] However, fighting continued, and by February 1993 the Georgian-held capital of Abkhazia, Sukhumi, was under threat and there were direct clashes between Russia and Georgia. Shevardnadze appealed for urgent international help and frequently accused Russian troops of assisting the Abkhazians.[55] A new ceasefire was agreed in July 1993 and the UN agreed to send military observers to verify compliance.[56] Georgians duly withdrew their heavy weapons and most of their troops from Abkhazia. However, before the UN observers had arrived to supervise the ceasefire, it had been broken by Abkhazians, and on 27 September they captured the regional capital, Sukhumi. Shevardnadze accused President Yeltsin of assisting Abkhazia and, in private at least, Russian soldiers admitted that notwithstanding the official policy of neutrality in the conflict, without their help an Abkhazian victory would be been impossible.[57] Nonetheless, Shevardnadze was forced to plead for Russian help to evacuate Georgian refugees from Abkhazia and to guard Georgian rail and sea links.[58] After a Transcaucasian

52. *Moskovskie Novosti*, 20 December 1992.
53. *Rossiskaya Gazeta*, 27 June 1992.
54. ITAR–TASS news service, 4 September 1992.
55. *The Guardian*, 10 July 1993.
56. *The Guardian*, 10 August 1993.
57. *Nezavisimaya Gazeta*, 23 October 1993.

summit meeting with President Yeltsin in October, Shevardnadze reversed Georgian foreign policy and announced that Georgia would join the CIS.[59]

The third conflict in Transcaucasia, over Nagorno–Karabakh, has proved to be impervious to Russian mediation efforts (and, for that matter, to those of the CSCE). There have been innumerable ceasefires, and Russia has participated in negotiating some of them, but all have been breached as soon as they have been agreed.[60]

Despite the scant progress in ending the violence in Transcaucasia, Yeltsin is convinced that Russia has a mission to keep the peace in the near abroad. In March 1993 he suggested to the UN that Russia should have the right to act, both unilaterally and with the CIS, to ensure security and stability in the former USSR, under the auspices of (and presumably with the financial support of) the UN.[61] Given Russian perceptions of the near abroad, and the non-Russians' fear of a resurgent Russian imperialism, the response has been understandably unenthusiastic. Russian troops are unlikely to be accepted as neutral peace-keepers in the near abroad. Moreover, it is not at all clear that Yeltsin and his advisers distinguish between peace-keeping and peace-making. There is little doubt, however, that Moscow will continue to see itself as the gendarme of the former Soviet Union. At the same time it is clear that, until the Russian military is firmly under political control, Moscow is likely to continue to be both troublemaker and peace-keeper in Transcaucasia. The oil resources of the Caspian Sea, and Moscow's determination that they should reach international markets by Russian pipelines, have raised the Russian government's stakes in Transcaucasia. Moscow's preferred route for Caspian oil requires safe pipelines through the Caucasian republics.

As long as there is conflict in Transcaucasia, therefore, Russian policy towards the area will be dominated by the need for peace. And if peace cannot be obtained by mediation and peace-keeping, Russia may well try to make peace, thereby essentially reverting to the methods it used in Transcaucasia in the nineteenth century.

58. When the Russian parliament was finally dissolved on 4 October, Shevardnadze accused it of aiding Abkhazia and shifted the blame from Yeltsin. *The Guardian*, 9 October 1993.
59. The newly elected President of Azerbaijan, Geidar Aliev, declared that Azerbaijan, which had previously attended CIS meetings as an observer, would also join as a full member.
60. E. Fuller, "Yeltsin brokers agreement on Nagorno–Karabakh", RFE/RL *Report on the USSR* (October 1991), 16–18.
61. S. Crow, "Russia seeks leadership in regional peace-keeping", RFE/RL *Research Report* 2 (1993), 28–32.

CHAPTER THREE
Turkey, the Black Sea and Transcaucasia[1]
WILLIAM HALE

Introduction: Turkey and the end of the Cold War

The collapse of Soviet power in eastern Europe, and the subsequent dissolution of the USSR, transformed the international situation of Turkey, like
that of all the neighbours of the former Soviet state. At the outset of these
changes, it was often concluded that Turkey had lost its former international importance, which derived from its value to the Western alliance as
the linch-pin of NATO defences in the eastern Mediterranean. Before long,
however, more positive reactions became the norm. As an example, in a
newspaper interview given in December 1989, the former premier Bülent
Ecevit pointed out that the transformation of Turkey's strategic situation
"should be a cause of satisfaction rather than regret" since the dramatic
reduction of the risk of war was bound to be a gain; on the other hand, new
dangers were likely to arise.[2] In fact, it soon became clear that the transformation of its international environment presented Turkey with a changed,
but not diminished, international role. This sometimes led to wildly exaggerated notions of its future international importance – including, for
instance, the idea that it would become a kind of regional superpower, in
a zone extending from the Adriatic to western China.

Since 1992, policy setbacks in Transcaucasia and the Balkans, as well as
mounting economic problems at home and an escalating conflict with
Kurdish insurgents in the southeastern provinces, have forced policy-
makers back to more modest and realistic assessments. Nonetheless, it still

---

1. In preparing this chapter, I must acknowledge my debt for valuable help and advice to
   Ambassador Özdem Sanberk, Mr Oktay Özüye, Ms Inci Tümay, Mr Candan Azer,
   Ambassador Ömer Ersan, and Mr Engin Soysal, of the Turkish Foreign Ministry. However, I must naturally take responsibility for any mistakes, and for the opinions
   expressed. I have also incorporated some material published separately in a contribution to David Menashri (ed.), *Central Asia meets the Middle East* (Boulder, Colorado: Westview, forthcoming). The text was originally prepared in the early spring of 1994. Some
   updating, up to July 1995, has been included in the footnotes.
2. *Cumhuriyet* (Istanbul daily), 27 December 1989.

seems fair to say that the end of the Cold War and of the USSR itself vastly increased the range of Turkey's foreign policy options, besides creating a new series of risks and instabilities. Where decisions had often been preset by Cold War rigidities, choices had now to be made, and the Turkish government, like others, had to be reasonably confident that it was making the right ones. In the aftermath of the formal dissolution of the USSR, it seems to have been generally assumed that the precedent set in the former satellites of eastern Europe would be repeated in the peripheral ex-Soviet republics – that is to say, that Russian power would be virtually ended. This expectation has clearly turned out to be wrong. Russia may be weak economically, but it is still the dominant power in a region in which the other ex-Soviet states are, if anything even weaker. Hence, a major task for foreign policy-makers – in Turkey, as in other countries – has been to come to terms with Russia's residual military power, and to try to assess its intentions and capacities.

Turkey's foreign policy: determinants, resources, strategies

As a preliminary, it seems worthwhile to outline some of the factors underlying Turkey's overall foreign policy strategies. To start with, Turkey's main strengths and weaknesses as an international actor can be summarized. On the assets side of the balance sheet, it has its geographical position, controlling the access of all the Black Sea states to the eastern Mediterranean, through the Bosphorus and Dardanelles, as well as land and air routes between eastern Europe and the Middle East. Its position as a longstanding ally of the West also gives it an advantage in dealing with third parties that most countries in the region do not possess. Although its economy has some severe weaknesses, it has shown a growth and diversity that contrast with those of all its neighbours, but for Greece. Turkey's economy may appear weak by the standards of northwestern Europe, but by those of the Balkans, the ex-USSR and the Middle East, it is successful and dynamic. In spite of frequent ups and downs, GNP has grown steadily by around five per cent per annum for most of the past four decades. The country is more than self-sufficient in food, and has adequate supplies of nearly all the basic industrial raw materials but for oil and natural gas.

On the military side, Turkey has a huge standing army, which could probably fight a successful defensive war against a conventional attack. However, in the last resort it would need the NATO nuclear umbrella if it were faced with war with a nuclear power. Besides its reliance on conscript soldiers, shortages of equipment would probably make it difficult for Turkey to sustain large-scale or long-term military operations outside its own borders. Like other regional states, it is also faced with a serious internal ethnic conflict, as the rebellion by Kurdish militants of the Kurdistan

Workers' Party (PKK) drags on. Economically, its high growth rate is offset by a high rate of inflation (and, hence, a weak though convertible currency) and reliance on continued inflows of foreign capital to maintain economic growth. Lastly, it frequently has tense relations with five of its eight neighbours (Greece, Syria, Iraq, Iran and Armenia) and no direct overland contact with any of the Muslim republics of the former USSR, but for the small Azeri enclave of Nakhichevan.

The effects of all these factors can be summed up by saying that Turkey probably has more room for manoeuvre than most states in the region but that, in the final analysis, it cannot allow its policies to drift too far out of line with those of the Western powers generally. In the context of Transcaucasian and Black Sea politics, Turkey would find it hard to intervene directly in Azerbaijan, except as part of a multilateral operation sponsored by the UN, NATO, or the OSCE. It could and probably would send a protective force to Nakhichevan, if the latter were directly attacked by Armenia, but on past form it would prefer to prevent this by diplomatic moves through Moscow. Its defensive strength, and membership of NATO, means that it does not have to fear direct aggression by any of its neighbours, assuming a reasonable degree of sanity on the other side. On the other hand, a hostile neighbour could exacerbate Turkey's internal problems by giving all-out support to the PKK (as Syria has done at times). Turkey strongly supports the independence of all states in the region, but it needs to avoid a head-on collision with Russia, partly because of its dependence on Russian supplies of natural gas, which is a vital source of pollution-free fuel. Economically, Turkey cannot supply the huge capital sums needed for the modernization of the economies of the former Soviet republics, but it can act as a conduit for Western capital and technology. If peace could be assured in Transcaucasia, then it could probably serve as an important trading partner and transit route for Georgia, Armenia and Azerbaijan. Finally, its territory sits astride the most direct route for potential oil and gas pipelines between Transcaucasia, Central Asia and southern Europe.

Since the end of the Cold War, it has sometimes been suggested that Turkey's new-found role in Western strategy in the Middle East (particularly in relation to northern Iraq) and its links with Central Asia might lead Ankara to abandon its orientation towards the West. However, there is as yet no clear sign of this; in fact, it is arguable that one of Ankara's main objectives in seeking a higher profile in the Middle East and the states of the former USSR is precisely because this increases the value of its friendship to the Western powers. Its new policy initiatives can thus be seen as complementary to its pro-Western alignment, rather than contradictory.[3]

---

3. This point is effectively argued by Paul Henze, "Turkey: towards the twenty-first century", in *Turkey's new geopolitics, from the Balkans to western China*, Graham E. Fuller & Ian O. Lesser (eds), 2 (Boulder, Colorado: Westview, for RAND Corporation, 1993).

As a sign of this, Turkey appears determined to work towards the goal of eventual membership of the European Union, in spite of the rebuff its first application received in 1989. Currently, its main efforts are directed towards the achievement of a customs union with the EU, which is due to come into effect at the beginning of 1996 (as of July 1995, implementation of this depended on ratification by the European Parliament). Viewed from Brussels, full membership of the EU for Turkey still looks very problematic, for both political and economic reasons. Nevertheless, it still seems likely that the Turks will renew their application some time towards the end of the century, assuming the customs union proves successful.

Lastly, the fact that Turkey has an elected government affects foreign policy in the political as well as economic spheres. David Vital suggests that, ideally, one of the chief functions of foreign policy-makers is the reconciliation of internal and external interests.[4] The process of foreign policy-making in Turkey is a vastly understudied subject; nevertheless it seems fair to say that Turkish political culture has traditionally supported a consensual approach to foreign policy questions. As Ferenc Vali argues, the gradual, if occasionally halting, liberalization of the political system has produced a more open debate on foreign policy than in the past. Nevertheless, he concludes, "the interest of the average Turkish citizen [has] remained skin-deep". At the same time, public opinion can be deeply stirred on foreign policy questions if they involve fundamental nationalist or religious beliefs.[5] In the present context, Turkish policy towards the conflict between Azerbaijan and Armenia has aroused just such reactions: hence, in this case, the job of reconciling external interests and domestic opinion has not been easy.

Black Sea co-operation: aims, experience and prospects

At first glance, the idea of working for greater economic co-operation between the countries of the Black Sea does not seem enticing. Even though the Iron Curtain is now a thing of the past, the countries of the region are beset by a series of ethnic and other political conflicts, both within the present states and between them. The inclusion of Armenia, Azerbaijan, Greece and Albania in the Black Sea Economic Co-operation project (BSEC) merely adds to the list of actual or potential conflicts. Economically, the problems seem equally daunting. With the exceptions of Turkey and Greece, all the actual or potential members are undergoing

---

4. David Vital, *The making of British foreign policy*, 20 (London: George Allen & Unwin, 1968).
5. Ferenc Vali, *Bridge across the Bosphoros: the foreign policy of Turkey*, 100 (London: George Allen & Unwin, 1968).

serious economic dislocation, as part of the process of intended transition to the market economy, so that levels of output have been falling (in some cases drastically) over the past five years. To add to the problems, transport links, especially those between Turkey and Greece on the one side and the former Warsaw Pact countries on the other, are barely developed, and the basic financial infrastructure for free market trading is largely lacking.

Turkey's interest in the proposal for closer links across the Black Sea is based on the expectation that, in spite of these daunting problems, it should be able to occupy an advantageous position in such a scheme, if it manages to produce tangible results. Politically, it gains from the fact that it has good relations with virtually all the other Black Sea states, tempered by periodically tense relations with Russia. An important case in point is that of Bulgaria, where the overthrow of the Zhivkov regime has overcome the problem of the Turkish minority in Bulgaria, unless Bulgarian ethnic chauvinism reasserts itself at some time in the future. Turkey and Bulgaria now have a treaty of friendship, co-operation and security, signed on 5 May 1992. Overall, Turkey's main interest is to promote a stable and reasonably peaceful external environment, in the hope that if the states of the region become more interdependent economically, then they will have an interest in soft-pedalling mutual disputes. Accordingly, it has actively sought the inclusion of Greece and Armenia in the project, although these are the two members with whom it is most likely to be in conflict. Ankara's calculation is that it would be better to have these states included and potentially co-operative than excluded and probably hostile.

Economically, Turkey may also have a good deal to gain from the project, at least in the longer term. In spite of the present dislocations, an important point of departure is the fact that the former Eastern Bloc countries have a lower share of world trade than of world output: hence, there should be good long-run prospects for increasing the international flow of goods and services. Compared with most of the other non-OECD countries, they have high levels of technical education, and a well developed industrial and transport infrastructure, besides large natural resources. Turkey's main advantage is that it has well established consumer goods industries as well as an agricultural surplus: in other words, it is in a position to export goods that the other Black Sea countries need to import. On the other hand, it imports industrial inputs – in particular, oil and natural gas – that the other regional states are or may be in a position to supply.

As a sign of the potential, Turkey's merchandise trade with Greece, Bulgaria, Romania and the former USSR rose in value from US$2300 million in 1990 to around US$4100 million in 1994, and its share in its total foreign trade from 6.7 per cent in 1990 to around 10 per cent in 1994. Within this, in 1994 the Russian federation accounted for 69 per cent of Turkey's total exports to the ex-USSR, and 71 per cent of imports.[6] Natural gas imports from Russia, which are delivered via a pipeline through Bulgaria, are easily the most important single item in this trade. These figures exclude the large amount of trade conducted by the suitcase traders – nearly all from eastern Europe and Transcaucasia – who have been flooding into Istanbul and Turkish Black Sea cities. In 1992, Turkey received around three million visitors from eastern Europe, the vast majority of whom came on shopping expeditions.[7] Almost certainly, big gains could be made if this currently unrecorded trade could be transferred to more normal commercial channels.

Turkey took the original initiative in launching the BSEC project in December 1990 – that is, after the collapse of the Warsaw Pact and Comecon, but before the dissolution of the USSR. On 19–21 December 1990 a preliminary meeting of representatives of Turkey, Bulgaria, Romania and the USSR met in Ankara and agreed to consider proposals for the free movement of persons, goods, capital and services between the participating states. Prospects for co-operation in infrastructure projects such as transport and telecommunications, and a Black Sea Development Bank, were also considered. It was decided to establish a permanent co-ordination committee, as well as a committee of ministers that would meet at least once a year.[8] Discussions continued during 1991, and survived the dissolution of the USSR, whose position was simply taken over by the Black Sea successor states, with Armenia and Azerbaijan added in for good measure.

Accordingly, a meeting of foreign ministers or their deputies from Turkey, Bulgaria, Romania, Moldova, Ukraine, Russia, Georgia, Armenia and Azerbaijan was held in Istanbul on 3 February 1992. A declaration was initialled, which was signed at a summit meeting held in Istanbul on 24–25 June, and attended by heads of state or government of Albania, Armenia, Azerbaijan, Bulgaria, Georgia, Greece, Moldova, Romania, Russia, Turkey and Ukraine. (Greece had been invited to join the grouping at the February meeting, and accepted: Albania also attended the June summit, and its accession was formally agreed to). The document agreed to at the summit was rather less ambitious than the 1990 declaration: rather than the establishment of free trade, the participants merely committed themselves to "reduce or progressively eliminate obstacles [to trade] of all kinds": instead of completely free movement of labour there would simply be free movement of businessmen. Joint projects in the fields of transport, energy, mining, and tourism would also be considered, as well as steps for environmental protection.[9]

A major problem in the search for greater economic co-operation is the

---

6. Data from *Briefing* (Ankara weekly), 4 May 1992, 20; 31 January 1994, 19.
7. *Doing business in Turkey* (1993, Istanbul: IBS Research and Consultancy).
8. *Turkey Confidential* (London monthly), January 1991, 21.
9. Declaration on Black Sea Economic Co-operation and Summit Declaration on Black Sea Co-operation. Texts kindly supplied by Turkish Ministry of Foreign Affairs, Ankara.

lack of financial intermediaries. In a bid to deal with this, the 1992 declaration committed the participant states to "consider the possibilities and
ways of establishing a Black Sea Foreign Trade and Investment Bank".
Decisions on the establishment of the bank where finally made at a meeting of the BSEC states in Sofia in December 1993, at which it was decided to
site its headquarters in Salonika, under a Turkish president. Meanwhile,
the BSEC secretariat would be established in Istanbul, under a Russian
director, with three deputy directors (Ukrainian, Romanian and Turkish).
In all this, Turkey was evidently anxious to counter criticisms that it was
aiming to dominate the organization, by carefully giving important roles
to the two countries – Greece and Russia – that were likely to be most sensitive on this point.[10]

In the reduction of mutual tariff barriers, the BSEC project faces the problem that Greece is already a member of the European Union. Turkey is
expected to establish a customs union with the EU in 1996, and will probably press for full membership thereafter. In effect, this means that neither
state can offer more favourable trading terms to the other BSEC countries
than those it already offers, or can be expected to offer, to the European
Union. Prospects are further complicated by the fact that other Black Sea
countries (in particular, Bulgaria and Romania) are likely to seek separate
trading arrangements with the Union. The 1992 declaration recognizes the
problem, by confirming that economic co-operation will not be developed
in a manner contrary to the participants' obligations towards the EU and
other international organizations, and that they will only work to freer
trade with one another "in a manner not contravening their obligations
towards third parties".[11] This apparently means that the BSEC states would
not apply tariffs on mutual trade at rates lower than those laid down in the
EU's common external tariff. For the moment, the problem is largely academic, since the process of reducing tariff and other trade barriers within
the BSEC region is barely in its infancy, but it could loom larger if the project
makes concrete progress.

Currently, most of this debate looks somewhat unreal, given the political and economic chaos in much of the region. Apart from continued conflicts in Transcaucasia, the nightmare scenario is a civil war in Ukraine, in
which Russia might well become involved. Even if this is avoided, there
are no clear signs that either Russia or the Ukraine will solve their internal
economic problems. Romania, Bulgaria, Greece and Turkey have a relative
degree of political stability, less acute internal conflicts, and stronger economies. Hence, it may be best to concentrate the BSEC project's efforts on
these states, at least in the short term. The full realization of the project,
embracing the ex-Soviet republics, could then be delayed until they have

---

10. *Turkish Probe*, 16 December 1993, 14.
11. Summit Declaration (see *n.* 8) paragraphs 7 & 13.

overcome their own problems. The BSEC scheme can help to soften regional conflicts, by providing a forum for mutual contacts, but it cannot solve them, and greater economic co-operation depends on a greater degree of political stability than has been seen since 1991.

Turkey and Transcaucasia

The ideological and emotional context that affects Turkish policy in Transcaucasia is complex, and at times ambiguous. On the one hand, most Turks feel a natural ethnic and religious affinity with the Azeris, reinforced by historical hostility towards the Armenians. On the other hand, pan-Turkism, in the sense of a political union between the Turks of Anatolia and those of Azerbaijan and Central Asia, has never enjoyed official support since the foundation of the Turkish republic in 1923. In 1921, Ataturk roundly declared that "neither Islamic union nor Turanism may constitute a doctrine, or logical policy for us. Henceforth, the government policy of the new Turkey is to consist in living independently, relying on Turkey's own sovereignty within her national frontiers".[12] No Turkish government since then has gone back on this commitment.

As a result, state-sponsored nationalism has sought to anchor the Turkish identity in Anatolia, rather than in the Turkic regions to the east. This emphasis has lost some of its force with the collapse of the USSR, since pan-Turkism now seems a slightly less unrealistic dream than it once was. Nevertheless, most of its adherents are still confined to the far right of Turkish politics, currently represented by the Nationalist Action Party of Alparslan Türkes. All the mainstream political parties of Turkey appear to accept the principle of developing cultural and economic links with other Turkic peoples, but draw away from the idea of political union.

The position of Armenia is also an extremely sensitive one for Turkey. Although there is no love lost between the two nations, Turkish policy-makers are keenly aware of the fact that there is a large Armenian diaspora in the West, especially in the USA, and that if Turkish policy were seen as being actively hostile to Armenia, this could cause a serious conflict between Ankara and Washington (or, at least, the US Congress).[13] One of

---

12. Quoted, Jacob M. Landau, *Pan-Turkism in Turkey: a study in irredentism*, 72 (London: Hurst, 1981).
13. At the beginning of 1990, Senator Robert Dole sponsored a resolution in the US Senate that sought to designate 24 April as a "national day of remembrance of the Armenian genocide of 1915–23" (quoted, *Briefing*, 5 March 1990, 3). This caused a serious rumpus in US–Turkish relations, since the Turks strongly dispute the claim that there was any organized genocide of the Armenians in the Ottoman Empire, and regarded the Dole resolution as a national slander. At the end of February 1990, the resolution was defeated in the Senate by a margin of three votes.

the main Turkish worries is that Armenia might move into the same position as that of Israel in the Middle East – that is, perceived as a Western outpost, enjoying virtually unconditional support from the USA, and a constant source of conflict between Washington and the other regional states. Alternatively, the Nagorno–Karabakh conflict might be converted into a Muslim–Christian confrontation, the very kind of polarization that Turkey, as an officially secular state, earnestly wishes to avoid. This point was emphasized by Süleyman Demirel, the then Prime Minister, during a visit to Washington in February 1992, when he warned that "a conflict similar to that in the Middle East might develop in the region ... Turkey is therefore impartial on the Azerbaijan–Armenian conflict ... The role of mediation may fall on Turkey, and we should be in a position to fulfil that role. In other words, both republics should continue to trust us".[14] Equally, in his public statements Demirel has emphasized that Turkey seeks to develop friendly relations with Armenia, but that full diplomatic relations could not be established until Armenia "adopts a peaceful stance in Azerbaijan", and Armenian forces withdraw from Azeri territory.[15]

Events since 1991 have put this policy to a serious test – partly because Armenia and Azerbaijan have carried on their conflict relentlessly, and partly because the press and public opinion in Turkey is clearly more sympathetic to the Azeris than to the Armenians. During most of 1990–1, the fighting in and around Nagorno–Karabakh stayed at the back of public consciousness, being overshadowed by the Gulf crisis, in which Turkey was directly involved. In November 1991, the outgoing Motherland Party administration under Mesut Yimaz announced that Turkey would recognize the independence of Azerbaijan, and this decision was confirmed by the successor government, under Demirel. On 16 December it was announced that Turkey would extend this, by recognizing all the new republics of the former USSR, as occasion arose. Meanwhile, a new crisis in Azeri-Armenian relations broke out in November, with the crash of an Azeri helicopter carrying senior government officials over Nagorno–Karabakh. Following this, Demirel sent an open message to the Azeri Prime Minister, Hasan Hasanov, warning him that Armenia and Azerbaijan "should avoid stands which might exacerbate the existing tension" failing which "irreparable damage may be inflicted to relations with neighbouring countries".[16] It also appears that, at about this time, the Demirel government was pressing Baku to cancel its withdrawal of the autonomous status of Nagorno–Karabakh, given that the withdrawal was almost certain to intensify the contest with Armenia.[17]

---

14. BBC *Summary of world broadcasts* (SWB) 14 February 1992. Ankara radio, 12 February 1992.
15. BBC *SWB*, 15 June 1992. Ibid., 14 June 1992.
16. BBC *SWB*, 28 November 1991. Ibid., 27 November 1991.
17. Graham E. Fuller, "Turkey's new eastern orientation". In Fuller & Lesser (1993: 78).

During 1992, the conflict between Armenia and Azerbaijan escalated, leaving the Turkish Government with the difficult job of continuing its policy of non-intervention. On 4 March, the Turkish press reported that some 500 civilians had been massacred by Armenian militiamen who had captured Khojali, an Azeri town in Nagorno–Karabakh. This report was later confirmed by British and American newspapers.[18] This awakened a storm of protest in Turkey, with demonstrators calling for a "Holy War" against Armenia. President Özal suggested that Turkey could cut off transit trade to Armenia and that "we should frighten [the Armenians] a little". Meanwhile, regular Turkish military manoeuvres in northeastern Anatolia sparked off protests from Armenia. However, a bellicose stand was not supported by Demirel, who criticized Özal's remarks as "very mistaken", since they would damage the government's efforts to find a peaceful solution.[19] Meanwhile, the government was raising the issue before the then Conference on Security and Co-operation in Europe (CSCE) and the Atlantic Co-operation Council, basing its case on a resolution passed by the CSCE on 28 February which confirmed that Nagorno–Karabakh is part of Azerbaijan and condemned the alteration of frontiers by force.

In May 1992, the Armenian-Azeri conflict passed two critical thresholds, amid the breakdown of several Iranian-brokered ceasefires. On 9 May, Armenian forces captured the town of Shusha, the last important Azeri stronghold in Nagorno–Karabakh, and opened a corridor between the Karabakh enclave and the official territory of Armenia. Meanwhile, the Armenians also attacked the separate Azeri enclave of Nakhichevan, capturing hills overlooking the Azeri village of Sadarak, close to Nakhichevan's frontier with Turkey. Official Armenian claims that these attacks were carried out purely on the initiative of local Armenian forces in Nagorno–Karabakh, or even by Kurdish irregulars, enjoyed little credence in Turkey or elsewhere. The Armenian offensive was accompanied by political chaos in Azerbaijan, as ex-President Ayaz Mutalibov, ousted from power after the fall of Khojali, briefly regained the Presidency on 15 May, but was then redeposed within 24 hours by forces loyal to the opposition Popular Front.

The attack on Nakhichevan caused particular concern in Ankara – partly because, unlike Nagorno–Karabakh, its territory directly abuts onto that of Turkey, and partly because its status is guaranteed under the Turkish–Soviet Treaty of 1921, Article 3 of which states that Nakhichevan "shall form an autonomous territory under the protection of Azerbaijan, on condition that the latter cannot transfer this protectorate to any third state".[20] In response, Bülent Ecevit, now on the opposition benches as leader of the small Democratic Left Party, urged that Turkey should send military

---

18. *Milliyet*, 4 March 1992; *The Economist*, 7 March 1992, 52.
19. *Milliyet*, 6 March & 14 March 1992.

equipment to aid Azerbaijan and that, if Armenia occupied all or a part of Nakhichevan, it had the right under the 1921 treaty to send troops into Nakhichevan.[21] The temperature rose further on 19 May, when the Turkish Commander of Land Forces, General Mühittin Fisunoglu, announced that "all necessary preparations" had been made, and that the army was awaiting orders from Ankara to act. Meanwhile, a strongly worded statement from the cabinet openly accused Armenia of "aggression and expansionism".[22] The US State Department also weighed in, by declaring that the administration "will not accept unilateral changes in the status of Nagorno–Karabakh, Nakhichevan, or any other territory, on the basis of military actions or violence".[23] There was also a strong reaction from Moscow, where Marshal Yevgeny Shaposhnikov, commander of the armed forces of the CIS, warned that any intervention by a third party could create the risk of a major war, since Armenia was a party to the CIS mutual security pact. Similar warnings were issued by Albert Chernishev, the Russian ambassador in Ankara.[24]

In the face of the mounting crisis, Prime Minister Demirel resisted strong domestic pressures, as well as appeals from Azerbaijan and Nakhichevan, for military intervention; as he put it: "No one can solve anything by force of arms. I say to those who ask us what we are waiting for: 'What do you want us to do? Is it such an easy thing to take up arms?' . . . You may capture land by force of arms but you won't be allowed to keep it."[25] Instead he put his main emphasis on behind-the-scenes diplomacy with both the USA and Russia. Accordingly, on 25–6 May, he paid an emergency visit to President Yeltsin in Moscow. This visit appears to have been a diplomatic success for Demirel. In their concluding communiqué, the two leaders recorded their "deep misgivings regarding the situation in Nagorno–Karabakh. The two parties concerned pointed out that the widening of the conflict beyond this region, the occupation of the town of Laçin [in the Armenia–Karabakh corridor] and the intensifying reports of clashes on the Armenian/Nakhichevan border are a source of special concern to them". They also confirmed their strong opposition to the altera-

---

20. Treaty of Friendship between Turkey and the RSFSR, 13 September 1921. Reprinted in J. C. Hurewitz, *Diplomacy in the Near and Middle East*, vol. II (???PrincetonNew York???: Van Nostrand, 1956), 95–7.

21. *Cumhuriyet*, 25 May 1992. Ecevit's interpretation of the 1921 treaty seems doubtful, although, as he pointed out, even if it were not accepted, Nakhichevan would still have the right to appeal for Turkish intervention, as a friendly neighbouring state. The parallel with Cyprus, which is sometimes suggested, also seems weak, since the Cyprus Treaty of Guarantee of 1960 specifically gives Turkey the right to intervene as a last resort (although only to protect the independence and territorial integrity of Cyprus).

22. Quoted, *Mideast Mirror* (London, daily), 19 May 1992.

23. Quoted, ibid., 20 May 1992.

24. Ibid., 21 May 1992; *Milliyet*, 20–1 May 1992.

25. BBC SWB, 14 May 1992. Ankara radio, 12 May 1992.

tion of borders by force, and committed themselves to co-operation in a wide range of fields.[26] This message seems to have got through to Yerevan: by 28 May, it was being reported that the guns overlooking Sadarak had fallen silent.[27] In effect, it appears that Armenia had been warned off making any outright attack on Nakhichevan.

After May 1992, Turkish influence in Azerbaijan appeared to be increasing, with the election of Abülfez Elchibey as President. During the summer of 1992, around 100 ex-officers of the Turkish army were reported to have entered Azerbaijan as advisers to the Azeri army, but the Turkish government carefully avoided sending soldiers or arms to Azerbaijan. Economically, the two countries advanced their relations. In particular, on 9 March 1993 they signed an outline agreement for the construction of an oil pipeline between Baku and Ceyhan, via Nakhichevan, to join the existing line between Kirkuk, in northern Iraq, and Yumurtalik, on Turkey's Mediterranean coast. A crucial but unsolved problem was how it could cross the strip of Armenian territory between Azerbaijan and Nakhichevan. One solution was to route it along the Iranian bank of the Aras river opposite to Armenian territory. However, Western oil companies, whose support would be essential, were said to be reluctant to give Iran a potential stranglehold over the project.[28]

Meanwhile, the fighting in and around Nagorno–Karabakh continued. On 28 March 1993 Armenian forces opened up a second corridor between the enclave and Armenia, through the town of Kelbajar, driving more Azeris from their homes. The UN Security Council reacted on 6 April by calling for an Armenian withdrawal from Azeri territory, but failed to condemn the invasion openly. Turkey also imposed a full economic embargo on Armenia. During June 1993, the situation deteriorated further, as Armenian forces made more advances. At the same time, President Elchibey was overthrown by an armed rebellion led by ex-Colonel Suret Husseinov, who had taken over large quantities of arms and ammunition from the departing ex-Soviet garrison at Ganja, in northern Azerbaijan. Outside observers found it hard to believe that the rebellion had not been promoted by Russia or, at the very least, by senior officers in the Russian army. As a result, Haydar Aliyev, another rival of Elchibey and a former member of the Politburo of the USSR, as well Chairman of the parliament of Nakhichevan since 1991, became Chairman of the Azeri parliament, and thus the acting President, with Husseinov as his Prime Minister.[29] He became the full President of Azerbaijan in October 1993.

---

26. *Milliyet*, 27 May 1992.
27. *The Independent*, 28 May 1992.
28. *Briefing*, 27 July 1992, 14; *Turkey Confidential*, September 1992, 10; *Milliyet*, 9 March 1993. See also *n.* 31, below.
29. *Briefing*, 14 June 1993, 14; 21 June 1993, 10–11.

Initially, the overthrow of Elchibey provoked sharp criticisms from Turkish political leaders. Whatever his faults, Elchibey had undoubtedly been a democratically elected President, and his removal had been carried out by brute force. However, Süleyman Demirel, who had succeeded Turgut Özal as President of Turkey after the latter's death in April 1993, made it clear that Turkey could and would not intervene in internal contests in Azerbaijan.[30] By the late summer, the Turkish government had reluctantly accepted the *fait accompli*. The pipeline project nevertheless became a major bone of contention. Soon after he came to power, Aliyev was reported to have cancelled the deal, in favour of an alternative route across Russian territory to Novorossisk, on the Black Sea. The Novorossisk route was strongly resisted by Turkey, since the oil would then have to be transported by tanker through the Bosphorus and Dardanelles, on its route to the Mediterranean. This would pose the risk of serious environmental damage, or possibly a catastrophic explosion, in the middle of Istanbul, Turkey's largest city. Apart from these strong environmental arguments, Turkey would also gain lose important political and economic advantages if the project for a pipeline across Anatolia were abandoned.[31]

In Azerbaijan, President Aliyev's political survival was likely to depend on whether he could recover the territory lost to the Armenians, and negotiate a reasonable settlement of the Nagorno–Karabakh dispute. On the

---

30. *Milliyet*, 23 June 1993.
31. Ibid., 2 August 1993; *The Independent*, 10 August 1993. Under Article 2 of the Montreux Convention, Turkey is obliged to allow free passage to merchant ships of all nations in peacetime. For the full text, see Harry N. Howard, *Turkey, the straits and US policy* (Baltimore: John Hopkins University Press, 1974), 292–9. However, a Turkish spokesman claimed that Turkey would be legally entitled to ban the passage of ships carrying potentially dangerous cargoes. It was expected that Turkey would forbid the passage of nuclear-powered ships, or tankers more than 150 metres long. *The Daily Telegraph*, 6 September 1993. The problem of deciding a route for a Baku–Turkey pipeline still remained unsolved at the time this book was being prepared for press in July 1995. By this time, President Aliyev had changed his position, and now backed the project, which had strong support from the United States. Hence, it seemed quite likely that it would eventually be built, either crossing Armenia (assuming there were a settlement of the Norgorno–Karabakh dispute) or Georgia. The alternative route, across a short section of northwestern Iran, appeared to be ruled out by the US embargo on economic dealings with Iran by US firms. In the short term, Azerbaijan was expected to start "early oil" production, with a limited export of around 70,000–80,000 barrels per day (b/d) in 1996 or early 1997. This would be exported by rail and existing pipelines, either across Russian or Georgian territory. Turkey had undertaken to buy all of Azerbaijan's "early oil" exports, if the latter route were chosen. Azerbaijan was not expected to reach full production of something like 750,000 b/d until 1998 or thereafter, by which time the trans-Turkey pipeline – if it were built – might become an attractive proposition. See Gareth Winrow, *Turkey in post-Soviet Central Asia* (London, Royal Institute of International Affairs, Russia and CIS Programme, 1995), 44–6, and Jeremy P. Carver and Greg Englefield, "Oil and gas pipelines from Central Asia: a new approach", *World Today* **50**(6), 119–21, 1994.

first score, the record during 1993 was one of almost unmitigated defeats for Azerbaijan. By early September the Armenians had captured virtually all the territory between Nagorno–Karabakh and Armenia proper, as well as the strong-point of Agdam, on the eastern side of the enclave. To the south, they had seized the towns of Fizuli and Jebrail, and were moving towards the frontier with Iran. If this move were completed, then it was expected that thousands of Azeri refugees would flee across the Aras into Iran, apart from the 100,000 or so who had already been driven from their homes by the previous month's fighting.[32] In mid-December 1993, the Azeris counter-attacked, recapturing a small amount of ground, but were reported to have suffered heavy casualties.[33]

The Armenian advances during 1993 brought another sharp rebuke from the UN Security Council, which on 30 July passed Resolution No. 853, confirming that Nagorno–Karabakh is part of Azerbaijan, and calling on the occupying forces – which were identified as Armenian – to withdraw immediately. The resolution was more toughly worded than its predecessor, but nothing was done to put it into effect.[34] During September 1993, further advances by the Armenians provoked Turkey into putting four battalions along its border on alert. More importantly, Iran also mobilized border units, and criticized the Armenian move towards Iranian territory. Iran was also forced to cope with an influx of Azeri refugees, fleeing across the Aras. The result was a potentially important shift in regional alignments. Up to this stage, Turkey and Iran had implicitly been ranged against one another, as Iranian policy seemed to show a tilt towards Armenia – mainly by keeping its border open for petroleum and other supplies. By the end of 1993, both Turkey and Iran were disturbed by Armenian expansionism, and the fact that it seemed to be supported by the reviving power of Russia. This rapprochement between Ankara and Tehran was marked by an unexpected visit to the Turkish capital by Iran's Foreign Minister, Ali Akbar Velayati, on 18–19 December, to be followed on 21 December by a previously arranged visit by Hassan Habibi, the Iranian first Vice-President. On the Turkish side, the main aim was to ensure joint action against the PKK, but there was also talk of reviving schemes for oil and gas pipelines from Iran to Turkey, and, more ambitiously, a gas pipeline from Turkmenistan to Europe, via Iranian and Turkish territory.[35] If these trends continued, then it seemed possible that, rather than confront one another as rivals for influence in Transcaucasia and Central Asia, Turkey and Iran might line up with one another against the resurgent ambitions of Russia.

By early 1994, similar considerations appeared to be affecting Turkey's

---

32. *The Independent*, 4 September 1993; *The Guardian*, 7 September 1993.
33. *The Economist*, 12 February 1994, 46.
34. *Milliyet*, 31 July 1993; *Briefing*, 2 August 1993, 13.

relations with Georgia. Since the dissolution of the Soviet Union, the two countries had enjoyed reasonably friendly relations, but Turkish attentions were mainly directed towards the war between Armenia and Azerbaijan, whereas Georgia was preoccupied by its internal chaos. Some Abkhazian emigrés have settled in Turkey, and have tried to promote an anti-Georgian stance by Ankara, but have had virtually no effect on government policy. In general, successive Turkish governments have recognized that it is important to maintain an entente with Georgia, as a regional counterbalance to both Russia and Armenia. These points were demonstrated in January 1994, when President Shevardnadze visited Ankara. Abkhazian demonstrators tried to enter his hotel, but were firmly dispersed by police. The Georgian President emphasized that the two countries had identical views on the Abkhazian problem, and the declaration issued by them confirmed their mutual respect for their territorial integrity, and the principle of non-interference in their domestic affairs. For his part, President Shevardnadze was apparently anxious to promote the idea that the BSEC organization should work towards regional disarmament, which would presumably be directed towards a reduction of Russian forces in the region. To this end, it was agreed that a special BSEC summit would be convened in Tbilisi in May or June 1994.[36]

The apparent rapprochement with Iran, and the entente with Georgia, nevertheless left Turkey with the task of adjusting its relationship with the Aliyev government in Baku, and avoiding a head-on collision with Moscow. For Ankara, the disturbing aspect of Elchibey's removal was that it appeared to have taken Azerbaijan out of Turkey's sphere of influence, and into that of Russia. On the other hand, it had not been an unmitigated loss from the Turkish viewpoint. President Elchibey had emphasized his closeness to Turkey, but his hostility to both Russia and Iran was a liability for Ankara, which needed to maintain workable relations with all the main regional actors. So long as Azerbaijan stayed out of the CIS, then Russia was likely to back the Armenians against the Azeris. Without supplies of fuel, arms and ammunition from Russian sources, the Armenians could never have launched their invasion of Azerbaijan. The Aliyev government's adherence to the CIS, which was formally ratified by the Azeri parliament

---

35. *Briefing*, 27 December 1993, 7–9; *Turkish Probe*, 23 December 1993, 2–3. In the summer of 1994, Turkey, Iran and Turkmenistan discussed plans for a pipeline to deliver natural gas from Turkmenistan to Turkey, via Iran. The pipeline would have a capacity of 15–25 billion m^3 per year, and would cost $8 billion to build. Similarly, in May 1995 the Turkish and Iranian ministries of energy and oil signed an outline agreement to build a gas pipeline with a capacity of 10 billion m^3 per year, from Tabriz in northwestern Iran, to Ankara. However, it was not clear whether these two projects would be connected, or how the necessary finance would be arranged: *Turkey Country Report*, 28 (London: Economist Intelligence Unit, 4th Quarter 1994); *Briefing* (15 May), 7, 1995.

36. *Turkish Probe* (20 January), 15, 1994.

in September 1993, fundamentally altered the factors in this equation since, in principle, Moscow now had an equal interest in maintaining good relations with both Baku and Yerevan. This consideration evidently underlay Russian attempts to broker a settlement between the two countries during the winter of 1993–4. Accordingly, in late September 1993 the Turkish government made it clear that it did not oppose Azerbaijan's adherence to the CIS, or even the stationing of CIS forces in Azeri territory.[37]

Meanwhile, President Aliyev was evidently anxious to mend his fences with Turkey. In a visit to Ankara in February 1994, he emphasized that Azerbaijan was determined to preserve its independence (by clear implication, from Russia) and to secure the complete withdrawal of Armenian forces from its territory. An Agreement for Friendship and Comprehensive Co-operation, which was signed by the two sides, also reaffirmed the existing agreements between them, referring specifically to oil and natural gas pipelines. This was taken as a sign that President Aliyev was now prepared to reverse his previous opposition to the Baku–Ceyhan pipeline project, although whether he would be able to square this with Azerbaijan's delicate relationship with Russia was still uncertain.[38]

For Turkey, the most ominous implication of all these developments was their effect on the diplomatic climate between Ankara and Moscow. The overthrow of President Elchibey, and the reassertion of Russian power in Georgia, suggested that President Yeltsin was now intent on promoting a Russian version of the Monroe doctrine in the "near abroad", in which the southern republics of the ex-USSR would be reduced to roughly the same status as that of the states of eastern Europe within the former Warsaw Pact. Ironically, this had meant that Turkey's relations with Moscow were now a good deal more tense than they had been during that later stages of the Cold War. The most open point of conflict was the Russian demand, voiced in late 1993, that NATO should accept a revision of the Treaty on Conventional Forces in Europe (CFE) to allow it to maintain a larger armed presence in Transcaucasia than had originally been allowed. Allied to this was the apparent Russian determination to exclude other powers from any role in policing a settlement between Armenia and Azerbaijan, assuming it could be arranged.

Turkey firmly rejected both these proposals, and was generally supported by the Western powers. At the NATO summit in Brussels on 10–11 January 1994, the principle that the CFE treaty could not be altered was confirmed, although the Turkish government apparently told a visiting Rus-

---

37. BBC *SWB*, 30 September 1993. Anatolia News Agency, 22 September 1993. See *n*. 31, above. Since this chapter was originally written, generally President Aliyev appears to have moved over to a more independent, and implicitly pro-Turkish, position (as of July 1995).

38. *Briefing*, 14 February 1994, 9.

sian military delegation at the end of the month that Turkey might be willing to consider some alterations when the treaty came up for renewal in 1996, assuming that Russia fully complied with all its stipulations up to that date.[39] Similarly, the CSCE (which has since changed its name to Organisation for Security and Cooperation in Europe, or OSCE) refused to endorse Russia's claim that it should be given the sole right to peace-keeping functions in the ex-Soviet republics.[40] This was reassuring, but it still left open the question as to whether the Western powers would be willing to give material support to either of these declarations. Without such support, it was hard to see how Turkey could prevent Russia achieving its own agenda, whatever its official undertakings under the CFE treaty, or its commitments to the OSCE. In the longer term, it was still possible that if a measure of political and economic stability were restored to Transcaucasia, then Turkey could develop mutually beneficial relations with both Armenia and Azerbaijan. Equally, the development of the economies of all the Transcaucasian republics would almost certainly strengthen their ties with the West, including Turkey, and help to release them from Russian hegemony. For the time being, however, this ideal outcome still seemed to be some way over the horizon.

---

39. Ibid., 31 January 1994, 10.
40. *Turkish Probe*, 3 February 1994, 13–14.

CHAPTER FOUR

Condemned to react, unable to influence: Iran and Transcaucasia

FRED HALLIDAY

The decline and collapse of Soviet power in Transcaucasia has proven to be one of the major challenges facing the government of the Islamic Republic of Iran (IRI), and one the long-term consequences of which will take many years to work through. Before the Gorbachev era, Iran, along with the rest of the world, had assumed that its northern frontier with the Soviet Union was secure and, economic interactions apart, closed. It faced turbulence on all three other frontiers – Iraq to the west, the Persian Gulf to the south, Afghanistan to the east – but on this northern frontier at least matters seemed to be settled, in a pattern established in the aftermath of the First World War, when the states of both Soviet Russia and Pahlavi Iran were created, and, after a period of initial conflict, and with the major interruption of the Second World War, fell into the pattern they were to exhibit till the late 1980s. The frontier itself was clearly defined. Neither Moscow nor Tehran were engaged in any significant interference in each other's internal affairs. The hegemony of each precluded the entry of other, disruptive, third parties. All of this was to change from 1985 and more particularly from 1988 onwards, with ambivalent results for the IRI.

Before proceeding to examine the historical record and contemporary situation more carefully, three general background considerations concerning Iran's relation to Transcaucasia may be worth making. The first is that history may be of limited relevance to explaining the contemporary post-Soviet situation. Although an examination of the past is an essential part of an analysis of the present, to examine causes, continuities and the legitimacy of claims, the past itself cannot provide an answer to present problems; its record is itself open to different uses and interpretations, and for all their invocation of historic justifications, the movements and actors of today may be responding much more to present concerns and opportunities than to the impulse of past wrongs and ambitions. This goes as much for the claims of Islamism and pan-Islamism as it does for nationalist movements. In some ways the past is an explanation for present patterns: the debates in Azerbaijan over national identity – the appropriate combination of the Turkish and the Persian – recollect in some respects those of the decades before the First World War. But there are many other things that the past cannot explain; for example, it has little light to cast on the apparent absence of Azerbaijani separatism in Iran during the 1980s and early 1990s, and it is of little guide in assessing how transnational economic factors, pertaining to energy, will affect the future of the area.

The second general consideration is that despite the existence over two centuries of the frontier between Transcaucasia on the one hand, and Iran and Turkey on the other, Transcaucasia is in many respects part of the Middle East, and more specifically of a broader area encompassing parts of northwestern Iran, northern Iraq and eastern Turkey. This is evident from history, where the mixture of peoples, empires and cultures corresponds little to more recent frontiers, and from the present where the form that the ethnic problem takes, namely inter-ethnic feuding, as distinct from anti-foreign nationalism, is common to the whole region.[1] The course of events not only in Azerbaijan but also in Georgia, and the kinds of legitimacy and mobilization practised by emergent political forces, have as much in common with the Middle East as with Russia: any student of Iranian or Turkish politics will find much to recognize in the language and style of, say, Zviad Gamsakhurdia or Abulfaz Elchibey.[2] The visitor to Baku is in a city at least as redolent of Tehran, Ankara or Baghdad as of Moscow.[3] Without conceding any determination or necessary continuity to such ideological forms, it is evident in Transcaucasia that elements of political culture, within and between ethnic groups, have been reproduced over the two centuries since Turkey and Iran ceded control to Russia.

The collapse of the Soviet frontier has, therefore, re-established a link with the rest of the Middle East that had, until 1921, been very alive, and had, before the late eighteenth century, not known significant Russian influence. This historical contiguity and connection suggest that one of the most important implications of the Transcaucasian conflicts is the impact these may have on the ethnic conflicts of this broader area. In one brutal respect, the map has been changed by the events of the early twentieth century: the elimination of the Armenian community in eastern Anatolia.

---

1. For an analysis that brings out the shared characteristics of the ethnic problem in all three Transcaucasian republics, see Ronald Suny, "The revenge of the past: socialism and ethnic conflict in Transcaucasia", New Left Review, November–December 1990. Ernest Gellner's observation on the different forms of the ethnic problem in the USSR merits recalling: "In the Baltic states, they hate the Russians; in the Caucasus, they hate each other; in Central Asia they hate whom the mafia tells them to hate". The common historical context in which nationalism emerged in the region is given in Firuz Kazem-zadeh, The struggle for Transcaucasia (Oxford: G. Ronald, 1951).
2. The symbolism of moustaches should not be underplayed: Takrit (birthplace of Saddam Hussein) and Gori (birthplace of Stalin) are but some hundreds of miles apart!
3. See, one account, Fred Halliday & Maxine Molyneux, "Letter from Baku", MERIP Middle East reports, January–February 1986.

What was the heartland of Armenia has now shifted eastwards, and irrevocably so, even if Armenian nationalists still include large parts of eastern Turkey in the territorial claim they make for the new republic. Nonetheless, the comparisons between the Azerbaijani/Armenian conflict and others to the south and southwest – Turkish/Kurdish, Azerbaijani/Kurdish, Kurdish/Arab, Arab/Turcoman – are striking enough.

The third preliminary point that merits noting, one in part derived from the past, is that for Iran the main importance of Transcaucasia is not an Islamic connection or identity, or even that of territoriality, but that of strategic balance and security, combined with the maintenance and, if possible, development of economic ties. Most specifically it involves the question of how the Transcaucasia region may be used by hostile powers, most obviously Russia or Turkey, against Iran. The concern is not so much to spread Islamism, let alone to re-establish dominion, but to protect the Iranian state.

With these points in mind, it is now possible to look in more detail at the three main components of Iran's relations with Transcaucasia: the historic record, the Azerbaijan question, and the development of involvement from 1988 onwards.

The historic record

The Czarist and early Soviet periods

From an Iranian perspective, the Russian domination of the Transcaucasia region is a recent, and, as it has turned out, rather transient occurrence. Before the late eighteenth century, Russia was not a power in the area: this 200-year influence contrasts with 3,000 years of Iranian involvement in what was, until the late eighteenth century, as much part of Iran as any other part of the area. With the break-up of the Soviet system in the late 1980s, the term Greater Iran – *Iran-i bozorg* – has started to be used, with historical, cultural and possibly economic overtones, but without any specific irredentist implications: Transcaucasia is certainly part of this Greater Iran. In pre-Islamic times, Iranian states ruled much or all of Transcaucasia, and under the early Islamic empires Persian culture, language, economic influence were strong. In the cultural sphere, the most prominent period was that of Caucasian lyrical poetry, epitomized in the world of Nizami, from Ganja, a figure revered in Iran and Azerbaijan to this day.[4] With the emergence of the modern Persian state around 1500, Transcaucasia was in large part ruled by the Safavi and later Qajar monarchies, the latter being themselves a Turkic dynasty. The prevalence of Shi'ism among the Azerbaijanis dates from this period and from the Iranian influence. Nadir Shah sought to reaffirm Iranian influence in this area in the mid–eighteenth century and what are now Azerbaijan, Georgia and Armenia were ruled by the Qajars in the 1790s; broadly speaking, Georgia was finally occupied by the Russians (in 1796), Azerbaijan was ceded in the treaty of Gulistan (1813) and Armenia and Nakhichevan in that of Turkmanchai (1828).[5] A protocol signed in 1829 defined the frontier between the two states, and was made more detailed in a protocol of 1883.

Since the 1820s the issue of the border, as such, was not a major factor in Iranian–Russian relations. The loss of the Transcaucasian lands was occasionally evoked in Iranian politics, as during the Constitutional Revolution, but more as index of what a weak Shah such as Fath Ali Shah could do than as the basis for an irredentist claim. On only one occasion in modern history did an official Iranian challenge to the frontier arise, namely during the Persian submission to the Versailles Peace conference in 1919. Tehran did not claim Georgia but did demand the return of what were, in effect, Armenia and Azerbaijan:

> In the North, the cities and provinces wrested from Persia after the Russian wars. We will cite Bacou, Derbent, Chakhi, Chemakha, Guendja (Elisabethapol), Karabakh, Nakhdjevan, Erivan. These provinces must be returned to Persia, for they had already formed part of Persia. The large majority of their inhabitants are Musulmans, and the generality of them are Persian in origin and race. In fact, from every point of view, historical, geographic, economic, commercial, religious, cultural, they are attached to Persia. Furthermore, a large portion of the inhabitants of these provinces have lately appealed to the Government of Teheran, to protect them, and they have expressed the wish to be restored to Persia.[6]

Improbable as this claim was, and without any resonance at Versailles,

---

4. Nizami's statue was erected by the Soviet authorities in Baku, and manuscripts of his *Khamsaname* displayed prominently in the national museum. On Nizami's place in Persian literature and the flowering of the Azeri school, see Jan Rypka, *Iranische Literaturgeschichte*, 193–205 (Leipzig: Otto Harrassowitz, 1959). In his *Azerbaijani poetry: classic, modern, traditional* Mirza Ibrahimov includes (without listing language of composition) both Persian and Azeri works (Moscow: Progress Publishers, 1970).

5. On the history of this period, see Muriel Atkin, *Russia and Iran* 1780–1828 (Minneapolis: University of Minnesota Press, 1980); Firuz Kazemzadeh, "Iranian relations with Russia and the Soviet Union, to 1921" and Gavin Hambly, "Agha Muhammad Khan and the establishment of the Qajar dynasty". In *The Cambridge history of Iran*, Peter Avery et al. (eds), vol. VII, "From Nadir Shah to the Islamic republic", 314–349, 104–143 (Cambridge: Cambridge University Press, 1991). The pattern of Iranian/Russian relations between Gulistan and Turkmanchai offers a bitter contemporary analogy: the attempt by the Iranians to re-open the conflict with the Russians was a result of pressure from militant clergy – resulting in a further defeat and loss of more territory. The comparison with Khomeini's misguided continuation of the war with Iraq after 1982, when the IRI could have secured a favourable peace, is indicative.

6. Kazemzadeh 1951, 266–7.

this proposal was revealing in certain respects: faced with a crisis of Russian power in Transcaucasia, Iran did not support the independence of these states, but rather their incorporation into Iran; Georgian territory was not included in the claim, but that of Armenia was. Once rejected at Versailles, this claim was dropped. Chapter 3 of the 1921 Soviet–Iranian treaty formalized the existing frontiers and allowed for some minor changes, by mutual agreement. Final detailed demarcation of the 797km long frontier took place in 1957, through the work of a joint boundary commission that, among other things, settled ownership of 805 significant islands lying in the Arax river.[7]

Less manageable was the issue of cross-border movements at periods of political upheaval on either side of the frontier. Prior to 1917 movement of people across the frontier was common, and Baku in Russian Azerbaijan attracted large numbers of migrant workers from Iran as the oil industry developed in the late nineteenth century.[8] During the constitutional revolution in Iran the upheavals in Tabriz brought in first support from Russian revolutionaries and then the counter-revolutionary intervention of Czarist forces. In this pre-1917 period, Baku was important for two other reasons: as a transit point for those making the journey from Tehran by boat and rail to Europe, and as a pilgrimage site.[9] In the conditions of weak or absent central government that endured in Iran before and through the First World War, there was in effect no political frontier between the two states: armies – Turkish, Russian, British – moved back and forth across the frontier. In 1920 the Bolsheviks recaptured Baku and then provided support to the insurrection in the neighbouring Iranian province of Gilan. Policy in Gilan followed a pattern of intervention similar in several respects to later Soviet moves into neighbouring areas of Central Asia–Sinjiang in the 1930s, Azerbaijan and Kurdistan in the 1940s, Afghanistan in the late 1970s: in each case the intervention was determined by strategic concerns, and terminated after a period of time, with dire consequences for Moscow's local revolutionary allies.[10] Only with the establishment of new central authorities in Tehran and Moscow, and the signing of their treaty of 1921, was this period of fluidity ended.

---

7. M. H. Ganji, "Some highlights on the historical developments of Azerbaijan boundaries". Paper presented to conference on Iranian Boundaries, Geopolitics and International Boundaries Research Centre, SOAS, 9 December 1991. The ability of the USSR and Iran to settle a border conflict running along a river, and within that to resolve the issue of disputed islands, is significant, if only by contrast with their inability to do so on other frontiers: the Iranians vis-à-vis the Shatt al-Arab frontier with Iraq, the Soviets in their dispute with China on the Ussuri river, where the question of disputed island territory was to lead to border clashes in 1969. In 1994 an additional Iranian/Azeri border commission was set up, but this was to deal with minor matters.

8. On the interaction of Russian Azerbaijan with Iran in this period, see chapter 2 of Sepehr Zabih, *The communist movement in Iran* (Berkeley: University of California Press, 1966).

9. Author's interview Boniatov, Azerbaijani Academy of Sciences, Baku, July 1984.

Although in Article 1 of the treaty the Bolsheviks renounced the impe-rial treaties imposed by the Czars, and the economic and legal concessions contained within them, this did not apply to the territorial stipulations of these treaties: Article 3 explicitly reaffirmed the border protocol of 1883.[11] The settlement of 1921 was also of political import, reflecting as it did both an entente between the two new regimes and their ability to reassert con-trol over all the territory they had inherited. Consequently, from 1921 onwards the frontier was to a large extent closed to population or political movement from either side, even if minor incidents and infiltrations con-tinued. The one exception was the movement of Iranian Armenians to Erevan after the Second World War, encouraged by Stalin. This post-1921 insulation of the frontier changed dramatically with the Second World War when, in addition to the invasion and occupation of Iran by Soviet forces, the question of Azerbaijan re-emerged.

The Azerbaijan question: 1945–6 and after

The most important and in the long run potentially uncertain issue in Iran–Transcausian relations concerns Azerbaijan, currently divided into an independent state in the north, with a population of around seven mil-lion, and a more populous region in Iran, comprising the provinces of east and west Azerbaijan, with populations estimated at around 15 million.[12] The issue of the Azerbaijani population of Iran is hard to evaluate since there are significant ethnic minorities in the Azerbaijani governorates – Persians, Kurds, Tats – and many Azerbaijanis live outside Azerbaijan proper, in Tehran and elsewhere; it has been estimated that between a third and a half of the population of the Tehran bazaar are Azerbaijanis.[13] Two centuries of separation between Russian and Iranian spheres of influence have left their mark on the language of the two populations of Azerbaijan, and there are some differences of vocabulary between them: for example, northern Azeris refer to the king as *kiral*, southerners use *shah*. However, their language is to most intents and purposes the same (in contrast to other divided peoples of the region, such as the Kurds and Armenians).

---

10. On the Soviet role in the Gilan movement, and its implications for broader Iranian pol-itics at the time, see Zabih 1966, 13–26; Shahpur Ravasani, *Sowjetrepublik Gilan* (Berlin: Basis, 1973) and Fred Halliday, "Revolution in Iran: was it possible in 1921?", *Khamsin* 7, 53–64, 1980.
11. Text of the 1921 treaty in Nasrollah Fatemi, *Diplomatic history of Persia 1917–1923*, 317–24 (New York: Russell Moore, 1955).
12. In 1992 a third Azerbaijani province, Ardebil, was created from east Azerbaijan. The official reason given was this was to highlight Ardebil's role in the history of Shi'ism in Iran but it may also have reflected security concerns.
13. The larger figure is put forward by even moderate (northern) Azerbaijani nationalists such as Gaidar Aliev.

Whatever the political options they choose, they continue to identify themselves as one people.

Here is not the place to provide an extended account of Azerbaijani nationalism north or south of the Arax river. Suffice it to say that from the late nineteenth century onwards this emerged as a current in both Baku and Tabriz, and it reached its first culmination with the weakening of both central governments in the First World War. The movement in Iran, led by Sheikh Mohammad Khiabani, was crushed in 1920; although supported by the Bolsheviks, it rejected communism and sought to improve its position within Iran by putting into effect the provisions for provincial autonomy in the 1907 constitution rather than to secede from it. The Azeri nationalist movement in Russia, by contrast, was sympathetic to Turkey and wanted complete independence.[14] This current movement was to re-emerge with the next crisis of Tehran's power, the Anglo–Russian invasion of 1941, which led to the establishment of the Azerbaijani republic of 1945–6. Subsequent events have obscured this episode; whereas on the one hand, the Tabriz republic was created as a result of great power rivalry attendant upon the end of the Second World War and the onset of the Cold War, and although its moment of inception and conclusion were dictated by Soviet diplomatic priorities, it was not *simply* the product of external manipulation. This becomes clearer by looking at it not in terms of international politics, but in that of the past half century of Azerbaijani history. For a variety of reasons resulting from the social and political changes within Iranian Azerbaijan in the inter-war period, a distinct Azerbaijani nationalism, led by the *Firqeh-i Dimukrat*, was able to develop in this period and to find expression in the Soviet-created republic, just as in the Kurdish republic a similar process occurred.[15] The Soviet withdrawal in March 1946 led in December to the reoccupation of Iranian Azerbaijan by the Shah's forces and suppression not only of the communist led movement there, but also of other, cultural, expressions of Azerbaijani culture and nationalism.

The Azerbaijani experience of 1945–6 is often regarded as simply a creation of external manipulation and as an attempt to split Azerbaijan off from the rest of Iran. But neither of these is strictly true: there was an endogenous factor that, however distorted, emerged during the Pishevari

---

14. On the Khiabani movement see Ervard Abrahamian, *Iran between two revolutions*, 112–3 (Princeton, NJ: Princeton University Press, 1982); Peter Avery, *Modern Iran*, 218–220 (London: Ernest Benn, 1967); and George Lenczowski, *Russia and the West in Iran, 1918–48: a study in big power rivalry*, 60–65 (New York: Greenwood Press, 1968). Both Avery and Lenczowski uses the term "separatism", but, as they make clear, Khiabani was not separatist in the sense of calling on Azerbaijan to leave Iran, only in the sense of calling for less central government control.

15. On the Azerbaijani movement at this time see chapter 8 of Abrahamian 1982, 388–415; Louise Fawcett, *Iran and the Cold War: the Azerbaijani crisis of 1946* (Cambridge: Cambridge University Press, 1992).

regime. Similarly, it is mistaken to see the Azerbaijani republic, either formally or informally, as an attempt to secede: it was, at best, an attempt to
acquire some greater autonomy for the Azerbaijanis within Iran as a whole,
at worst, an attempt by Moscow to create a region under its control within
Iran in order the better to manipulate and ultimately dominate the regime
in Tehran itself. As already suggested, it bears comparison with the USSR's
other Central Asian excursions in Gilan, Sinjiang, Afghanistan: in all cases,
Moscow acted according to its own strategic dictates, but the occasion to
do so was in part the result of indigenous radical forces emerging.

The issue of Azerbaijani nationalism is all the harder to evaluate because
of what occurred, or rather did not occur, within the region during the revolution of 1978–9. In one word, nothing happened. There was no revival of
the nationalism of the 1940s, and no apparent resistance to the Islamic
republican regime in Tehran on a specifically Azeri basis. One faction of the
Islamic movement, the Islamic People's Republican Party, led by Ayatollah
Sharriat-Madari, had strong following in Azerbaijan, and revolted against
the central government in December 1979: but this revolt was not widely
supported, and was more religious than ethnic in character, pertaining to
differing interpretations of the Islamic revolution. Similarly, one of the
more prominent liberal opponents of the clerical direction in the revolution, Rahmatollah Moghaddam-Maraghe'i, was elected from east Azerbaijan. He was one of the only independent delegates in the first *Majlis*, but
was soon forced into exile and no distinctive movement emerged.[16] Since
1979, although there has been considerable and overt resistance among
other ethnic groups – Kurds, Arabs, Turcomans, Baluch – the Azerbaijani
regions of Iran have been quiet. In an upheaval in which many dogs
barked, Azerbaijani nationalism is the one dog that did not, at least during
the first 15 years after the Islamic revolution. It had widely been assumed
that such a movement would recur in the event of a new upheaval in Iran
and, within the bounds of state-to-state propriety, Soviet policy had also
sought to promote an idea of a separate Azerbaijani nation.[17]

This lack of Azeri nationalism in itself requires some attempt at explanation, not least by contrast with what was the case in the 1940s. It is not
possible to be sure about counter-factuals, but several factors appear to
have contributed to this contrast between the incidence of Azerbaijani
nationalism in the two most recent periods of upheaval in Iranian politics.
The most important is the change in Iranian society as a whole between the

---

16. Moghaddam-Maraghe'i's political platform was above all one based on defence of pluralism and democracy, not Azerbaijani particularism (author's interview with
Moghaddam-Maraghe'i, Tehran, August 1979). On his critique of the IRI see Shaul
Bakhash, *The reign of the ayatollahs*, 81–4 (London: I. B. Tauris, 1985).
17. David Nissman, *The Soviet Union and Iranian Azerbaijan: the use of nationalism for political
penetration* (Boulder, Colorado: Westview Press, 1977).

1940s and the 1970s, a process by which the population of Azerbaijan was to a considerable extent integrated into the economy and polity of Iran as a whole. To a certain extent, the Azerbaijani elite had always been important in Iran, from the Safavi and Qajar dynasties through to the commercial and administrative elites of the Reza Khan regime. In the 1940s Azerbaijan was, if anything, more developed than the rest of Iran, and, in the context of the Iranian–Soviet dispute over oil concessions, it may have appeared probable that an autonomous Azerbaijan could have acquired direct access to some of this oil wealth, just as Baku to the north had done. By the late 1970s this differential, and potential advantage, had gone. What the increasing prosperity of the post-war period did was to broaden that integration, diffusing oil money into Azerbaijan, but tying the region more closely to Tehran and giving Azerbaijani merchants and officials a greater participation in Iran's economic and political system. The changes accompanying the Islamic revolution did not alter this: Azerbaijanis were prominent members of the new political elite, whereas the commercial elite continued to include many Azerbaijanis.[18] The form that Azerbaijani assertiveness took was not that of demanding separation but of vaunting their power at the centre: a similar phenomenon could be identified in some other distinctive areas where secession was not an issue, such as Bavaria or Crete. The fundamental reason for the failure of Azerbaijani nationalism to emerge in the late 1970s was, it seems, rational calculation: incorporation into the central regime, politically and economically. Whether this was under the Shah or under Khomeini, inclusion was preferable to the risks of separation.

Three further factors may have contributed to this outcome. The first was that, despite its overall dictatorial character, the Islamic regime did offer something for Azerbaijanis. The new constitution provided some cultural and linguistic rights denied under the Shahs, with the result that books and newspapers could now be published in Azeri.[19] The politics of the IRI certainly had an element of chauvinism within them, and some of this was Persian in character: but it was above all a Shi'ite chauvinism, so that the Kurds and Arabs, who were predominantly Sunni, felt excluded from the new regime in a way that the Azeris did not. Moreover, the predominant view among Azeris was not that they were a separate "nationality" or "minority", but were a "people", comparable to the Persians – a *khalq* rather than an *aqaliyyat*.[20] On an impressionistic level, it would seem

---

18. Among Azeris in the new regime: Hojjat al Islam Khamene'i; Mehdi Bazargan, Ayotollah Khalkhali, Ayatollah Musavi-Ardebili.

19. On the suppression of Azeri culture under the monarchy see Reza Baraheni, *The crowned cannibals* (New York: Vintage Books, 1977).

20. A prominent early exponent of this view was the Iranian Azeri writer Ahmad Kasravi. Kasravi saw himself an Iranian nationalist, and had broken with Khiabani on the issue of provincial autonomy (Abrahamian 1982: 113).

that Azeri sentiment was directed more against the supposedly rival, but inferior, Kurds, than against Persians; indeed the main form of political conflict in the Azerbaijani region during the Islamic revolution was that of clashes between Kurds and Azeris in western Azerbaijan, around Urumiyeh, rather than of anti-Persian mobilizations.[21] Finally, the apparent hiatus between the 1940s and the 1970s may have something to do with a straightforward political lesson – the movement for Azeri autonomy of the 1940s was manipulated and destroyed, it was a failure. Just as within Iran as a whole the Mosadeqist and Tudeh movements were discredited in the eyes of a younger generation, in addition to being repressed after 1953, so the Azeri movement was not waiting to be reborn after its defeat in 1946: it had in effect been discounted precisely because of what had happened in that period. When expressions of Azerbaijani nationalism began to emerge in the late 1980s, in support of the movement emerging in northern Azerbaijan, this took the form not of a statement of separatism, nor even of autonomy from Tehran, but of a demand for greater support by Tehran for Baku, *vis-à-vis* the USSR and Armenia.

Tehran and the post-Soviet system, 1988–93

In this context the Islamic revolution was to have remarkably little impact on the course of Iran's relations with the USSR, as far as they concerned the Caucasus; in other areas, such as Afghanistan, the treatment of the Tudeh Party, and trade, there were significant developments, but not here. An area of potential uncertainty was opened up by Iran's attempts to revise the 1921 treaty, with regard to Articles 5 and 6: these gave the Russians the right to intervene in Iran if hostile third parties were active there. Moscow refused to acknowledge Tehran's right to do this, arguing that it was not possible to renounce part of a treaty; but this remained a political wrangle, rather than a diplomatic or legal issue. Neither side saw fit to question the broader provisions of the treaty in practice, especially with regard to territorial provision. The *status quo ante*, as far as relations with Transcaucasia were concerned, therefore continued. All this was to change in the late 1980s with the gradual weakening of Soviet control in the Transcaucasia region, leading up to the dissolution of the USSR in late 1991 and the emergence of three independent states in Azerbaijan, Georgia and Armenia. Despite its hostility to Soviet communism, and rhetorical appeals to the Muslims of the Caucasus and Central Asia, the Islamic Republic did not encourage the breakup of the USSR. In common with almost all outside powers, Iran did not

---

21. During a conversation I had with a group of young Azeris in Tehran in 1979, I asked whether they would not like provincial autonomy. The answer was: "We might, but then the Kurds would get it too".

anticipate fragmentation and, moreover, as we shall see, had reason for being concerned about it. In general, the weakening of the USSR was a result of changes at the centre, in Moscow, and if any region of the former Soviet Union contributed to it, it was the Baltic states. Indeed, one can say that it was the pattern set by and in the Baltics that did more than anything to accelerate the end of Soviet power in Transcaucasia.[22] There was, of course, the particular aggravation of the dispute around Nagorno–Karabakh, which from 1988 onwards led to clashes between Baku and both Erevan and Moscow, and to demands by some nationalists in these states for independence. But neither local pressure nor urgings from outside (Iran included) were the main factors in the final retreat of Soviet power.

For their part, post-revolutionary Iranian politics, despite their repressive character, are not monolithic, in the way that those of Iraq or the former Soviet Union have been. Official statements, issuing from the president's office or the foreign ministry, are often at variance with what particular religious leaders, members of the *Majlis* or newspapers are saying. Transcaucasia has been no exception, but although some radical leaders advocated a more forward policy based on Islamic solidarity, Iran's official role in this period of transition was cautious and reactive. First, while criticizing Moscow at the ideological level, most remarkably in Khomeini's letter to Gorbachev, and while militantly opposed to the Soviet intervention in Afghanistan, Iran wanted to avoid any charge of encouraging secession in the USSR itself. The reason was obvious: as a multi-ethnic country, Iran did not want to encourage similar demands, and forms of interference, against its own state. Moscow had, in the 1940s, backed the movement in Kurdistan and Azerbaijan, and had intermittently attacked the IRI's policies in Kurdistan in the period 1979–81. Thus, right into the latter part of 1991 Iran was calling for changed conditions for Muslims within the USSR, not for independence: for example, official Iranian reaction to the military intervention in Baku in January 1990 supported the desire of the Azerbaijanis to express their Muslim identity, but blamed the trouble on Western government involvement and Western state incitement, and restated Iran's commitment to non-interference in the internal affairs of other countries.[23] Secondly, Iran wanted to maintain its economic ties with the USSR and to use the changed circumstances of the Soviet Union for its own benefit: when Rafsanjani visited the USSR, taking in both Moscow and Baku, in late June 1989, the main purpose of his visit was to sign agreements on economic and technical co-operation. He pointedly declined,

---

22. See Anatol Lieven, *The Baltic revolution* (London: Yale University Press, 1993). However, there were many considerable informal links between Baltic and Transcaucasian opposition groups in the late 1980s.
23. *BBC summary of world broadcasts*, part iv: the Middle East and North Africa, 22 January 1990, ME/0998, A/1; 23 January 1990, ME/0669 A/1; 26 January 1990, 1 ME/0672i.

during his visit to Baku, to make anti-Soviet political statements (and one may assume that his hosts did not take him to a central square to see the statue of the woman tearing off her veil). Thirdly, Iran was concerned from the beginning that any lessening of Soviet influence in this area would be replaced by an increase in Turkish influence, and by extension in American influence. Radical critics of the Iranian government position were particularly keen on this theme: thus Ayatollah Musavi-Ardebili, himself an Azerbaijani, in a speech in April 1992 was to denounce Turkey's role in the Caucasus and Central Asia and he accused it of being subservient to the USA.[24] The thread running through much of Iran's policies towards Transcaucasia and Central Asia since the late 1980s was the anxiety about a Turkish–American presence growing as Soviet power withdrew. Tehran gave the impression of wanting to avoid an all-out competition with Turkey, and both sides had more common interests, not least in the area of trade and transit, than they had issues in dispute: but Iran left little doubt that, if it has to choose between Moscow and Ankara, it would choose Moscow – the comparatively recent, more distant and more ineffectual competition. Fourthly, Iran was concerned about the potential cost to it of a major crisis in Transcaucasia, be this between states and ethnic groups or through outbreaks of violence between political factions, as occurred in all three states. Having faced the influx of over a million refugees from Iraq and Afghanistan, Tehran did not want to see a third tide of refugee movements coming in from the north. In January 1990, during the first outbreak of Azerbaijani nationalism along the frontier, Iran allowed up to 40,000 Soviet Azerbaijanis to enter Iran on visits, but it sought to resolve this issue with the Soviet authorities, and pointed out that the 1921 treaty allowed for such limited cross-border movements.

It was these broad considerations that guided Iranian policy in this area. Before 1991, Iranian policy evolved in relation to two particular issues: Nagorno–Karabakh and internal Azerbaijani politics. On the Nagorno–Karabakh conflict, Iran sought to adopt a neutral position, appealing to both sides to settle their differences peacefully. It condemned all attempts to alter frontiers by force, but also condemned the forcible movement of populations. If Iran condemned the Azeris for some of their actions in the conflict, it also condemned the Armenians, first for sabotaging the May 1992 ceasefire accord, and secondly for appearing to threaten the Azeri enclave of Nakhichevan later in the month. At times Iranian policy appeared to one of blaming both sides, as in a semi-official *Tehran Times* editorial in March 1990 that can have given little comfort to either party:

The two ethnic groups do not even appear ready to utilize the favourable political situation now prevailing in the USSR after sev-

---

24. *BBC SWB ME*/1377 A/5–6, 27 April 1992.

enty years of political repression . . . Internecine wars between ethnic races and nationalists are unacceptable to any central government. Continuation of violence and bloody clashes only justifies Moscow's use of force to quell the disturbances.[25]

At other times, Iran stressed that it was the only external power capable of acting as a broker between the two sides. Most notably, in the agreement reached by all three parties – Iran, Armenia, Azerbaijan – in May 1992, Tehran sought to bring peace to the rival factions. But whereas in public it expressed optimism and commitment towards such a process, Iranian diplomats were pessimistic in private about the prospects of a quick peace, and thought the Nagorno–Karabakh issue would continue to blaze for years to come.[26] The best they thought they could do was to shorten the time needed for the fire to burn itself out. The high point of Iranian diplomatic involvement came in May 1992, when the presidents of both Armenia and Azerbaijan signed a tripartite agreement on a ceasefire in Tehran, as well as separate agreements between each and Iran on economic cooperation. The latter two demonstrated the extent to which Iran would have benefited from increased economic relations with these two, particularly in the field of energy, and if implemented, would have given Iran considerable access to their markets.[27]

Iran's main area of concern, for the religious, cultural and historic reasons already given, was Azerbaijan itself. As long as the USSR existed (i.e. up to late 1991) Iran at no point called for the incorporation of northern Azerbaijan into Iran, nor did it call for the independence of Azerbaijan from Moscow. Beyond appeals to Islamic sentiment in Azerbaijan, Iran took up a critical stand when it felt the Soviet authorities were repressing political forces in Baku, notably in January 1990. When expressions of Islamic sentiment were made, Tehran reported these favourably and the impression given in Tehran was that Islamic sentiment in Azerbaijan was growing. Iranian media endorsed those in Azerbaijan who wanted to go from the Cyrillic to the Perso-Arabic script, rather than to the Latin.[28] Despite their cautious and sympathetic policy as far as developments inside Azerbaijan were concerned, the Iranian authorities must have realized, however, that neither the communist forces of Ayaz Mutalibov, nor the Popular Front opposition, saw their main salvation in imitating the IRI. Concerned above all to limit the impact of events in Azerbaijan on Iran,

---

25. *BBC SWB* ME/0727/A/1, 31 March 1990.

26. Interview with diplomat from Iranian embassy, London, May 1992.

27. Texts of all three agreements *BBC SWB* s/1377 c/6, 11 May 1992.

28. *BBC SWB* ME/1325/A/6, 10 March 1992, reporting an appeal to the Azerbaijani parliament by the Tabriz arts society protesting at the decision to adopt the Latin script. The Tabriz arts society denounced this as an example of colonialist cultural influence.

they adopted a cautious, benign, but not too intrusive attitude to the new political forces emerging. The victory of the Popular Front in the spring of 1992 was a disappointment to Iran, not least given the anti-Iranian statements of the Front's presidential candidate Elchibey; but Iran's position, as expressed by its ambassador to Baku, was that in the end Azerbaijan was closer to Iran than to Turkey – they were best advised to remain close to their brothers (i.e. the Iranians) than to their cousins (the Turks).

The evolution of these two issues – Nagorno–Karabakh and politics in Azerbaijan – indicated how little Iran could expect to influence, let alone benefit from, the collapse of the USSR. Combined with the turn of events in Tajikistan, where Islamist forces sympathetic to Iran were routed with great loss of life in late 1992, events in the Caucasus seem to have led to some rethinking in Tehran and to a realization of the limits of the IRI's appeal. It was noticeable that in February 1993 Rafsanjani, when asked about events in Tajikistan, merely voiced regret, but stressed that Iran would not interfere, only express an opinion.[29] A similar loss of optimism was experienced in the face of events in Afghanistan, where the Islamist coalition fell apart after the collapse of the Najibullah regime in April 1992, and the pro-Iranian Hizb-i Vahdat forces became the target for attack by the troops of Gulbuddin Hekmatyar. As far as Transcaucasia was concerned, Iran could only sit and wait.

It was events themselves that produced some changes in Iran's position. In Azerbaijan, matters took a dramatic turn in June 1993 when the regime of Elchibey was ousted in a military uprising that led to the return to Gaidar Aliev as president. Although Iran had to some extent been able to normalize relations with Elchibey's regime, matters had not gone far, and the Popular Front government continued to repeat charges that Tehran was siding not just diplomatically but also militarily with Erevan, by supplying weapons and training forces. In general, Elchibey's government appealed for help from the West on the grounds that it was faced with a "totalitarian" menace to the south similar to the communist threat that had earlier faced the West.[30] Iran reacted cautiously at the official level, but there is evidence that it continued its support for Islamist elements in Azerbaijan, and that it encouraged opposition among the Talish minority in the southern part of the country, near the Iranian frontier. It is not known whether Iran played any role in the return of Aliev to power, but there can be little doubt that it welcomed it, and signs of an improved relationship could soon be seen. During his period as ruler of Nakhichevan Aliev had maintained separate, bilateral, relations with Tehran and had been careful not to antagonize the IRI.[31]

---

29. *BBC SWB ME*/1603/A/6, 3 February 1993.
30. Speech to Royal Institute of International Affairs, London, by Dr Asim Molla-Zade, Deputy Chairman of the Experts Advisory Council, 23 February 1993.

This shift in relations with Azerbaijan coincided with change in its policy on the conflict with Armenia. Although Iran had been disappointed by the failure of its peace effort in 1992, it had continued to take a neutral stance and offer mediation. In the spring of 1993, however, Iran became much more outspoken in its criticism of Armenian military advances, repeating its call for the return of Armenian forces from territory they occupied in Azerbaijan, and its insistence that there could be no forcible changes of frontiers. A Tehran radio commentary also warned of "signs of possible interference by third countries in the conflict" and called for a positive response to appeals from Elchibey for assistance. The issue of assistance was most pertinent to the treatment of Azeris who had fled the combat zone and who were in increasing numbers approaching the Iranian frontier. Iran, with the agreement of the Baku government, set up camps inside Azeri territory, and by November of 1993 claimed to be caring for over 40,000 of these, with the capacity for up to 100,000.[32] When, in October and November, Armenian forces made further advances into Azeri territory outside Nagorno–Karabakh, Iran took an even harsher tone: it called for international assistance to help Azerbaijan, and, together with Turkey, made a joint appeal to the UN Security Council to condemn Armenian "aggression". Tehran's anxiety was all the greater because, in addition to the fact that the Armenian forces were approaching the frontier with Iran, they had also captured and, so Iranian sources claimed, looted the Khoda Afarian dam, a joint Azeri–Iranian project, while at the same time shelling Iranian frontier areas. Tehran warned that this might "jeopardize" relations between the two countries.[33] There was, however, little Iran could do: it was clearly nervous about the immediate impact of the extension of the war, but also its broader consequences, including the undermining of the newly installed Aliev regime in Baku. Beyond that lay the question of how continued conflict in the Transcaucasian region would encourage Turkey and Russia to play a greater role: Russia had, by the latter half of 1993, evolved a new security doctrine involving a more active role in the "near abroad", already evident in Georgia and Tajikistan, and Turkey's mood was changing, as a result of developments in both Bosnia and Azerbaijan. The intersection of Transcaucasian conflict with the broader strategic triangle – Moscow–Ankara–Tehran – therefore continued.

---

31. A further issue in the Azeri/Iranian story was the question of oil and in particular of the pipeline that would be built to get Azeri oil to the West. Three options presented themselves: north, through Russia to the Black Sea; west, through Georgia, and/or through Turkey; south, through Iran. The last appeared more attractive given the political problems with the other two, but was strongly opposed by Turkey and not welcomed by Western oil firms.
32. *BBC SWB ME*/1845 MED/7, 13 November 1993.
33. *BBC SWB ME*/1859 MED/7, 30 November 1993.

Limits on Iranian policy

If Iran's policy was in general reactive, Tehran's ability to influence the course of events in Transcaucasia was also limited by several factors. First of all, the two main issues on which it sought to formulate policy – the Nagorno–Karabakh dispute and political developments in Azerbaijan – were ones in which it had little influence. There was no strong pro-Iranian or Islamist current in Baku, and indeed most forces there located themselves on a spectrum between Moscow and Ankara. The course of the debate on Azerbaijani political identity seems to have retrod the path covered in the late nineteenth-and early twentieth-century discussions, when those espousing a Persian identity were overcome by those looking to a modern, secular, Turkey.[34] With the growing power of the Popular Front, crowned by its electoral victory in June 1992, Iran's weakness was confirmed, not least because the Front, for perhaps short-term reasons, sought to make anti-Iranian militancy one of its policies. The return of Aliev in 1993 gave little greater leverage, even assuming his hold on power endured. As far as Nagorno–Karabakh was concerned, neither party paid much heed to Tehran, except where it thought there might be some immediate benefit in so doing. The Armenians realized they had something to gain by having normal relations with Tehran and trying to use the IRI to offset Turkey: but there was little love lost between the two capitals, and Armenia was certainly not going to heed Iranian appeals when it did not want to. The May 1992 ceasefire agreement was killed off by an Armenian offensive a few hours after it was signed. By 1993 Tehran had become far more critical of the Armenian stance. For their part, the Azeris considered the Iranians to be disloyal and to have sided with the Armenians.

However, there were further limits from within Iran itself. Foreign policy-making in the IRI has since the inception been centralized in the top leadership, with the foreign ministry acting as technical and administrative back-up to decisions taken by the leaders – since 1989, comprising Rafsanjani, as president, and Khamane'i, as *rahbar* or spiritual leader. In this sense there is no overt popular or democratic input into the foreign policy process. Key elements of foreign policy are off limits to public discussion: up to 1988, the conduct of the war with Iraq, since 1979 relations with Israel and the USA. But domestic considerations and influences do play their part on some issues, Transcaucasia included. On the one hand, with the emergence of the Nagorno–Karabakh and Azerbaijan issues from 1988 onwards, a distinctive pro-Azerbaijani note could be detected. Some politicians of Azeri origin began to speak out in favour of more support for

---

34. On this earlier debate see Tadeusz Swietochowski, *Russian Azerbaijan 1905–20: the shaping of national identity in a Muslim community* (Cambridge: Cambridge University Press, 1985).

Baku, and even to speak in Azeri in the *Majlis*. But this was as much as anything part of a wider power-play within the regime, not a distinctive expression of an Azeri current. This became clearer in 1991 when strong opinions in favour of Azerbaijan were expressed, not by Azeris as such but by proponents of the more "radical" line, opposed to what were seen as the equivocations of Rafsanjani and the "pragmatists". Ali Akbar Muhtashami, former minister of the interior and a leader of the Tehran Militant Clerics Association, tried to use the January 1990 clashes in Baku to mobilize support, accusing Gorbachev of combining the policies of Lenin, Stalin and the White House in an attack on Islam and calling for Muslims to carry out reprisals; Abdul-Karim Musavi-Ardebili used the same events to call for Islamic revolution in the Caucasus, and in 1992 was one of those who denounced the even-handed policy on Nagorno–Karabakh as a betrayal of struggling Muslims.[35] It was not, therefore, issues within Transcaucasia, so much as the symbolic importance with which they were invested, that determined how these forces reacted.

On the other side, there were domestic factors favouring support for Armenia, or at least a consistent neutrality. One was the desire not to encourage an Azeri nationalism that could have a demonstration effect on Iran. The other was the desire to maintain good relations with the Armenian community in Iran; estimated at 120,000 in the early 1990s, down from around 170,000 at the time of the revolution, it remained a significant commercial element in the country that the IRI leadership did not want to lose, as they had already lost the majority of the Jews. If Iran was to take advantage of the collapse of the USSR to increase influence in Transcaucasia and Central Asia, it would do so as much by economic links, in which the commercial class would play a leading role, as through the appeals of "Islam".[36]

Policy guidelines

Thus, condemned to react, but unable to influence, Iran was forced by the evolution of forces beyond its control to evolve a policy towards Transcaucasia in the period from 1988 onwards. Its situation was in some respects similar to that of European states faced with the crisis that evolved in Yugoslavia from 1991: a mixture of diplomatic initiative, prudential insulation, wary concern at the strategic intentions of others. Iran did not take any major initiative in Transcaucasia involving, for example, a revision of the Soviet/Iranian frontier, or direct political let alone military interven-

35. *BBC SWB ME*/0698/A/2, 26 February 1990; ME/1389 A/6, 25 May 1992.
36. A Persian visitor to Baku in 1992 was surprised to see pictures not of Khomeini but of Fath Ali Shah (d. 1834), the last Persian ruler of Azerbaijan.

tion. It continued to shape policy in response to what occurred across the frontier, and this would probably continue to be the case. However, some broader policy lines were clear and would in all likelihood endure, whatever the particular turn of events in Transcaucasia itself.

- Iran held to the view that the successor states to the USSR were bound by the treaty obligations of the latter. This pertained most obviously to the frontier, but also the range of economic and technical agreements signed prior to December 1991. Whether or not the successor states would be able to meet these obligations was another matter: but the principle of inheritance of obligations stood.
- Within Transcaucasia itself, Iran was opposed to a policy of revision of frontiers, unless this was by mutual, peaceful, agreement of all parties concerned.
- Iran was not in favour of Azerbaijani unification, be this by the incorporation of northern Azerbaijan into Iran, or the secession of Iranian Azerbaijan to join its now independent neighbour.
- Iran's main concern in Transcaucasia was the growth of Turkish, and therefore American, influence. Although it would be mistaken to see Iran's relations with Turkey in this period as inevitably set on a collision course, elements of contest coinciding with a degree of understanding and accommodation, the stage was certainly set for a long-run competition for influence in the whole of the former USSR, including Azerbaijan. How explosive this would prove to be depended on a range of strategic and internal factors that lay well beyond Transcaucasia itself.
- Events in Transcaucasia and in the former USSR more generally aroused hopes, illusions, aspirations in Iran, be it of a return of some former Iranian sphere of political influence, of Islamic revival, or of economic opportunity. Most of these proved to be short-lived, not least because Iran had a limited amount to offer. Dreams of Greater Iran therefore gave way to other, more restricted, expectations. In the end, Tehran's main concern in this region, after 1991 as before, under the IRI as under the monarchy, was stability: regular and beneficial economic agreement, secure frontiers, absence of destabilizing political influences be these refugees or secessionists. Iran had an obvious economic interest in developing areas of common concern in the Caspian, as well as in continuing forms of trade, especially gas pipelines, with Russia itself. This, rather than the shaping of the new regimes within its three former dominions across the Arax river, was the dominant consideration in Iranian policy towards Transcaucasia.

CHAPTER FIVE

The Armenian presence
in mountainous Karabakh

CHRISTOPHER J. WALKER

Historic Armenia constitutes an elevated plateau buttressed by formidable mountain systems. The severe geography, and resultant harsh climate, has enabled the Armenian people to survive invasion and foreign domination, and has assured a continuity of population. At the eastern end of the Armenian plateau, around Lake Sevan (which has an elevation of 1,916m) the mountainous aspect of the landscape is at its most pronounced. This region comprised the ninth and tenth provinces of Armenia: Siunik and Artsakh. Northeast of Artsakh, where the mountains decline to the valley of the Kura, lay the province of Utik; and east of the southern end of Artsakh, towards the confluence of the Kura and Arax rivers, lay Paytakaran, a province that also included land south of the Arax.[1]

The elevation of the plateau of historic Armenia was also a major factor in determining the social system; mountain and valley dwellers live differently from plains people. In essence, the typical Armenian social structure was of a federation of local dynastic princes, known as *nakharars*, which both pre-dated and survived the various monarchies of Armenia. In the east the *nakharars* were the descendants of tribal chieftains (Armenian and non-Armenian) of considerable antiquity. Their authority ensured strength and continuity in Armenian society, although their conflicts with monarchy (which was seldom superior to them) sometimes weakened the State. They usually had wide powers of raising taxes and administering the law. Beneath the princes, and subject to them, were a landed gentry (*azat*) and a peasantry (*shinakan*).[2]

---

1. R. E. H. Mellor, *Geography of the USSR*, 123 (London: Macmillan, 1964); Paul E. Lydolph, *Geography of the USSR*, 150–2 (New York: John Wiley, 1964); Theodore Shabad, *Geography of the USSR*, 409–10 (New York: Oxford University Press, 1951). The authors of these works concur in the opinion that geographically mountainous Karabakh is an extension of the Armenian plateau.
2. C. Toumanoff, *Studies in Christian Caucasian history*, 33–273 (Washington DC: Georgetown University Press, 1963); and the references to Toumanoff in R. H. Hewsen, "The meliks of eastern Armenia: a preliminary study", *Revue des Etudes Arméniennes*, NS IX, 286–329, 1972. I am greatly indebted to Hewsen's pioneering study; and to the late Edward Gulbekian for his comments on the first third of this paper.

Mountainous Karabagh

With the passing centuries, the number of princely households throughout Armenia diminished. Among the longest survivors (and here the mountain systems interrelate with historical detail) were the princes of eastern Armenia, specifically those of Siunik (modern Zangezur and Nakhichevan) and Artsakh (sometimes known as Pokr Siunik or small Siunik, modern Karabakh). Siunik encompassed all of the shoreline of Lake Sevan, except the northernmost part (which belonged to the Ayrarat region), and stretched south as far as the Hagar (Akera) and Vorotan rivers. Artsakh encompassed the territory of the Nagorno–Karabakh Autonomous Oblast (NKAO) and extended, as a long and slim band of territory, almost as far again to the northwest, beyond the River Akstafa, and the southeast as far as the River Arax.[3]

The highest parts of both Siunik and Artsakh are without vegetation, but the land receives abundant rainfall. "No country in all Armenia, Georgia or Persia is so fertile as that of Carabagh, where one pound of seed produces 110 of grain . . . It is the properest country to carry on war in, and to maintain liberty with ease. They have another valuable advantage over others, that the corn continues good for ten years, and remains as fresh as the new grain . . . As for all sorts of fruits, they are in abundance; silk, cotton and wool in great plenty. In other places the fuel is chiefly the dung of cows, sheep, or horses; but in Carabagh it is wood, for there is no village without a forest near it."[4] So wrote Emin Joseph Emin, who might have

---

3. Hewsen 1972, 287–8; see maps on pages 8–9 in M. A. L. Cuneo, P. Cuneo, S. Manoukian, *Armenian architecture/Documenti di Architettura Armena 19* (Milan: OEMME Edizioni, 1988).

added to his list of regional produce vegetables and walnuts, and pointed out that the fruits included apricots, plums, peaches, pears, grapes, pomegranates and figs. The wine of the region has a strong, distinctively herby bouquet. Artsakh and Siunik were without cities and almost without trade routes, and contained only a few towns. In their place there existed, and still exists where possible, a rich village life.

The spoken language of today shows a gradual change as the villages extend farther from Erevan and the Ararat valleys;. The villagers of western Siunik speak the Erevan dialect, that is, standard eastern Armenian, whereas in eastern Siunik, and in parts of Lori and Pambak in northern Armenia, as well as throughout Artsakh/Karabakh, the dialect of Karabakh is spoken. This is characterized by ten vowels, three diphthongs and 33 consonants, as well as by a stress on the penultimate syllable, in contrast to the pronunciation of both eastern and western Armenian, where the final syllable is usually stressed.[5]

Was Artsakh (the modern Karabakh) ever part of the third major nation in what is today Transcaucasia, Caucasian Albania? For the most part, Caucasian Albania (in Armenian, Ał vank – that is Aghvank or Aghouank) only stretched a short way south of the Kura River. If there was a disputed province of ancient Armenia, it was Utik (which contained the town of Partav, at one time Caucasian Albania's capital, and the southern valley of the Kura), and not Artsakh, the more mountainous region corresponding to Karabakh and Shahumianovsk today. Following the partition of Armenia in AD 384, Artsakh, Utik and Paytakaran became part of the Sasanid Persian province of Arran (or Albania), a proportion of the people remained Armenian, and the local monarch remained a member of the Arsacid dynasty, a kinsman of the dynasty that had ruled Armenia since AD 53.[6]

Caucasian Albania converted to Christianity at about the same time as Armenia, that is, early in the fourth century. Grigoris, the grandson of St Gregory the Illuminator, was a bishop in eastern Armenia when appointed bishop of Caucasian Albania. He is buried at Amaras, the site of the oldest church in Karabakh in the Hadrut region. Ecclesiastical proximity was mirrored by theological stance: the Church of Caucasian Albania for the most part adhered to the Christological viewpoint of the Armenian church, rejecting the conclusions of the Council of Chalcedon (AD 451). Nor was the influence of Armenia on Albania only ecclesiastical. Armenian culture became important in Caucasian Albania and, by the eighth

---

4. [Emin] Joseph Emin, *The life and adventures, 1726–92*, 307 (London: Baptist Mission Press, 1792). Reprinted Calcutta 1918. Hewsen 1972, 289.

5. Hewsen 1972, 289 and fn 17.

6. Patrick Donabedian & Claude Mutafian, *Le Karabakh*, 16–20 (Paris: GDM, 1989). English version in Christopher J. Walker (ed.), *Armenia and Karabakh: the struggle for unity*, 73–5 (London: Minority Rights Group, 1991); also Toumanoff 1963, 128–9.

century, Armenian appears to have been spoken throughout much of the region. (The only surviving traces of the Caucasian Albanian language are fragmentary inscriptions dating from the sixth–seventh centuries.) Artsakhian was a recognized dialect of Armenian by the eighth century, according to the grammarian Stepannos Siunetsi.[7]

In the eighth century Armenia was recognized (as Arminiyya) by the Arabs as an extensive administrative province; the east of this province was the scene of fierce fighting between the caliphate and the Khazars. By the tenth century, Caucasian Albania had disappeared as a State, although it survived into the early twentieth century as an ecclesiastical term signifying an eastern administrative diocese of the Armenian church, whose spiritual centre was at Echmiazdin.

The Seljuk Turks invaded and conquered much of eastern Armenia in the eleventh century. At the same time, new princely families emerged in Artsakh (which began to be known as Khachen), who were probably descendants of the earlier dynasts, notably the Orbelians. They included Hasan Jalal Dawla [Dovle] whose family was later known as Jalalian. With the defeat of the Seljuks by the Georgian king, David the Builder (1121), and under the benevolent shadow cast by his great grand-daughter, Queen Tamar, who allied herself with the Armenian Zakarian family, Christian culture expanded throughout the region. The majority of the 1600 Armenian architectural monuments that exist today in Nagorno–Karabakh were built at this time, most notably the monastery of Gandsasar (1216–61), which became the ecclesiastical centre of the region.[8]

The term "Karabakh" dates from the thirteenth century, probably from the time of the Mongol invasions. It is a Turko–Persian term, meaning "black garden", and probably signifies the rich dark earth that is the characteristic soil of the region. In administrative terms, it denoted a large area taking in all Artsakh and Siunik.

Following the death of Timur in 1405, Caucasia and western Persia were contested between the Timurid ruler Shah Rukh and the Turcoman dynasty of the Karakoyunlu, whose most able leader was Kara Yusuf (1406–20). During the rule of Kara Yusuf's fifth son, Jahan Shah (1440–67), the Armenian people appear to have gained a higher profile, notably when, under this monarch, the governor of Erevan permitted the re-establishment of the Armenian Catholicosate in Echmiadzin in 1441. It was almost certainly Jahan Shah who, taking prudent measures to strengthen border regions, established a set of small buffer States at the northeastern edge of his realm, in the lands of Artsakh and Siunik. The local Armenian rulers of these "Statelets" were confirmed in authority, privileges were

---

7. Donabedian & Mutafian 1989, 18, 76.
8. Ibid.; David M. Lang, *The Georgians*, 111 (London: Thames & Hudson, 1966); Cuneo et al. 1988, 104.

restored to them, and they were granted local autonomy and given the title of *melik* (*malik*, Arabic for king or sovereign). The principalities were expected to take up arms on his behalf. The enemy against whom he was defending his realm was almost certainly the growing power of Safavid Persia, although the dynasty that ended the rule of the Karakoyunlu was that of the rival Turcoman confederation of the Akkoyunlu, which in turn ruled for only 35 years before being ousted by the Safavids.[9]

Jahan Shah appears to have streamlined the principalities of eastern Armenia by reducing the territories in number but increasing them in size. In mountainous Karabakh, the shake-up led to the establishment of five melikdoms, known as the *Khamsayi Melikner* (*khamsa*, Arabic for five).

From north to south, these were known as: Gulistan (Iranian, meaning "country of roses"), which was situated outside the modern NKAO, in what is now the Shahumianovsk region, and extended in the north from the River Ti or Kurak-get (or -chai), on which the town of Getashen is situated, to Mount Mrav in the west, to the east by the edge of the mountain range, and to the south by the neighbouring melikdom, Jraberd. The ruling family in Gulistan was that of Melik Beglarian (alternatively, Melik Abovian).

Jraberd (Armenian for "water fortress"), the smallest of the five, was situated in the valley of the River Terter (or Tartar), the northernmost river in NKAO, where a reservoir is sited today the southern boundary was the River Khachen. Its leading family, resident in Jraberd castle, was that of the Melik Israelians, descendants of the Prosh (or Proshian) family who had built the celebrated monastery of Ayrivank or Geghard (mid–thirteenth century), not far from Erevan. They eventually lost the region to the Mirzakhanids and the Atabegians.

Khachen (Armenian *khach* for cross), the neighbouring melikdom, was the largest: it stretched almost to Lake Sevan in the west, and south to the river Meghri-get or Ballu (Gargar on modern maps). The monastery of Gandsasar was situated in Khachen. In the south it took in Khankend, the modern Stepanakert. The Hasan–Jalalians, the oldest family of the region, indigenous to the area, and as a princely family traceable back to the thirteenth century, ruled in Khachen.

South of Khachen lay the small territory of Varanda, originally part of its southern neighbour, Dizak, and only given a separate identity in the early sixteenth century. The ruling family, confirmed in that capacity by Shah Abbas I, was that of the Melik Shahnazarians. In the territory of Varanda lies the modern town of Shushi (or Shusha). Farther south lay Dizak (or Thizak), ruled from their castle at Togh by the Melik Avanians. Their realm stretched from the Dizapaiti mountains to the River Hagar in the west, the lowlands in the east, and the valley of the Arax to the south.[10]

---

9. *Cambridge history of Iran*, vol. VI, 163–76 (Cambridge: Cambridge University Press, 1986); Hewsen 1972, 297–9.

These melikdoms were the most significant. The meliks' social status has been described by W. E. D. Allen as "that of clan chieftain rather than of hereditary territorial magnate", indicating a situation "comparable to that of the chieftains of the Scottish highlands rather than . . . the fruit of primogeniture in England, France or Spain". Other Armenian melikdoms were set up around Lake Sevan, in Ghapan in southern Siunik, in the plain of Ararat (the Aghamalian family were the hereditary meliks of Erevan), as well as in the north in the Georgian marchlands. Many of such leaders were merely village headmen given a title to confirm their loyalty, much as honours are given out in Britain today. What distinguished the meliks of mountainous Karabakh was their family continuity, dating from a much earlier time.[11]

It is very hard to assess any even approximate population statistics. All we have to go on are inflated figures given in a letter of 1699 from the representative of the meliks, Israel Ori, addressed to the Elector Palatine. His figure, for the whole of Siunik and Karabakh, was 192,000. A more realistic estimate, made for the year 1800, has put the population at around 50,000.[12]

The meliks had been confirmed in their positions with the intention of providing efficient fighting forces, a practice very different from that in Ottoman Turkey, where the narrower interpretation of Islam insisted that the Christian nationalities were disarmed, considered second class, and assigned non-military roles. By contrast, the meliks were expected to furnish troops, and each melik had between 1,000 and 2,000 troops at his command. These troops were divided into companies, each commanded by a *yüzbashi* (Turkish for centurion or captain).[13]

Following the destruction of the Akkoyunlu by the Safavids, the new rulers of Persia (against whom the melikdoms appear to have been established) confirmed the meliks in their power and privileges. The whole of eastern Armenia came under the dominion of Persia, where it remained (apart from brief incursions by the Ottomans) until the Russian conquests of the early nineteenth century.

The Safavids established hereditary Shi'ite khanates in much of the region. Close to the area of the Karabakh melikdoms were those of Karabakh (that is, lowland Karabakh: Ganja), Erevan and Nakhichevan. The melikdoms were to some extent dependent on the khanates, and suffered and declined in the early years of Safavid rule. However, Shah Abbas I (1586–1628), who created New Julfa as an Armenian suburb of Isfahan,

---

10. Hewsen 1972, 299–301.
11. W. E. D. Allen (ed.), *Russian embassies to the Georgian kings*, vol. I, 70 (Cambridge: Hakluyt Society, 1970); Hewsen 1972, 293–4.
12. Ibid., 291.
13. Ibid., 298.

was on good terms with Armenians throughout his realm, once they were where he wanted them to be, and although there is no record of him visiting a melik of Karabakh, he did pay a visit to Melik Shahnazarian of Gegharkunik in the village of Mazra in 1606. By this time the Shahnazarians had become the dominant melikdom of the region. Shah Abbas confirmed their privileges, and increased their lands and title to take in much of Varanda.[14]

Under the yoke of Shah Abbas's successors, the meliks of Karabakh fell on bad times, and in a letter to Pope Innocent XI they expressed both exasperation with the dissension and greed of their own clerics, and anger at the injustice of their Muslim rulers grown intolerant. In consequence they sought submission to Rome. However, the prime mover of this plan to free mountainous Karabakh, Israel Ori – almost certainly a descendant of the Melik Israelians of Jraberd, since he is described as a descendant of Borhosch, that is, Prosh – died in 1711, and nothing more came of his plans.[15]

Armenian military strength came into focus again in 1722 in the Caucasus, at the time when the Safavid dynasty collapsed under pressure from the Afghans, and Peter the Great made his emblematic but ineffectual entry into Caucasian affairs. In a time of great turbulence and complexity, an Armenian by the name of David-Bek came to the fore. He was neither a melik nor a member of a princely family, and his story pertains more to Siunik than to Karabakh. He was an extremely able Armenian soldier and leader, from Mtzkheta in Georgia, who arrived in Karabakh and Siunik in 1722. Fighting from the fortress of Halidsor (near Ghapan), he united the melikdoms of Siunik into a kind of republic, and inflicted defeats on the Ottoman Turks in 1725 and 1729. Independence lasted only until 1730, but the memory of it lived on.[16]

At the same time, at the northeast end of the melikdom highlands, the Armenians were showing a spirit of independence. The English historian Jonas Hanway, writing in 1726, relates:[17]

> The winter had passed without any action worth notice, except that of Savi Mustafa, who marched out of Ganja of which he was governor, and dispersed the Armenians in the neighbourhood of Shamakie [Shamkhor]. These people taking advantage of the present circumstances, formed themselves into a kind of republic, which, as we have mentioned, distinguished itself by the total defeat of a body of

---

14. Ibid., 302.
15. J. Saint-Martin, *Mémoires historiques et géographiques sur l'Arménie*, vol. II, 470–85 (Paris: Imprimerie Royale, 1818).
16. Hewsen 1972, 305–6.
17. Jonas Hanway, *The revolutions of Persian . . .* , vol. II, 252 (London: T. Osborne, 1762).

six thousand men, whom Abdallah Basha had sent against them the preceding summer. It was not long too before they had their revenge also of the governor of Ganja. It was their custom to assemble in great number during Easter, in a plain in that neighbourhood. Having received intelligence that the Turks had formed a design to surprise them on this occasion, they took their measures, and not only defended themselves, but also drew the Turks into their defiles, where they obtained an easy victory over them.

However, the eighteenth century was to see the decline and fall of Armenian supremacy in the mountains at the eastern end of their plateau. It did not come at once: Armenians prospered under Nadir Shah, and he extended some of the privileges of the meliks, releasing the Shahnazarians from dependence on the sirdar of Erevan; he also appointed Melik Avan of Dizak governor of all the melikdoms. But in the disturbed period following his death in 1747, the Armenian principalities of Karabakh fell into decline. At this time a Turcoman shepherd named Panah, of the tribe of Djivanshir, became chieftain of his people, and sought to seize control of Karabakh. The Djivanshir had been used to using mountainous Karabakh as pasture in summer, when the lowlands of the Karabakh steppe became hot and malarial, but they never gained control of any part, until dissension between the meliks gave them the opportunity. This occurred because the Shahnazarian family was in dispute with the Hasan Jalalians, whom the other meliks supported. Shahnazar found an ally in Panah. Together they built a fortress at Shusha, defying the other meliks, and with the aid of the local khans they gradually took lands from the neighbouring melikdoms. Wars ruined the region until a truce of 1760, which recognized Panah as lord of Karabakh. On his death in 1763, the struggle was renewed by his son Ibrahim: the meliks were slain, dispersed and dispossessed. (It seems that two representatives of melikial families entered the service of the Russian army: Avan II of Dizak, at the time of Peter the Great, and around 1800 Prince Valerian Grigorievich Madatov, a kinsman of the Beglarians.) By the time the Russians under Prince Tsitsianov conquered the region in 1805, only Shahnazar, and the Atabegians, newcomers in Varanda, were living as meliks. Armenian dissension had assured non-Armenian overlordship, despite the fact that the people of mountainous Karabakh continued to be predominantly Armenian.[18]

Despite the end of the melikdoms in the eighteenth century, the spirit of independence that lingered there was one of the elements that (together with work of the Mkhitarist fathers, and of the Armenian writers in Madras and Calcutta) gave inspiration to the Armenian emancipatory struggle. Following Israel Ori, Joseph Emin spent some years in the 1760s

---

18. Hewsen 1972, 325–6.

in Karabakh, seeking the freedom of his people and looking to Erek'le, king of Georgia, as an ally. His autobiography makes clear the unbowed spirit of the people.

After Tsitsianov's conquest of Karabakh, the region was recognized as part of the Russian empire by the Treaty of Gulistan (1813). Initially the Russians confirmed the existing Islamic rulers in their roles as khans and beks, but in 1822 these titles were abolished, and in 1840 Karabakh became part of Caspian province. From that time to 1991 the people of mountainous Karabakh, despite being Armenian, have always been administratively united with Turko–Islamic peoples, and have had to struggle for recognition of their Armenian identity. In 1846 Karabakh was incorporated into Shemakha province, renamed Baku province in 1859. In 1868 it was included in the province of Elizavetpol, which was the new name for Ganja, known in Soviet times as Kirovabad. Here it remained until the First World War and the collapse of the Russian empire.[19]

Shusha, which was important by reason of the fortress built by Panah and Shahnazar, became the capital of Karabakh and (after Tbilisi and Baku) the third most important cultural centre in Transcaucasia. Five Armenian journals came to be printed from Shusha, and many books and five churches were built in the course of the nineteenth century, as well as three mosques. From 1865 it became a centre for the development of the Caucasian theatre, and an Armenian theatre was built there in 1891. But the Armenian nature of Karabakh was not recognized by the Russian autocracy. The nucleus for a reborn Armenia, and the region which was from 1828 to 1840 designated as the Armyanskaya Oblast, was Erevan and Nakhichevan, not mountainous Karabakh, despite the long-established Armenian presence there.[20]

Armenians prospered for much of the nineteenth century in Transcaucasia, but, following the death of Alexander II, the Caucasian viceroyalty was abolished, and the post was downgraded to that of governor-generalship, which was given into the mean and divisive hands of Prince G. Golitsyn. Armenian schools were closed, the church's autonomy was violated, and measures against Armenians reached a climax with the strife encouraged by the regime between Tatars (as the Azerbaijanis were then known) and Armenians. Shusha was twice the scene of conflict, in August 1905 and July 1906, when violence against Armenians was legitimized by the regime; but the people were able to set up efficient self-defence and protect themselves. After 1906, an uneasy calm prevailed until the First World War.[21]

---

19. J. F. Baddeley, *The Russian conquest of the Caucasus*, 69, 90 (London: Longmans Green, 1908); "Nagorno–Karabakh", *Great Soviet encyclopaedia* [English edn], vol. 17 300c, vol. 31, 574d (New York: Macmillan, 1983).
20. Donabedian & Mutafian 1989, 36 and 85.

What was the root of the Azerbaijani/Armenian hostility, which the regime was able to exploit? Partly it was an age-old struggle of the Muslims of the plain seeking to dislodge the Christians of the highlands (a pattern similar to the struggles in Zeitun, Sasun and to some extent Mount Lebanon); partly it was a reflection of Tatar jealousy at Armenian commercial success in Baku under the tsars (although Tatars like Taghiev partook of that success); partly too it was the first beginnings of the emergence of the violent and destructive secular ideology of pan-Turkism, which sought initially to unify Anatolian Turkey and eastern Transcaucasia across an extinct Armenia: an ideology whose adherents understood the formidable problems posed by the fact that the Armenians held the highlands between the two.[22]

At this time too, the Armenians were unsuccessful in seeking the reorganization of the administration, with a view to separating the Armenian mountains from the Tatar plains. If such a change had taken place, it would have seriously weakened the Tatar pastoral economy, since the Muslim shepherds needed to alternate between highland and lowland with their flocks.[23]

Early in 1918, the Armenians and Tatars of mountainous Karabakh were, as they had been for the duration of the war, living in relative peace. Both communities at this time owed allegiance to a bi-racial council, which paid homage to the authorities in Tbilisi. But the situation changed with the invasion of Transcaucasia by the Ottoman army in May: dormant antagonisms came to the surface. The division of the region into three independent States at the end of May 1918 increased the tensions. The Karabakh people rejected the demand of Azerbaijani sovereignty over their region put forward by Nuri Pasha, commander-in-chief of Ottoman forces in the Caucasus. The first assembly of Karabakh elected its own People's Government of Karabakh in August 1918, which was unconnected to the Azerbaijani State. The Second Assembly, unimpressed by the Ottoman victory in Baku, voted similarly in late September. A Third Assembly, meeting in late September, was urged by the mayor of Shusha, Gerasim Melik Shahnazarian, to let the Turks and Tatars in. These entered (with 5,000 Turkish troops) in early October, promising peace and justice, but arresting leaders and intellectuals, and erecting a gallows in the central square. However, it was only days before Ottoman Turkey lost the war.[24]

Shusha had submitted before the armistice, but the mountain districts

21. Ibid.; Christopher J. Walker, *Armenia: the survival of a nation*, 2nd edn, 71–8 (London: Routledge, 1990) and references thereto.
22. See Jacob Landau, *Panturkism: a study of irredenta* (London: Hurst, 1981); Zarevand (pseud.), *Touranie unifiée et indépendante* (Athens: Editions Les Armeniennes, 1989).
23. Richard G. Hovannisian, *The republic of Armenia: the first year, 1918–19*, 81 (Berkeley: University of California Press, 1971).
24. Ibid., 85.

remained unsubdued. There the structure of the melikdoms re-emerged, and the people looked to the Armenian partisan leader Andranik (Oza-nian), then fighting with his well trained irregulars in Zanzegur. Moun-tainous Karabakh issued an appeal to him for help. After hesitation and delay, Andranik eventually set out in mid-November and, after a fierce battle with Tatar irregulars, he was in command of the heights, and the way to Shusha lay before him. But as he was about to move into the town, he received a message from Major-General W. M. Thomson, commander of Allied forces in Transcaucasia, requesting him to cease military activity, since all issues would now be solved at the Peace Conference of Paris. Andranik had implicit faith in the Allies, and acceded. But the Peace Con-ference was to solve no problems for the Armenians, and the separation of mountainous Karabakh from the body of Armenia can be said to derive from the day on which Andranik laid down his arms, trusting the word of an Allied officer.[25]

Since the diplomats and negotiators ignored the issues, the decisions of the military were those which had most impact. General Thomson and his successor, Colonel D. Shuttleworth, showed a partiality to the Azerbai-janis' claim to the Karabakh, and paid no heed to the democratic aspira-tions of the population. Their tilt to Baku reached a bizarre climax when in early 1919 Thomson approved Azerbaijan's choice of Dr Khosrov Bek Sultanov as governor of Karabakh – a man whose pan-Turkish views were known to the British, and who was a friend of the leading Ittihadists in Ottoman Turkey (with which the Allies had recently been at war).[26] To the Armenians this appointment virtually constituted a continuation of the genocide perpetrated by the Ittihadists in 1915. Presumably the main points that recommended Sultanov to the forgetful British were that he was a landlord, that he kept "order", and that he was not a democrat – issues that may have reflected the position of some upper class British mil-itary families in Ireland at the time.

Throughout early 1919 conflict over the administration of Karabakh continued, with the British insisting on the installation of the Azerbaijani governor, and the representatives of Jraberd, Khachen, Varanda and Dizak expressing strenuous opposition. A Fourth and Fifth Assembly of Kara-bakh stressed the popular refusal to acquiesce in alien military control. The British, short-tempered and mostly ignorant of history and historical sen-timent, lost patience, and virtually gave the green light for the Sultanov family to demonstrate its "traditional" method of showing authority: a massacre of 600 Armenians took place, which centred on the Armenian village of Khaibalikend on 5 June 1919.[27]

25. Ibid., 88–90.
26. Ibid., 162.
27. Ibid., 175–82.

Despite an outcry, Britain was able to reinstate Sultanov in his office. By the time of the Seventh Assembly of the Karabakh Armenians, the people were exhausted and dispirited, and they agreed on provisional inclusion within the Republic of Azerbaijan (22 August 1919).[28] Within weeks the British had withdrawn from almost all the Caucasus. It was left to Colonel J. C. Plowden, British military representative in Erevan, to frame an epitaph for British policy in Karabakh, expressing a view not common among his fellow officers:

> The handing over of Karabakh to Azerbaijan was, I think, the bitterest blow of all. Karabakh means more to Armenians than their religion even, being the cradle of their race, and their traditional last sanctuary when their country has been invaded. It is Armenian in every particular, both financially, militarily, and socially.[29]

Conflict in Karabakh was renewed in late 1919 and early 1920, centring on the dispute between the Armenians and Sultanov, whose rule, while ostensibly posing as the rule of law, was characterized by violence and lawlessness. Sultanov insisted on the deletion of the word "provisional" from the aforementioned agreement of 22 August 1919. The Armenians were divided in their response. A stock of arms was built up on both sides and the Armenians decided to forestall a Tatar attack by staging a rising, which was mismanaged. The Tatar army entered Shusha on 4 April 1920, and sacked the Armenian part of the town, slaughtering the inhabitants. Henceforward, until May 1992, Shusha was an overwhelmingly Azerbaijani town.[30]

Bolshevik forces entered Baku on 27 April 1920, and for the next seven months the struggle for mountainous Karabakh took on an ideological perspective. In the negotiations conducted between the government in Erevan and the Bolshevik representatives in the Caucasus, Karabakh (along with Zangezur and Nakhichevan) was one of the three disputed territories. An alliance was developing between Bolshevism and Kemalism, the latter representing, as regards Armenians, a milder version of the Ittihadism that had destroyed the Armenian people in 1915. The Bolsheviks for their part needed to control the disputed territories, in order to funnel funds and materiel to their allies, the Kemalist Turks. But this did not mean total support for the Azeri–Tatar viewpoint on territory, and the

---

28. Ibid., 186.
29. Gerald J. Libaridian (ed.), *The Karabakh file: documents and facts*, 155 (Cambridge Mass: Zoryan Institute for Contemporary Armenian Research and Documentation, 1988); Artin Arslanian, "Britain and the struggle for mountainous Karabakh, 1918–19", *Middle Eastern Studies* **16**, 92–104, 1980; Sir Edward Grey to Cox, August 1919. FO371/4159 piece 145863, Public Record Office (PRO), Kew.
30. Donabedian & Mutafian 1989, 51 and 98–9.

Bolshevik commissar for foreign affairs, G. V. Chicherin, opposed the more extreme manifestations of Baku's chauvinism. For the moment, mountainous Karabakh was denied complete inclusion in Azerbaijan.[31]

By an agreement between Armenia and the Bolsheviks of 10 August 1920, Erevan, seeing no end to the conflict, permitted the Bolsheviks to occupy Karabakh and most of the disputed territories. This signalled a vigorous protest from the British, which was ironic, in view of the support that Britain had given throughout early 1919 to forces intent on undermining Armenian sovereignty in Karabakh and Zangezur.[32]

The Kemalist invasion of Armenia in September 1920 led to the collapse of independent Armenia and to the country's sovietization, which occurred when the 11th Red Army entered Erevan on 2 December 1920. Immediately, the leader of Soviet Azerbaijan, Nariman Narimanov, cabled Erevan: "As of today the border disputes between Armenia and Azerbaijan are declared resolved. Mountainous Karabakh, Zangezur and Nakhichevan are considered part of the Soviet Republic of Armenia". Stalin hailed Narimanov's generosity. But were the Bolsheviks sincere? Simon Vratsian, in his history of the Armenian republic, was convinced that the expressions of fraternity and generosity were a hoax. The territories, with the exception of Zangezur, remained in Baku's orbit. The Bolshevik leaders were keen to keep Turkey on their side, since they expected its imminent sovietization. Some of them, too, sought to punish Armenia for adopting a pro-Allied stance.[33]

The matter of Karabakh was discussed in the first half of 1921, by the Kavburo. An agreement seems to have been reached on Karabakh in Armenia's favour on 12 June 1921, with the assent of Baku. However, some weeks later the Kavburo was still discussing the future of the territory, which had apparently not been resolved in June. It was proving a contentious issue. There were two more meetings on 4–5 July. Stalin was present at both of them. On 4 July, discussion centred on whether to treat all of Karabakh as a unit, or to treat the mountainous part as separate from lowland Karabakh. The latter option was eventually chosen, and the meeting decided to include mountainous Karabakh in Armenia, and to carry out a plebiscite there. (Those in favour of this resolution included G. K. Ordzhonikidze, A. Miasnikian, Yu. P. Figatner, S. M. Kirov and A. M. Nazaretian; Narimanov opposed, and so, apparently, did Stalin.) The matter was raised again the next day with Ordzhonikidze and Nazaretian dissenting from the resolution agreed upon in the previous meeting, stressing the importance of reaching inter-ethnic peace. The earlier decision was overturned, and, citing the economic linkage between upper and lower

---

31. Walker 1990, 283–4.
32. Ibid., 290.
33. Libaridian 1988, 34–5.

Karabakh, the region was declared an autonomous region in Azerbaijan, with Shusha as its administrative capital.[34]

This was the origin of the Nagorno–Karabakh Autonomous Oblast (NKAO). At the time, the population was about 92 per cent Armenian. (The Armenian population of Zangezur was about 60 per cent and that of Nakhichevan 40 per cent). The Armenian percentage has been cited as somewhat smaller before the First World War, but that figure took in several lowland districts, and even so had always shown a clear Armenian majority.[35]

The final administrative arrangements for NKAO took place in July 1923: it was to be an autonomous Armenian region forming part of the Azerbaijan SSR, with Khankend as its centre. (The town was renamed Stepanakert, in honour of Stepan Shahumian). Connection with Armenia and Erevan was severed. Financially and technically it was dependent on Baku, and although it was initially designated as an Armenian region, this adjective was finally dropped from the AO's official name, reflecting a pervasive Azeri–Tatar dislike of minorities, especially territorial ones.[36]

On two issues the boundary of NKAO was a further disappointment for Armenians. In the first place, the northwestern part of Karabakh, the former melikdom of Gulistan (Shahumianovsk today, containing Shahumian, Khanlar and Dashkesan), was placed outside the designated region of NKAO, even though there was an Armenian majority there. It was sited within Azerbaijan proper, with no special status. Secondly, a Lachin corridor was deliberately established to separate Karabakh from Zangezur. (The Armenian villages between the two had been destroyed before sovietization). NKAO constituted a region of 4,161 km², which constituted 4.91 per cent of the total territory of the Azerbaijan SSR. New names were given to the regions of the AO. Jraberd became Martakert, Khachen was divided between Armenian Stepanakert and Azerbaijani Shusha, Varanda became Martuni, and Dizak Hadrut.[37]

It was not long before protests began to occur in Karabakh. An Armenian fleeing from the territory to Iran told of the existence of a political society called "Karabakh to Armenia", which had distributed thousands of leaflets proclaiming that slogan in all parts of the region in November 1927, and attacking the complacency of the Armenian communists. The year 1929 saw increased pan-Turkic activity in Azerbaijan (something that was occurring in Turkey at the time, with further Armenian deportations); the Armenians responded by stressing their claim to Karabakh. The party

---

34. Ibid., 36; also USSR archives, Moscow. Protokoli nos. 11 and 12, TsPA IML, f. 64, op. 1, d. 1, 11. 117–18, 121–22 [communicated by Ronald Suny].
35. PRO FO371/3659 piece 97452.
36. Libaridian 1988, 37.
37. Donabedian & Mutafian 1989, 59–60 and 109–11.

secretary in Erevan in 1930–5, Aghasi Khandjian, worked for the retrocession of Karabakh and Nakhichevan to Armenia. As a result he was shot by Beria in July 1936. In 1936 the Stalin constitution was introduced, which separated the three Transcaucasian republics, which from 1922 to 1936 had been one unit; the effect was further to distance mountainous Karabakh from Armenia.[38]

The Azerbaijani authorities in effect ran an apartheid system in Karabakh, and the Armenian population decreased as a result. On sovietization it had constituted about 92 per cent; by 1926 it was just over 89 per cent; and in 1979 it was 75 per cent. The population figures for 1979 show approximately 120,000 Armenians out of a total of 160,000. Shusha's Armenian population had been 40,000 at the turn of the century; by 1929 that population was 5000. (By contrast, though, the new capital, Stepanakert grew from 3,000 in 1929 to over 60,000 in 1991. This new town was designed by Alexander Tamanian, the creator of modern Erevan, and was laid out with traditional Armenian architectural motifs). But the use of the Armenian language in education was chauvinistically restricted by the Azerbaijani authorities, and television programmes were in either Russian or Turki. Health clinics were for Azerbaijani villages, not Armenian. Armenian historical monuments in Nagorno–Karabakh were systematically ignored and left untended. Azerbaijani historians tried to prove that the people were not Armenian at all, but Caucasian Albanian, and therefore Azerbaijani.[39]

Hope re-emerged during the Khrushchev thaw that the situation of Karabakh would change. The Armenian party secretary, Hakob Zarobian, was thought to be personally sympathetic. In 1963 (according to some, 1964) a petition from the Armenians of mountainous Karabakh was submitted to Khrushchev. It detailed the subtle and chauvinistic policies imposed by Azerbaijan on the Autonomous Oblast (which in fact was hardly autonomous at all), designed to destroy the Armenian culture and language, and to encourage Armenians to leave the region. Economic coercion was used by Baku to make life as hard for the people as possible. The Azerbaijani regime compelled Armenian economic enterprises to be dependent on Azerbaijani ones, situated some way away in Azerbaijan proper, usually in Aghdam. Construction in Stepanakert had to be controlled by officials in Mingechaur, 120km away. No roads had been constructed in 40 years, and agriculture and stockbreeding had been left undeveloped. All the measures "deprived the Armenian population of its livelihood and wellbeing, and forced it to abandon its own ancestral homeland". At the same time, the Armenian decline had made it possible to repopulate the area with Azerbaijanis, in accordance with Baku's policy.

---

38. Libaridian 1988, 40.
39. Ibid., 41.

Things were worse in the Shahumianovsk region, outside NKAO. The petition ended by asking for mountainous Karabakh and adjacent regions to be incorporated into Armenia, or made part of the Russian Soviet Federative Socialist Republic (RSFSR), and for the Armenians of Karabakh to be treated in accordance with Lenin's policy on nationalities.[40]

Nothing happened, and in 1967 the people of Karabakh addressed another appeal, this time to the government and party officials of the Armenian party in Erevan. This stressed the degree of anti-Armenian violence and lawlessness that the authorities were permitting in mountainous Karabakh, demonstrated by the fact that it was always possible for an Azerbaijani murderer of an Armenian to get off with a light sentence. When the people tried to protest, Stepanakert was filled with soldiers and secret policemen, who persecuted and terrorized the people, attacking them as traitors and spies. Only Armenia itself could help find a way out for the people.[41]

Again nothing happened. Ten years later Sero Khanzatian, a member of the executive committee of the Writers' Union of the USSR and author of a popular historical novel entitled *Mkhitar Sparapet*, addressed a letter to General Secretary Leonid I. Brezhnev (15 October 1977). Much of the language of this document is cloudy and soviet, but Khanzatian makes the point that the people of mountainous Karabakh never accepted separation from the motherland, and quotes a statement by Lenin on national injustice, which the inclusion of Karabakh in Azerbaijan manifestly constituted. The letter made no impact, beyond being noticed in the *New York Times*.[42]

It was the sense of national injustice and the fact that the inclusion of Karabakh in Azerbaijan seemed to violate the essence of any reasonable policy on nationalities (including Lenin's), which gave impetus to the vast protests that took place in 1988.

Initially the status of Karabakh did not feature among the topics of *perestroika*. Change indeed came slowly in Armenia; despite the launch in 1985 of the movement for change, nothing happened in Armenia until 1988, except for a few demonstrations and statements by small groups. In June 1987 Gorbachev had indirectly criticized the corruption operating within the Armenian Communist Party, a cause taken up by *Pravda* in January 1988.[43] But the issues that really stirred the people were industrial pollution, the protection of the environment, and the status of mountainous Karabakh (and to some extent Nakhichevan).[44]

---

40. Libaridian 1988, 42–5.
41. Ibid., 47–8.
42. Ibid., 49; Walker 1990, 397.
43. BBC *summary of world broadcasts*, SU/0054 B/2–B/6, 21 January 1988. I am grateful to Caroline Cox for her comments on the following section.
44. *Asbarez* newspaper (Glendale, California), 23 January 1988.

These issues had been aired in small demonstrations in Erevan in September–October 1987. They were all (to the Armenians) issues of equal merit; none was more or less important. But the issue of Karabakh tapped a sense of deep national injustice. It symbolized three things: first, the fact that the Turks had not been punished for the mass killings of Armenians in 1915 (Armenians often equate Turks with Azerbaijanis, calling them both "Turks"); secondly, the betrayal of Armenia by the Western allies in 1918–20, and, thirdly, the unsatisfactory territorial deal of the Transcaucasian republics under Soviet rule, out of which (of the major nationalities) the Armenians had come off worst.[45]

It was Abel Aghanbekyan, Gorbachev's economic adviser, who, in speeches in London and Paris in November–December 1987, voiced the national injustice felt by the Armenian people, and spoke on the likely retrocession of Karabakh and Nakhichevan to Armenia. But it soon appeared that he had spoken out of turn. For no decision was made at the top. (The notion that Aghanbekyan spoke on orders from Gorbachev in order to stir the people up with the intention of giving them nothing, and thereby leading them to war with their neighbours, is too fanciful to be worth serious consideration.) The issue became a live one and it appeared to be within the limits of discussion. The Armenians gained two effective spokesmen in Zori Balayan, a native of mountainous Karabakh, and Sergei Mikoyan, son of the famous "Old Bolshevik", namely A. I. Mikoyan.[46]

Things remained quiet in Armenia following the demonstrations of October 1987. It was in mountainous Karabakh itself that political activity re-emerged. In sessions of the regional soviets on 11–12 February 1988, motions were passed calling for the Autonomous Oblast's incorporation into Armenia.[47] This was a direct and unprecedented challenge to the *status quo*. None of the participants – Moscow, Baku or even Erevan – expected decisions to be made in Karabakh. They liked to feel that between them they fixed the politics. A decision taken in Stepanakert was like an uprising of slaves.

News of these decisions reached Erevan on 15 February 1988; the fact that it took three days for the news to travel indicates the lack of contact between Armenia proper and the enclave. Demonstrations had been planned in Abovian, a new town to the north of Erevan, largely populated by exiled and unemployed former residents of Karabakh. With the news, the focus of the demonstration shifted from the environment to Karabakh. On 18 February 1988, 20,000 people demonstrated. The number grew to 50,000 the following day.[48]

---

45. Edmund M. Herzig, "Armenians". In *The nationalities question in the Soviet Union*, Graham Smith (ed.), 152–4 (London: Longman, 1990).
46. *Armenian Mirror Spectator* (Watertown, Mass.), 5 December 1987.
47. Ibid., 5 March 1989; personal interview with Armen Aivazian, Erevan, May 1989.

Back in Karabakh, the members of the Stepanakert soviet undertook another bold stroke of defiance of the *status quo*. On 20 February 1988, the regional soviet of Karabakh voted "to transfer the Autonomous Oblast of Mountainous Karabakh from the Azerbaijani SSR to the Armenian SSR, [and] at the same time to intercede with the Supreme Soviet of the USSR to reach a positive resolution regarding the transfer of the region from the Azerbaijani SSR to the Armenian SSR".[49]

Again, the news took time to reach Erevan. A demonstration on the Green issue drew more participants than one on Karabakh. But Moscow was worried about the spirit manifesting itself in Stepanakert, and, in a statement reflecting the bureaucratic conservative nature of communism, *Tass* dubbed those calling for change "extremists".[50]

Erevan heard of this designation with disappointment, but the spirit of the people was roused, and they demonstrated through the night of 21–22 February 1988, ending their march in front of the headquarters of the Armenian Supreme Soviet. Moscow despatched two politburo men to Erevan, and two representatives to Stepanakert. All appealed for calm.[51]

But the situation became the reverse of calm and the first of the really massive demonstrations took place in Erevan. From all corners of Armenia the people came to protest, on foot, on horseback, or by car. All came to express the vast pent-up but denied national pride of Armenia. They converged on Opera square, which, although not in the very centre of Erevan, holds a large space. Two points were of significance. One was that the demonstrations were peaceful; there was no violence. The other was that the demonstrators carried placards of Gorbachev. They continued to believe that discussion of the status of mountainous Karabakh was within the scope of *perestroika*.[52]

The issue of Karabakh was twice discussed in Moscow, in March and July 1988, the second time at the presidium of the supreme Soviet. The upshot was that no change was permitted. Article 78 of the Soviet constitution was invoked, which said that there had to be mutual agreement between republics over changes of sovereignty. The points at issue in Karabakh, about the suppression of the Armenian language and culture, denial of identity, and the legal, economic and social pressure from Baku to make the Armenian population leave – everything that can be put under the heading of "national injustice": these were not discussed. Andrei Sakharov felt that in the presidium debate Gorbachev was clearly biased against the Armenians and in favour of the Azerbaijanis. At the same time, the issues

48. Personal interview, Erevan, May 1989.
49. Libaridian 1988, 90.
50. Ibid., 98–9.
51. Ibid., 94; *Armenian Mirror Spectator*, 5 & 19 March 1988.
52. Walker 1990, 400.

were not addressed by the Armenian proponents of the Karabakh cause, who took refuge in turgid and windy "sovietic" rhetoric that failed to identify the points at issue. If one reads the speeches, one almost comes to the conclusion that the Armenian intelligentsia was colluding in negating the possibility of change for the people of mountainous Karabakh.[53]

Two Azerbaijanis had been killed in the course of demonstrations in Karabakh and, as a result of this, and of the insolence of claiming territory, there was an organized pogrom of Armenians in the Caspian town of Sumgait on 28–29 February 1988. Officially, 32 people were killed, but that figure was widely disbelieved, and access to death certificates has shown a considerably larger figure. The legal procedure of prosecuting the killers was observed to be very flawed. Eventually one Azerbaijani from the lower echelons was convicted. At once a fierce outburst of intercommunal violence took place – this was November 1988 – which assumed the proportions of an exchange of populations: 180,000 ethnic Armenians living in Azerbaijan left for Armenia and 150,000 ethnic Azerbaijanis living in Armenia left for Azerbaijan. (Some Armenians left for other parts of the USSR, especially Ashkhabad, Tashkent and Dushanbe.) There was also anti-Armenian ethnic strife in Kirovabad.[54]

Although the severe Armenian earthquake of 8 December 1988 did not affect Karabakh physically, it was powerful shock to the whole Armenian people and it weakened their struggle for a better deal for Karabakh. Moreover, two days later, in an act of remarkable cynicism, Gorbachev arrested the members of the Erevan-based Karabakh committee, which had been set up to co-ordinate activities.

On 13 January 1989 the authorities responded to the demands of the Armenians of Karabakh and their supporters (such as Sakharov, who had proposed the scheme back in July 1988) by taking Nagorno–Karabakh out of control of Baku, and putting it under Moscow's direct administration. The special administrator was to be Arkady Volsky. Volsky was a decent and humane person, a good example of an imperial proconsul. He acknowledged that the incorporation of Karabakh and Nakhichevan in Azerbaijan in the 1920s had been a mistake. However, he also realized that his hands were tied. When Moscow voted 50 million roubles for development in Karabakh, the money was despatched (in accordance with Soviet practice) via Baku. Not surprisingly, given the hostility of Baku to the Armenians of Karabakh, the money got no further. The special administrative status ended in November 1989, having achieved almost nothing, and Baku started to issue threats that included an end to the separate status of NKAO, and the renaming of Stepanakert as Khankend.[55]

---

53. Text of Supreme Soviet debate in BBC SWB SU/0210 B/1-B/17, 22 July 1988; Andrei Sakharov, *Moscow and beyond*, 54–5 (London: Hutchinson, 1991).

54. Walker (1990: 401–5).

Karabakh was the catalyst for change within Armenia, but nothing changed for the people of Karabakh themselves. Azerbaijani sentiments of fury at not being in control reached fever pitch in Baku in January 1990, when Azerbaijani mobs looted and murdered ethnic Armenians and destroyed their homes. So great was the extremism of the mob that they even pursued Armenians fleeing to the airport, in order to try and kill them. Russian tanks rolled in, in a heavy-handed sovietic manner, and an action that could have been mounted as the protection from the centre of a vulnerable minority soon took on the appearance of a typical example of crude military communism.[56]

In mid–1990 the communists were defeated and ousted in Erevan. A Moscow–Baku axis was formed as a result, with a view to saving some communist rule in Transcaucasia. The Soviet regime, embittered by its defeat in Armenia, took punitive military action in April and May 1991, in collaboration with the Azerbaijani OMON or interior ministry forces. Twenty-four Armenian villages were attacked, some inside NKAO and some situated in the Shahumianovsk district. Thousands of people were brutally deported. Getashen and Martunashen were sacked, and ethnically cleansed.[57]

The Armenians sought resolutely to turn away from communism, which seemed the worst evil to them. Their views were articulated in the referendum on independence held in September 1991, in which Armenia voted overwhelmingly for secession from the USSR. At the same time, quadripartite talks were held at Zheleznovodsk in the north Caucasus on the issue of Nagorno–Karabakh, between Presidents Yeltsin, Nazarbayev (of Kazakhstan), Mutalibov and Ter-Petrosian. A reasonable compromise was reached, and a document signed detailing a ceasefire, an end to the blockades, an exchange of prisoners and the opening of lines of communication. (Both Armenia and Nagorno–Karabakh had been blockaded since mid-1989 with catastrophic effect on the economic activity, and indeed livelihood, of the people of both the republic and the Autonomous Oblast). However, no ceasefire resulted, and Baku's blockade remained in place, with crippling effect. There appears to have been no political will involved in the implementation of the Zheleznovodsk agreement, and it lapsed.[58]

In September 1991 the people of Karabakh, tired of the threats that surrounded their region, made a pathfinder declaration of independence, confirmed in a real declaration in January 1992. The territory was proclaimed a separate diplomatic entity, the Republic of Karabakh, which included the Shahumianovsk district. This declaration has led to heated dispute within Armenia itself, on the issue of recognition or non-recognition.[59]

---

55. Sakharov (1991: 53, 87).

56. *The Times* (1990: 15 and 16 January).

57. *Armenian Mirror Spectator*, 11 May 1991.

58. Ibid., 28 September 1991.

Conditions within Karabakh continued to be bitterly fought over. The Azerbaijani minority held on to its positions tenaciously and let the Baku authorities use their towns and villages to attack the Armenian majority unceasingly. The places of greatest danger to Armenians were a village and a town: Khojalu, from which the Azerbaijanis could control the airport of Stepanakert, thereby tightening the blockade on the Karabakh people; and the town of Shusha, whose Armenian minority had been forced out in 1988, and which was now a ghost town even for Azerbaijanis, and only used as a strategic position for launching GRAD missiles upon the civilian housing of Stepanakert. On some days as many as 400 GRAD missiles rained down on Armenian multi-storey apartments. The Armenians had no access to GRAD missiles.

In a controversial action, the Armenians took control of Khojalu in February 1992. Allegations of a massacre of the civilian population of the town were made, but several events surrounding its capture were not widely reported: first, the Armenians warned the people of Khojalu that they were planning to take the town, and told them to quit, but their own Azerbaijani militia leaders appear to have prevented them from leaving; secondly, a week after the capture of the town the Armenians invited the Azerbaijanis to claim their dead. Neither of these open actions is characteristic of a group seeking to carry out a massacre.[60]

By contrast, disturbing details were revealed in an investigation of April 1992 of some killings of Armenian villagers in Maragha, northern Karabakh. Bodies exhumed from shallow graves had clearly been decapitated and burnt. Forty-five Armenians had been killed. These details went largely unreported.[61]

Iran was, in early 1992, showing that it was keen to have a resolution to the conflict on its northwestern borders, which had implications for a section of its own population. Consequently, Tehran launched an initiative, and after a lengthy process induced the leaders of Armenia and Azerbaijan to sign a peace agreement on Karabakh in May 1992. On the very day of its signature it was invalidated by the Armenian seizure of Shusha (which ended the GRAD bombardment of Stepanakert), and by Armenian forces puncturing a hole in the Lachin corridor, creating a vital landlink between Armenia and Karabakh. It appeared that the actions of the fighters in Karabakh were strongly influenced by the Dashnak party, well known for its militant stance, and that they were to some extent in opposition to the policy of the government in Erevan, which took the view that diplomacy could work.[62]

---

59. See *The Republic of Karabakh* (Washington DC: the Armenian assembly, 1992).
60. *Nezavisimaya Gazeta*, 2 April 1992.
61. Eyewitness report by Caroline Cox, communicated in May 1992.
62. *Armenian International Magazine*, vol. III (June 1992), 13.

Parallel negotiations, conducted under the auspices of the Conference on Security and Economic Co-operation (CSCE), continued in Rome, Minsk and Vienna, with little success, bogged down in procedural disputes about the status of representatives of mountainous Karabakh, with Baku unwilling to give recognition to delegates from Stepanakert. However, the process continued, despite meagre results.

The military position was from 1992 to 1994 somewhat fluid. The election of a Popular Front government in Baku under Abulfaz Elchibey in June 1992 brought ideological Turkism to power there. It was smarting from a sense of loss of control, a dangerous mood for an ideology. Soon, in secret collaboration with some volunteer Turkish officers (who discreetly resigned for the purpose), Azerbaijan undertook a widespread assault on the villages of mountainous Karabakh. Mardakert province fell quite rapidly, but thereafter progress was slow. In August 1992 Azerbaijani forces seized the town of Ardsvashen (plus 46 km^2), territory of the Republic of Armenia, not of the former NKAO. By the late summer of 1992 the pro-western Elchibey regime had created 20,000 Armenian refugees from villages in mountainous Karabakh. In September 1992 President Nazarbayev of Kazakhstan tried, at a summit in Alma-Ata, to persuade the leaders of Armenia and Azerbaijan to end hostilities, but with no success. The condition of the villagers remained precarious and bad throughout the following winter, although they registered some successes in downing Azerbaijani SU–24 and SU–25 bombers.[63]

There were, however, several military reverses suffered by the Azerbaijanis during the spring of 1993. It became clear that the Azerbaijani army had some basic operational defects, and that the Armenians of mountainous Karabakh would fight courageously in defence of their homes. By March 1993, self-defence forces of the Nagorno–Karabakh Republic had retaken around 25 villages in the Mardakert province. The Karabakh army proved to be a more competent and mobile fighting force than the army of Azerbaijan, which despite initial successes soon appeared inept, showing the weaknesses typical of a conscript army whose frontline troops were, in this instance, largely members of Muslim minorities from within Azerbaijan. In April 1993 Nagorno–Karabakh forces broke out from the borders of the Autonomous Oblast and took Kelbajar, a strategic position from which the Azerbaijanis were at the time seriously threatening the Lachin humanitarian corridor.[64]

The Azerbaijanis responded with further attacks against the Martuni and Hadrut districts, and against Goris district in Armenia. Further Nagorno–Karabakh advances secured villages near Fizuli, another site of Azerbaijani shelling of Nagorno–Karabakh and southern Armenia. By late

---

63. *Transcaucasus: a chronology,* vol. I, no. 9, 12 (September 1992).
64. Ibid., vol. II, no. 5, 12 (May 1993).

June 1993, Nagorno–Karabakh forces had freed all but a 6 km strip of land along mountainous Karabakh's eastern border, and had seized those positions in Azerbaijan proper from which assaults had been launched upon their land.[65]

In battle formation Azeri–Turkish officers only took up second-line positions. Their prudence for their own welfare proved the downfall of the Azerbaijani army as a fighting force, and it melted like snow in April–May 1993, leading to a rebellion within Azerbaijan and the collapse of the regime of Abulfaz Elchibey (June 1993). The rebel leader Surat Husseinov came to power, in uneasy collaboration with the former communist Haidar Aliev. This two-man executive signified a tilt back to Russia and away from Turkey and "the West".

The significance of the end of the Elchibey regime for both Armenia and Nagorno–Karabakh was that it indicated the end, for the time being, of the overt pan-Turkist vision (supported by the oil companies and to some extent by the more privatized sections of Western governments), which had brought about the possibility of close collaboration and possible unity between Azerbaijan and Turkey, over a defunct Armenia and Nagorno–Karabakh.

Nevertheless, Azerbaijan was still capable of launching attacks, and there were assaults on Stepanakert (21–23 July). Azerbaijani officials agreed to meet representatives of the Republic of Nagorno–Karabakh on 24 July, initiating a three-day ceasefire. But Azerbaijani attacks continued on the Hadrut and Martuni districts in early August, and in response Nagorno–Karabakh forces seized artillery positions in Fizuli, from which Armenian villages had been shelled. The UN Security Council voted for immediate unconditional withdrawal of Nagorno–Karabakh forces from the recently seized areas of Azerbaijan (18 August). On that day, attacks by Azerbaijani aircraft on the Ghapan district of Armenia left 7 villagers dead and 34 wounded, and Baku attacked villages in the Martuni district with cluster-bombs. These assaults were not addressed by the Security Council. On 19 August Nagorno–Karabakh forces seized the Azerbaijani town of Jebrail (Dzhebrail). A further advance by Nagorno–Karabakh forces confirmed their possession of Fizuli (23 August). With each new Nagorno–Karabakh advance, a quantity of war materiel was recovered.[66]

A serious development was recorded in early September 1993 with the report of the presence of 600 Afghan *mujahidin* mercenaries in the Azerbaijani army. Later assessments put the figure at between 1,000 and 1,500. Eight Afghans were killed in combat with Nagorno–Karabakh forces. Further bilateral agreements between Baku and Stepanakert achieved temporary ceasefires. However, these were broken on 23 October by Azerbaijani

---

65. Ibid., vol. II, no. 7, 12 (July 1993).
66. Ibid., vol. II, no. 9, 12 (September 1993).

attacks on Hadrut, as well as on some of the territory in control of Nagorno–Karabakh forces. Nagorno–Karabakh forces counter-attacked uncompromisingly and seized a further 40 km area of territory along the Arax river.[67]

The foreign minister of Nagorno–Karabakh, Arkady Ghukasyan, issued a statement on 5 November 1993 that spelt out the issues for peace as seen by his government and people. Real peace had to concern itself with three main topics (he believed): the political status of Karabakh, the lifting of the Azerbaijani-imposed blockade of Armenia, and the withdrawal of Karabakh forces from their positions within Azerbaijan. He also saw bilateral negotiations between Baku and Stepanakert as holding out the best prospect for peace, since to date only these had brokered remotely effective ceasefire agreements.[68]

Whether the bravery and competence of the Nagorno–Karabakh forces is sufficient to gain their territory a permanent recognized status is yet to be decided. Foreign diplomatic negotiators can hardly fail to take into account the fact that mountainous Karabakh is not an inalienable part of Azerbaijan, but has always been – most obviously in 1919–21 – a disputed territory, and that nowadays, when the dialogue is of democracy and human rights, the wishes of the great majority should be the deciding factor. However, the pervasive pro-Turkish slant of Western governments, and the influence of the oil lobby, are immensely strong opposing elements and, when measured against them, the wishes of the people to determine their own future may be held to be of little import. Foreign chancelleries of even the most democratic countries do not regard democracy for mountainous Karabakh with enthusiasm. The strategic importance of Turkey and the mineral wealth of Azerbaijan are of far greater significance. So it is likely to be some time before a solution is found to the Nagorno–Karabakh question.

67. Ibid., vol. II, no. 10, 12 (October 1993).
68. Ibid., vol. II, no. 12, 12 (December 1993).

CHAPTER SIX

The republic of Azerbaijan: notes on the state borders in the past and the present

SULEJMAN ALIJARLY

The province of Azerbaijan is a term of the Middle Ages. It is used in contemporary sources (Mir Yahya Qazvini, Iskander bek Munshi, etc.) in reference to the whole of Azerbaijan: although the province has been very variable in its geographical connotations over time, the whole is generally held as consisting of the northern (Republic of Azerbaijan) and the southern (Iranian Azerbaijan).

This land lies between the main Caucasus range and the mountain chain Kurtdag, from which the Little Zab River, a tributary of the Tigris, takes its waters. Here runs the 36th parallel. This is the southernmost boundary of the lands of Azerbaijan.

According to al-Ya'qubi, an Arab author of the ninth century, Arran (the lands of northern Azerbaijan by the confluence of the Arax and Kura) represents Upper Azerbaijan (Azerbaijan al-ulya), stretching as far as Barda and Derbent.[1] An important note of precision is made by Ibn Hauqal, who lived in the tenth century. On the map of Azerbaijan that he drew, the western coast of the Khazar (Caspian) Sea to the city of Derbent belonged to this country.[2] According to the information of al-Tabari (838–923) and Ibn al-Athir (1160–1233), Maslam ibn 'Abd al-Malik, leader of the Caliphate, moving in a march against the Turks, reached Al-Baba (Derbent) in the district of Azerbaijan.[3] Al-Kufi (731–798), one of the early Arab authors, includes in the country of Azerbaijan the towns Baylakan and Sheki along with Barda; Qudama ibn Jafar, writing at the end of the ninth century, even mentions Barda as the capital of Azerbaijan.[4] Ibn al-Fayih and Yaqut, who also take the northern border of the country as far as Barda, name Zenjan as its southern frontier and Arzinjan as its southwestern.[5]

---

1. Zija Bunijatov, *Azerbaijan in the 7–9th centuries* (Baku: Elm, 1989), 136–7, in Azerbaijani.
2. Ibid.
3. N. M. Velikhanova, "The change in the historical geography of Azerbaijan as a result of its capture by the Arabs". In *Historical geography of Azerbaijan*, Ziya Buniyatov (ed.), 53 (Baku: Elm, 1987).
4. Velikhanova, 53.

Azerbaijan

It is the contention of this author that during the course of the next millennium the geographical co-ordinates of Azerbaijan, about which Arab scholarship reports in the eighth to tenth centuries, underwent relatively minor change.

In the sixteenth century the Azerbaijani lands, existing as a metropolate of the Safavid empire, formed three *beglerbekates* (governorships): Azerbaijan proper, the centre of which was the city of Tabriz, the first capital of the state; Karabakh, with its centre in Ganja; and Shirvan.[6] This administrative state structure, which existed for 200 years, exercised a significant influence on the subsequent political history of the country. On this basis there developed in the 1740s the Azerbaijani feudal state structures known as the khanates of Sheki, Karabakh, Kubin, Urmi, and Nakhichevan. The territory of the Karabakh khanate, for example, equated to the extent of the

---

5. Ibn Khordadbekh, *Book of ways and countries*. Russian translation, commentary and essay by N. Velikhanova (Baku: Elm, 1986), 289.

6. I. P. Petrushevskiy, *Essays on the history of feudal relations in Azerbaijan and Armenia from the sixteenth to the beginning of the nineteenth century* (Leningrad: Leningrad State University, 1949), Cg. II.

former *beglerbekate*, with the exception of the town of Ganja. Among the state activists of the eighteenth century who most clearly perceived the national interests of Azerbaijan was Fatali-khan, governor of the Kubin khanat. He came out determinedly against the idea of forcefully splitting off the western lands of the country (together with the town of Ganja) to the advantage of Georgia.[7]

Azerbaijan was recognized as an established entity, even by the leaders of a country that maintained active foreign policy intentions towards it. Thus, the Russian representative in Kakheti, S. D. Burnashev, wrote that the lands of Azerbaijan in the north bordered Georgia, in the east the Caspian Sea and the province of Gilan, in the south Iran, and in the west Turkey. Along with the cities of Tabriz, Maragha, Urmija, Khoj, Ardebili and Meshkin, the areas of Baku, Shemakha, Sheki, Ganja, Shusha and Nakhichevan also belonged to Azerbaijan.[8]

During the course of 1600 years, the lowland and upland confluence of the Kura and Arax, including the Karabakh and Nakhichevan provinces, were a component part of the state structures upon the territory of Azerbaijan. Some sources have traced the establishment of this all-inclusive structure of Azerbaijan to the late fifteenth century. The writings of an Armenian historiographer certainly reckon that this period was significant for Transcaucasia in a territorial sense. "In 387 Armenia was split into two unequal parts: the western districts . . . went over to Rome, whereas all the other parts – more than three-quarters of the territory of Armenia – to Iran. Moreover, in the western part of Armenia there was no king appointed, and it was incorporated into the provincial system of the Roman Empire".[9]

Up until the ninth century, taking into account the 200 year rule of the Caliphate between the seventh and ninth centuries, the lands referred to as Ancient Arran could not have been under the domination of Armenia either *de jure* or *de facto*. This question has received exhaustive treatment in historical works, based on contemporary sources (Greek, Caucasian Albanian, Arab and Armenian).[10]

The quality of the testimony of the great historical and geographical literature of the Arabs needs no commendation. The state apparatus of the Caliphate afforded Azerbaijan special strategic importance. This was demanded above all by the interests of the rivalry with the Khazar kaganate, the war that lasted intermittently some 150 years. In order to create

7. A. Tsagareli, *Seals and other historical documents of the eighteenth century, touching upon Georgia*, vol. II, part II (St Petersburg, 1902), 17–24, in Russian.
8. *Description of the districts of Azerbaijan in Persia and their political situation* by officer and cavalryman Burnashev in Tbilisi 1786 (1793, Kursk), 4, in Russian.
9. H. G. Nersissian (ed.), *History of the Armenian people* (Erevan: Armenian Academy of Sciences, 1980), 96, in Russian.
10. Bunijatov, 1965; F. J. Mamedova, *The political history and historical geography of Caucasian Albania* (Baku: Elm, 1986), in Russian.

for itself a strong shield before the Khazars, the Caliphate engaged in the migratory politics of colonization and resettled in Azerbaijan the population of entire districts of Aravi. One of the main cities of Azerbaijan, Barda (the former capital of Arran) was transformed into the residency of the Caliphate's local representative. Therefore, for a long period Arabs gathered significant information on Barda and its environs, precisely that which later constituted the province of Karabakh.

In Arab sources the question of Karabakh is treated to all intents and purposes quite uniformly – as a province of Arran. The report of al-Mas'udi, writing in the tenth century, can be counted as fundamental. He wrote: "The mountains of Abu-Musa [Karabakh], which belong to Arran, are settled by tribes from the peoples of Arran".[11] The report of the Armenian author Vardan is important, where he describes the establishment in Ganja of the rule of the Sheddadid Fazlun I (Patlun, according to Vardan) at the end of the tenth century. The author also reports that Fazlun I (985–1030) incorporated into the composition of Varda, Baylakan and Khachen (the basic part of upper Karabakh),[12] the main lowland and upland regions of Karabakh. The same Vardan also writes that Fazlun took control of the town of Dvin as well, laying upon Armenia a tax of 3000 dinars. The assertion that at the beginning of the eleventh century Khachen and Gardman were included in the Bagratid kingdom of Ani (the Armenian state formation from 885 to 1045)[13] is difficult to reconcile with the evidence. Perhaps one can speak of the war episode, but no more than this, because Fazlun I, minting his own money in Ganja and in command of a significant military force, held northern Azerbaijan in his own sphere and scored a victory over the Khazar *kaganate*. It is difficult to suppose that he would have accepted the loss of his kingdom's metropolis. This is even more the case as other contemporary sources, including the Qasida of the Azerbaijani poet of the eleventh century Qatran of Tabriz,[14] report Arran and Siunik being under the power of the Sheddadids, even after Fazlun. Moreover, the kingdom of Ani was annulled by Byzantium in 1045, whereas the Sheddadids ruled Arran right up to 1088, when Ganja came under the power of the Seljuk emperor Melik-shah.

According to the sources, Karabakh remained in the administrative political structure of Ganja, even during the next century. The author Mkhitar Gosh (1130–1213), in mentioning Khachen, writes of its capital Ganjak.[15] In an anonymous text written at the beginning of the thirteenth

---

11. Citation from Velikhanova, 48; Prince Isai Abu-Musa ruled a large part of Arran, together with the town of Baylakan in the 1830s.
12. Vardan, *Universal history* (1861, Moscow), 125–6, in Russian.
13. Nersissian, 126.
14. M. X. Sharifli, *Feudal states of Azerbaijan in the second half of 9–11th centuries* (Baku: Elm, 1978), 203, in Azerbaijani.

century in Persian, the author states "This district [Khachen] is difficult of access, among mountains and forests; it belongs to the region Arran".[16] The same applied in the case of the district of Chiljabjurt (Jalpert), governed by the Ganja emir of the state of the Atabeks (Ildenizids) of Azerbaijan, since the district of Jalpert was in the region of Barda.[17] In collective historical works between the fourteenth and sixteenth centuries, such as Nuzhat al-Qulub, Zeyl-e tarikh-e gozide, Takmilat al-akhbar, the upper part of historical Karabakh is generally referred to in no way other than as "Karabakh of Arran". Just such a state of affairs in essence is fixed also by Arakel Davrizhetsi, the Armenian author of the seventeenth century, according to whom Karabakh is the land of the Caucasian Albanians: "Then the vardapet set out for the land of the Albanians, to Karabakhn . . ."[18] Precisely through the strength of the tradition of state rule formed over centuries, Karabakh became in the system of the Safavid Empire (1501–1736) one of the three Azerbaijani *beglerbekates*, the administrative centre of which was the town of Ganja.[19]

The state administrative identification of Karabakh in an historical retrospective corresponds to the following schema:
- 387–705: Arran, Gardman principality, capital Barda
- Seventh to ninth centuries: rule of the Caliphate
- End of ninth century to beginning of tenth century: Arran, Gardman principality
- 985/6–1088: Arran, state of the Sheddadids, capital Ganja
- 1088–1225: part of the states of the Seljuks and Atabek-Ildenizids, in the administrative governance of Ganja
- Beginning of thirteenth century to end of fourteenth century: rule of the Mongols
- 1410–1500: part of the states of the Qara and Al-Qoyunlu, in the administrative governance of Ganja
- 1501–1736: part of the Safavid state, administrative unit was the Karabakh *beglerbekate*, Administrative centre Ganja
- 1747–1822: the independent Karabakh khanate, capital Shusha

During the course of the 14 centuries adduced in the schema, with the exception of the existence of the previously mentioned kingdom of Ani,

15. Mkhitar Gosh, *Albanian chronicle*. Russian translation and commentary by Z. M. Bunijatov (Baku: Academy of Sciences, 1960), 12.

16. N. D. Miklukho-Maklaj, "Geographical works in the Persian language". In *Uhenye zapiski Instituta Vostokovedeniia* AN SSR, T. IX (1954, Moscow & Leningrad: Academy of Sciences of the USSR), 204–5.

17. Al-Nasavi, *Biography of Sultan Jalal ad-Din Mankburn*. Russian translation and essay by Z. M. Bunijatov (Baku: Elm, 1973), 204.

18. Arhak'el Dawrizhets'i, *Book of history,* Russian translation, introduction and commentary by L. A. Khanlaryan (Moscow: Nauka, 1973), 226.

19. Petrushevskiy, 122–4.

Armenia was not represented on the map of Transcaucasia in terms of its own statehood, which removes the basis for any further attempt to interpret the facts differently.

Furthermore, Arabic historical and geographical literature in particular fixes the fact of statehood in Azerbaijan. Yaqut al-Hamavi, having visited several towns in Azerbaijan in 1213 and 1220, wrote "[this] is a huge land and great state".[20] Such a conclusion had in view not merely an evaluation of the frontiers of the state of the Azerbaijani Atabeks, who, by the way, minted money also in the capital of Arran, Ganja. According to the observation of another mediaeval encyclopaedist, Hamdallah Kazvini, at the time of the Atabeks of Azerbaijan and of the khakans of Shirvan, this was one of the richest countries of Asia Minor, along with Iraq and Iran. In particular, budget revenues recorded by these authors flowing into the state treasury, reveal the significance of Azerbaijan as a state (Table 6.1).[21]

As to the question about who was the creator of these huge riches in Azerbaijan, Hamdallah Kazvini provides precise ethnic information with

Table 6.1 Budget revenues (million dinars).

Great Armenia	2
Georgia and Abkhazia	5
Rum Sultanate	15
Azerbaijan	25
Persian Iraq	25
Arabian Iraq	30

reference to the large towns: "[t]he people of Tabriz . . . speak in their own Turkic dialect; in Maragha the people here are white-faced Turks; Khoj is famous as a Turkic area . . . [22]

The eighteenth to nineteenth centuries hold a special place in the history of Karabakh. In connection with the annulment of the Karabakh *beglerbekate*, the town of Ganja and its environs were split, gaining semi-independent status. But the Karabakh khanate, formed in the wake of this, was also no less based on the lands of ancient Arran. This is a natural triangle, formed by the lower course of the rivers Arax and Kura. Here is what the historian of the Karabakh khanate, Mirza Jamal Jevanshir Karabagi, wrote at the start of the nineteenth century:

> As is described in the old historical [books], the borders of the Karabakh *vilayet* are the following: in the south the River Arax, from the

20. Jakut al-Hamavi, *Mudjam al-Buldan. Hamdallah Qazvini. Nuzhat al-Kulub.* Russian translation by P. K. Khuze, I. P. Petrushevskiy and Z. M. Bunijatov (Baku: Elm, 1983), 7.
21. Ibid., 37–62.
22. Hamdallah Qazvini, *Nuzhat al-Kulub*, 47–9.

Khudaferin bridge as far as the Sinix körpi, which is today found on the territory of the Magalov Kazakh, Shamsaddin and Demirchi-Hasanli. Bureaucrats of the Russian state call it the Red bridge; in the east the river Kura, which joins with the River Arax by the village of Javad and later flows into the Caspian Sea; in the north the River Gëran serves as the frontier of Karabakh and Elizavetpol (Ganja) as far as the River Kura, and the Kura, stretching along the frontier, extends to the River Arax; in the west the high mountains of Karabakh, named Kjushbek, Sadvarty and Erikli . . . The Karabakh *vilayet* is part of the country of Arann . . .[23]

The Karabakh khanate, despite the contention of Armenian authors, was not a semi-independent Persian khanate, nor its leader a direct appointee of the Persian court.[24] Right from the start of the existence of the khanate in Karabakh the inevitability of a long struggle with Iran was perceived, which had no desire to reconcile itself with the loss of the former Azerbaijani *beglerbekates*. This also explains the bitterness that was occasioned by the question of building a capital for the khanate. In the State Council of the khanate it was stated "[w]e must surely perish unless we construct a more secure fortress against them, and thus is it not preferable to found another castle in an inaccessible place of our domains, so that, in case of need, we might also receive help from one of the khanates that are our [Azerbaijani] neighbours?"[25]

The threat from Iran brought about a union of all the patriotic forces in the land of Karabakh – Turk and Armenian. Everything was dependent on this. Within the composition of the khanate a single coalition formed, incorporating even the Armenian *meliks* – the Vardan Shahnazar, to whose daughter Ibrahim-khan was married, the Khachen Mirza-khan, and also the chiefs of the Erimankants monastery, elevated by the ruler of Karabakh to the [Caucasian] Albanian (Ganja) catholic throne. However, the Armenian *meliks* of Dizak, Gulistan, and Chiljabjurt were in opposition to the khanate and sowed the seeds of civil conflict. As regards the position of *meliks* they "represented in themselves forces which wished to consolidate the feudal dismemberment of Karabakh". In the conditions of the second half of the eighteenth century this was extremely dangerous. Divided forces could easily be dominated by more powerful neighbours – Iran and Turkey.[26] The regime of the *meliks* was also negatively evaluated by General A. P. Ermolov, Russian Supreme Commander in the Caucasus.[27] Dur-

---

23. Mirza Jamal Jevanshir Karabagi. *History of Karabakh*. Russian translation, introduction and commentary by F. Babaev (Baku: Academy of Sciences, 1959), 63.

24. Nersissian, 183; Z. Balayan, *Hearth* (1984, Erevan), 42.

25. Mirza Jamal, 127.

26. Leviatov, 145.

ing the second decade of the eighteenth century, the self-styled warriors went over to the side of the Qajar, the sworn enemy of the freedom of the peoples of Transcaucasia. But against the enemy a coalition of patriotic forces arose, which was led by Ibrahim-khan. Lieutenant General Kishmi-shev of the Russian service and of Armenian origin wrote:

> . . . the patron of Karabakh did not limit himself to the defence of the castle (Shusha) but took all measures in general to strike a significant blow against his opponent. Convinced that his hatred towards the tyrant was shared by his subjects, he declared a people's war, thanks to which he was able only to expel the Persians from his domain.[28]

This was explained by the fact that the Karabakh and Kubin khanates, in practice holding under their power the whole of north Azerbaijan, found themselves in a position that was incompatible in relations to the Qajars. Both Azerbaijani khanates were in an anti-Iran coalition. At first, the leading role was taken by the Kubin khanate, having drawn up a joint defence pact with Eastern Georgia against aggression from Iran. Far sighted Fatali-khan (the ruler of the Kubin khanate) had long noticed the shadow of Qajar aggression on the southern horizon of Transcaucasia, and was preparing Azerbaijan for battle.[29] This is how the union between Fatali-khan and King Erek'le of Kakheti was formed. After the death of Fatali-khan, the sworn union of Eastern Georgia was formed with the Karabakh khanate. The allies did what they could to aid each other. For the military needs of Erek'le financial assistance was made available from the Karabakh treasury to the tune of 120,000 roubles. The main division of the Persian army, consisting of 8,000 *sarbaz*, was annihilated at Askeran by the joint Georgian–Azerbaijani forces. King Erek'le wrote the following to his appointee on the Caucasian line by the Russians: Agha Muhammad-shah lay siege to the castle of Shusha for more than a month, but the people there . . . inflicted a great loss upon him. For this reason he was unable to come out in battle against us.[30]

Then there followed the famous cavalry march of the Persians on Tbi-lisi. Together with several Azerbaijani ruling khans, the opposition Arme-nian *meliks*, Mezhlum and Abov, crossed over to their side; it was these who began to lead the Iranian military in the direction of Tbilisi.[31]

27. Documents gathered by the Caucasian Archaeological Commission, under the supervi-sion of A. Bergé, vol. VI, part I. Report 1273, in Russian.
28. S. O. Kishmishev, *Campaigns of Nadir-shahn . . . and the events in Persia after his death* (Tbilisi: A. A. Mikhel'son, 1889), 255, in Russian.
29. O. P. Markova. Russia, *Transcaucasia and foreign relations in the eighteenth century* (Mos-cow: Nauka, 1966), 220, in Russian.
30. Tsagareli, 13.
31. Leviatov, 171.

There can hardly be any dispute as to which of these forces can be evaluated positively from a historical perspective. Nonetheless, in recent Armenian publications the Azerbaijani feudal state – the Karabakh khanate – is reduced to the status of being a representative and vassal of the shah, and the opposition vassals of this khanate are glorified as warriors.

The weakness alone of this argument requires that its proponents should resort to a different criterion of evaluation; to be exact, to look at events through the prism of Russo–Caucasian relations:

> Thought is occasioned only by the how certain scholars try to prove that Panah-khan and his successors were the initiators of the unification of Karabakh and Zangezur with Russia. The question must be asked – from whom were they seeking protection? Well, people of Karabakh and Zangezur (under these terms are understood only as Armenians, although the demographic evidence adduced below paints a different picture), this is clear! They were seeking liberation from the Turkish yoke. As for the so-called khans, whose yoke were they wishing to reject? Isn't it true that the khans didn't conceal that their one sworn enemy was the Russians? And all of a sudden the khans voluntarily decided to enter the composition of Russia. Isn't such falsification a little insulting in the first place to the Russian people, whose sons in their thousands were sacrificed in unending battles, caused by khans and pashas?

> ... But how on earth could a handful of nomad newcomers all of a sudden decide voluntarily to incorporate another's land into the composition of Russia?[32]

This quotation expresses the *credo* of an entire literature. But such manifest exploitation of the Russian theme, although corresponding perhaps to the intellect of a sub-officer in pre-Slavic times, still does not bring us anywhere near the truth. Was not a whole packet of documentary sources published over 100 years earlier by Adolphe Bergé in Documents of the Caucasian Archaeological Commission on the interrelations of the Karabakh khanate with Russia? Many are in the original language with contemporary translation. According to the published collection of the Imperial Russian Historical Society, diplomatic relations which the great poet Vagif, grand vizier of the Karabakh khanate, conducted in St Petersburg, led in 1783 to the following edict of Catherine II: "As for Ibrahim-khan, if no difficulty or doubt is met in taking him into Russian protection, it seems possible to adopt for guidance that which was done with King Erek'le ...". The edict was not executed by G. A. Potemkin, although good

---

32. Balayan, 43.

relations with the empress continued. A year later she wrote to Potemkin:

> The letters of Ibrahim-khan are written with much greater politeness than the Turkish or other Persian ones when they have reached me. Please inform me who he is. How did he become khan? Is he young or old, strong or weak, and are the Persians inclined towards him?

In July 1784 the empress bestowed upon Musa Sultan, the Karabakh ambassador, the honour of being the representative of a sovereign friendly state, commanding that an artillery salute be given, and that he be shown all the fountains and sights of Peterhof, "all worthy curiosities, especially our fleet".[33]

As for the bilateral treaty regarding the transference of the khanate (not Karabakh, but precisely of the khanate) into the power of Russia, it was signed on 14 May 1805 in Kjurek-cha. Entitled the Sworn Declaration, it was signed by Ibrahim-khan of Shusha and Karabakh and by the All-Russian military infantry General Pavl Tsitsianov,[34] empowered for the purpose by Tsar Aleksandr I. It is pointless to search in this treaty for the Armenian names of Karabakh or Zangezur.[35]

Within the limits of its own state borders, the Karabakh khanate remained in the composition of Russia as a vassal state, preserving its own internal institutions and establishments, but without the right of external relations. In 1822 the khanate was abolished. So what system of state administrative dependency was introduced this time? Is it possible that a realignment of dependencies of the melikate of Karabakh occurred, that is, of the upper and lower parts of Armenia? The fact is that, during the course of war between Iran and Russia during the mid- to late 1820s, the latter gained control over even the Erevan khanate. Disregarding the absolute majority of the Turkic population, the khanate was refashioned into an administrative unit with national nomenclature, called the Armenian district, into the composition of which was assigned even the khanate of Nakhichevan. An edict of Nikolai II of 21 March 1828 declared: "[b]y the power of the treaty concluded with Persia, we command that the Erevan

---

33. Central State Military Historical Archive of Russia, fund 52, list I/194, act 72, lines 130–1, in Russian.
34. Documents collected by the Caucasian Archaeological Commission, vol. II (1846, Tbilisi), document 1436, 702–5, in Russian.
35. As Halliday outlines briefly in Chapter Four, the turn of the nineteenth century witnessed the permanent incorporation of the Transcaucasian territories within the Russian Empire and the permanent retraction of Persian control from the region, the result of a series of decisive military victories inflicted upon Tehran by St Petersburg. These territorial gains were ratified by treaty. The 1813 Treaty of Gulistan saw Azerbaijan ceded to Russia, and the 1828 Treaty of Turkmanchai extended formal recognition to the inclusion of Armenia and Nakhichevan within the territorial limits of the Russian Empire.

khanate and the Nakhichevan khanate, annexed to Russia from Persia, henceforth in all deeds be known as an Armenian district and that it be included in our title".[36] Thus, when the emphasized goodwill towards the national expectations of the Armenians and the Armenophilia of the Russian authorities received political expression through an imperial edict, the frontiers and territorial integrity of Karabakh were not transgressed. In the place of the abolished khanate was formed Karabakh province, subordinated to a military district of Islamic provinces. The capital of the former khanate, Shusha, became the residence of the head of the district (drawn from the number of Russian generals). In governmental circles there was no question of identifying any part of Karabakh as Armenian. This explains the fact that in an official publication put together by the imperial ministries of foreign affairs, internal affairs, war and finance Karabakh is included in the make-up of the Islamic provinces.[37]

The Russian Empire, incorporating into its bosom the Karabakh khanate, did not start to tear it out of the administrative state complex of the remaining khanates of north Azerbaijan.

Subsequently, the administrative territorial governance of Karabakh altered according to the following schema:
- 1822–40: The Karabakh province is in the make-up of the region (Okrug) of Islamic provinces.
- 1841–4: The Shusha district (the former Karabakh province) in composition of the Caspian territory (Oblast).[38]
- 1846–67: The Shusha district is in the make-up of the Shemakha (from 1859 the Bakin) Guberniate.[39]
- 1867–1918: The Shusha district is in the composition of the newly established Elizavetpol Guberniate.[40]

---

36. Collection of documents relating to the examination of the history of the Armenian people, part I (Moscow, 1833), 178–9, in Russian.
37. V. Legkobytov, *Survey of the Russian domains in Transcaucasia in statistical, ethnographic, topographic and financial relations*, parts I–IV (St Petersburg, 1836), in Russian.
38. By a law of 10 April 1840 Transcaucasia, with the exception of Mingrelia, Svanetia and Abkhazia, was divided into the Georgian–Imeretian Guberniate (consisting of 11 districts) and the Caspian territory (consisting of 7 districts), incorporating within it most of the area of northern Azerbaijan. Together with the transformation of the Karabakh province into the Shusha district, the former Azerbaijani provinces were recast into the corresponding districts, with the exception of the Shirvan province, on the basis of which were created two districts – Bakin and Shemakha. The Armenian territory was abolished. The Erevan, Nakhichevan and the newly formed Aleksandropol districts were incorporated into the Georgian–Imeretian Guberniate. To it were quite arbitrarily assigned the lands of northern Azerbaijan – the Elizavetpol district with the Kazakh and Shamshadil wards and the Belokan district, fashioned out of the Jaro–Belokan territory and the Ilisu sultanate. See *Complete complex of laws of the Russian empire*, vol. XV, 13368, in Russian).
39. Ibid., vol. XXIV, 23303.

- 1919–20: The Karabakh General Guberniate, encompassing the Zangezur, Shusha, Jevanshir and Jebrail districts, in the make-up of the Azerbaijan Democratic Republic. The status of the General Guberniate was recognized by representatives of Entente – commander of the British Expeditionary Force to Baku, General Thomson, and agent of the Council of the Entente, Colonel Haskell. Moreover, at the demand of Thomson an end was put to the excesses of the infamous General Andranik, who was expelled from the borders of Karabakh.[41]
- 1920–22: The Shusha, Jevanshir and Jebrail districts of the Ganja Guberniate in the make-up of the Azerbaijan SSR.

From 1923 The Shusha district and some parts of the Jevanshir and Jebrail districts were transformed into the Nagorno–Karabakh Autonomous Region (Oblast) in the composition of the Azerbaijan SSR.

Thus, over a period of 1600 years, Karabakh as a whole and its upper section (Nagorno) in particular formed part of Azerbaijani state formations or represented of themselves an administrative unit of the Azerbaijani provinces. Despite the contention of Armenian authors, they were never ancient Armenian lands, unified with or handed over to the Azerbaijan Republic in the 1920s. On the contrary, the incontrovertibility of the historical facts forced the Bolsheviks of the Lenin–Stalin cohort, as well as the departments of the Tsarist empire 100 years earlier, to leave Karabakh in the make-up of Azerbaijan.

Moreover, after the establishment in Transcaucasia of communist power on the bayonets of the Red Army, powerful forces were set in motion. The Caucasian Bureau of the Central Committee of the Russian Communist Party (Bolshevik) passed a decree on the transference of the upper part of Karabakh to Armenia on 4 July 1921. However, exactly 24 hours later this was annulled, and the resolution was passed which has become today standard reading:

> Starting from the requirement of national peace between the Muslims and the Armenians and of the economic link between upper and lower Karabakh and of its permanent link with Azerbaijan, Nagorno–Karabakh is to remain within the borders of the Azerbaijan SSR, although it is to be granted wide autonomy . . .[42]

Forced to abandon the idea of wrenching Karabakh away from Azerba-

---

40. Ibid., vol. XI, 45260. The Zangezur, Jevanshir and Jebrail districts were soon formed in the make-up of the Elizavetpol Guberniate out of the lands of the former Karabakh khanate. The Shusha district was split up but stayed as the kernel of upper Karabakh.

41. Richard Hovanissian, *The republic of Armenia: the first year, 1918–9* (Berkeley: University of California Press, 1974), 169–70.

42. Documents and materials on the history of the formation of Nagorno–Karabakh Autonomous Region of Azerbaijan SSR, 1918–25 (Baku, 1989), 90–2, in Russian.

ijan, the supreme Red legate in the Caucasus, S. Ordzhonikidze, put into effect the idea of autonomy. This was not out of fellow feelings towards the Armenians but through the force of imperial interests ("I well appreciate that in certain political circumstances we may have need of Armenia"). He conducted the dialogue with the independent Azerbaijan SSR exclusively in the language of diktat: "I require Azerbaijan to pronounce the autonomy of these regions, but this must emanate from Azerbaijan . . ."[43]

Matters took on such a scandalous character that Lenin appointed another underling, First Secretary S. Kirov, under whose chairmanship in September 1921 the Central Committee of the Communist Party of Azerbaijan passed the following resolution: to ask the Kav (Caucasian) Bureau to re-examine its decision on the division [into an autonomy] of Nagorno–Karabakh, not to announce any autonomy pending this.[44] But things did not work out that way. Baku was able to withstand Ordzhonikidze's pressure for only one and a half years. In June 1923 the Regional Committee of the Russian Communist Party demanded in the form of an ultimatum that Nagorno–Karabakh be detached into an autonomous region within one month,[45] and the implementation of the decree of the Azerbaijani Central Committee on the formation of the autonomous region of Nagorno–Karabakh from 7 July 1923.

Protagonists for annexation utilized a demographic argument by which Karabakh was characterized as 98 per cent Armenian.[46] Also, Dr Tessa Hofmann set about propagating arguments for annexation, when referring to this phase of the Karabakh drama. Famous for her many publications on Armenia,[47] Hofmann published an abusive paper in *Tribunal of the People*, censuring the Turkish republic for the 1915 tragedy, which had nothing to do with that republic. However, her statement on the demographic situation in Karabakh appeared no less staggering than the contention cited earlier of Balayan to the effect that the Armenian population was predominant throughout the whole of history – the resettlement of 50,000 Armenians from Iran apparently did not apply to Karabakh.[48]

To return to the historical sources, the first special household description of the Karabakh province was carried out by the Russian authorities in 1823, immediately after the abolition of the khanate. The enquiry fixed the number of households at 18,963, of which 1559 families (or 8.4 per cent)

43. Citation in Ë. Namazov, "Zangezur wedge", *Baku worker*, 29 November 1990, in Russian.
44. *Documents and materials on the history of Nagorno–Karabakh*, 97
45. Ibid, 149.
46. Balayan, 43.
47. In one book alone Hofmann was the author of articles dealing with 13 questions: Tessa Hofmann & Gerayer Koutcharian (eds), *Armenien Völkermord, Vertriebung, Exil, Menschenrechtsarbeit für die Armenier 1979–1987* (Göttingen, 1987).
48. For my polemic with Dr Tessa Hofmann on this question, see Bergland Karabach, *Utopien und wahrheiten* (Ankara: Azerbaycan Kültür Dernegi, 1989), in Turkish and German.

fell to the share of the 5 Armenian melikates (Talysh, Chilaburt, Varanda, Dizak and Khachen).[49] Admittedly, this tells us almost nothing about the ethnic composition of Karabakh.

The late 1820s marked a watershed for Karabakh. As a result of the Russo–Persian Treaty of Turkmanchai of 1828, many Armenians from Iran and later from Turkey were resettled in Karabakh and other provinces of Azerbaijan. Clause 13 of Paskevich's instructions provided to settle most of them in the areas of Nakhichevan and Erevan, "because of the particular desire to ensure the growth of the Christian population here".[50] It was planned to send to Karabakh the residents of only three border villages. But scarcity of land and resources in the first two promises changed the initial plan. By order of the same Paskevich of 24th April 1828, an absolute majority of 5000 Armenian families who had arrived in Arax were settled in Karabakh. Moreover, in this connection, with the lack of the state lands in Nakhichevan, many of the settlers designated to this province were sent to Karabakh. As a result, of the 41,245 Armenians (8,249 families) who arrived from Iran in the first three to five months, approximately 30,000 settled in Karabakh.[51]

The Russian writer A. S. Griboedov, author of the idea of resettling Armenians, has left an important testimony on the given question:

> Also we . . . argued quite a lot over the suggestions as to what should be done with the Muslims [Azerbaijanis] in order to reconcile them to the burden they are currently bearing, which will not be long-lasting, and to eradicate from them their misgivings regarding *the Armenians permanently taking control of the lands where they were first allowed to go.* [my emphasis][52]

Griboedov, as befitted a man who had received appointment to the post of Minister Plenipotentiary of Russia to Teheran, had recourse to veiled phrases. More unfettered in the expression of his opinions was the St Petersburg author, N. Shavrov (admittedly, a rather obscure source), who wrote:

---

49. Central State Research Archive of Azerbaijan 1, 24, 141, 226 with the general title: Description of the Karabakh province, carried out in 1823 at the command of Ermolov, supreme commander in Georgia. Tbilisi, 1866.

50. C. F. Neumann, *Geschichte der Uebersiedlung von vierzig tausend Armeniern, welche im jahre 1828 aus der persischen Provinz Adarbaidscan nach Russland auswanderten. Nach dem russischen und armenischen originale frei bearbeitet und kit einer einleitung versehen* (Leipzig, 1834), 79–86.

51. Neumann, 72, 91–108; K. Beydilli. 1828–9: Osmanli–Rus savasinda dogu Anadoludan Rusyaya gocurulen ermeniler. *Turk Tarih Belgeler Dergisi*, Cilit XIII, Sayi 17 (Ankara, 1898), 376–82.

52. *Deeds*, vol. VII, report 618; A. S. Griboedov, *Works*, vol. II (Moscow: Pravda, 1971), 341. See "Note on the resettlement of Armenians to our regions". It is unclear as to whether Griboedov's remarks apply specifically to Karabakh, or to Erevan or Nakhichevan.

... we began our colonizing work not with settling Russian people in Transcaucasia but with the settlement of others ... Then after the end of the war in 1826–8, during the two years 1828–30 we resettled in Transcaucasia more than 40,000 Persian and 84,000 Turkish Armenians and settled them in the best public lands in the Guberniates of the Elizavetpol and Erevan, *where the Armenian population was insignificant*, and in the Tbilisi Guberniate in the districts of Borchalo, Akhaltsikhe and Akhalkalaki. For their settlement more than 200,000 desiatins of public land were set aside and more than 2 million roubles worth of private land was purchased among the Muslims. The mountainous part of the Elizavetpol Guberniate and the shore of Lake Gökchä [the Turkish term for Sevan] were settled with these Armenians. It is essential to bear in mind more than 124,000 Armenians officially resettled were resettled here together with many of the unofficial ones, so that the general number of the resettled significantly exceeds 200,000 persons.[53] [my emphasis]

Such a state of affairs resulted in the fact that, of 1.3 million Armenians resident in Transcaucasia at the start of this century, over one million, in accordance with the source cited, "do not belong to the number of native dwellers but were [re]settled by us".[54]

From this it is clear that the dividing line of the 1830s was the time when the demographic situation in the area began to undergo a radical shift as a result of Tsarist politics. In full agreement with this, the summary household description of 1832 revealed more than a fourfold increase in the percentage of the Armenian population in the Karabakh province – 34.8 per cent[55] compared to 8.4 per cent in 1823. Naturally, we are not dealing with a case of demographic explosion during these two to three years.

The demographic situation did not change in Karabakh alone but everywhere throughout Transcaucasia. Table 6.2 illustrates the percentage balance of Azerbaijanis and Armenians in the nineteenth century.

To take the data on Karabakh for the period of the First World War, then according to *The Caucasian calendar*, published each year by the chancellery of the imperial legate in Tbilisi, the correlation of the two nationalities in

---

53. N. N. Shavrov, *The new threat to Russian business in Transcaucasia* (St Petersburg: Russki Eksport, 1911), 63, in Russian.
54. Ibid., 64.
55. *Survey of the Russian authorities in the Caucasus*, part III (St Petersburg, 1836) Table B, in Russian. See also A. G. Dekanskiy, "The economic situation of the state peasants of the Shusha and Jebrail districts", *Materials for the study of the economic situation of the peasants in Transcaucasia*, vol. IV, part I (Tblisi, 1885), 230–1, in Russian. Even Armenian historiography admits that Armenian resettlers were placed in Karabakh, although only to a certain degree. See V. A. Parsamyan, *History of the Armenian people, 1801–1900*, part I (Erevan: Aiastan, 1972), 51, in Russian.

Table 6.2   Change in the percentage balance of Azerbaijanis and Armenians in the nineteenth century (%).

	1823[1]		1832–5[2]		1886[3]		1897[4]	
	Az.	Arm.	Az.	Arm.	Az.	Arm.	Az.	Arm.
Karabakh province (later Shusha district)	91	8.4	64.8	34.8	41.9	57.9	45.3	53.3
Nakhichevan province (later Nakhichevan district)	86.5	13.5	50.6	49.4	56.8	42.2	63.7	34.4
Armenian region (former Erevan khanate, later Erevan Guberniate)	76	24	46.2	53.8	37.4	56	37.7	53.2

Sources:
1. Description of Karabakh province in 1823, prepared by the command of Ermolov, 1866.
2. Survey of the Russian authorities in Transcaucasia, 1836.
3. Code of statistical data on the population of Transcaucasian area, extracted from local household lists, 1886.
4. First universal census of the population of the Russian empire, 1897.

1915 was respectively expressed by the figures (Azerbaijanis) 43.5 per cent to (Armenians) 52.5 per cent, and in 1917 as 40.2 per cent to 52.3 per cent. And so the passage about the number of Armenians reaching 96–98 per cent in Karabakh one of the historical regions of Armenia remains wholly upon the conscience of the authors of similar mystification. The percentage balance of the Karabakh Armenians right up to 1917 never exceeded 53 per cent. The tragedy came later. During the years 1918–20 there was a mass liquidation of Turks by the bands of Andranik, Tevan, Dro and their ilk in practically all regions where they lived in joint communities. Sources are by no means unanimous on the extant of the ethnic cleansing that occurred in these years. According to the investigation by one of the Armenian historians (A. Lalayan), during the 30 month existence of the Armenian Republic 200,000 Azerbaijanis were liquidated, as a result of which their number was reduced from 260,000 to 60,000 persons.[56] Also, in Baku the Dashnaks from 31 March to 3 April 1918 massacred 12,000 Turks,[57] and more than 20,000 from the towns of Shemakha, Kuba and Lenkoran.

The second phase of ethnic cleansing at the expense of the Azerbaijanis in both Armenia and Karabakh, proceeded under the cloak of communist dictatorship. In 1950 Stalin by a single stroke of the pen sanctioned the deportation from the Armenian SSR of more than 100,000 Azerbaijanis. Covert forms of ethnic cleansing began to be harmonized with legal ones.

Authors sympathetic to the argument that Karabakh constitutes one of the historical regions of Armenia deny the fact that this area is one of the

56. A. A. Lalayan, "The counter-revolutionary essence of the party of the Dashnaks", *Historical Notes*, Academy of Sciences USSR, vol. II (1938, Moscow), 80, 104, in Russian.
57. *La République d'Azerbaidjan du Caucase* (1919, Paris: Délegation de l'Azerbaïdjan à la Conference de la Paix à Paris), 19.

historical hearths of the Turkic culture of Azerbaijan. Dr Tessa Hofmann made her own infamous contribution when she wrote categorically: "In the history of Azerbaijan Karabakh never played a role as a centre of culture".

The great poet Vagif lived and worked on the land of Karabakh, and its presence infuses the whole of his output. Karabakh is the homeland of the classics of national culture and science: Khurshid Banu Natavan, Qasim bek Zakir, Nejef bek Vezirov, Abdrahim bek Haqverdiev, the brothers Uzeir bek and Zulfugar bek Hajïbeyli, Jabbar Karyagd-ogli, Sadiqjan, Bulbul, Fikret Amirov, Rashid Beybutov, Mirza Adïgözäl bek, Mirza Jamal Jevanshir, Ahmed bek Jevanshir, Mir Mohsun Navvab, Firidun bek Köchärli and others. It is sufficient to say that Adolphe Bergé, the German orientalist who was famous in Russia, published in Leipzig in 1867 in the original Azeri *A collection of poets popular in the Caucasus and in Azerbaijan*.[58] In this volume the names of Karabakh poets predominate, which gave the basis in 1903 for Firidun bek Köchärli to call it a monument of Karabakh poetry.[59] This corresponded to the state of affairs which Karabakh occupied in the cultural life of Azerbaijan in the second half of the eighteenth and first half of the nineteenth century. In the middle of the last century in the town of Shusha the literary unions Mejlis-i uns and Mejlis-i Khamushan, encompassing 30 writers, were active. The great dramatist, Mirza Fatali Akhundov, who lived in Tbilisi, kept in touch and corresponded with their leading members.

The town of Shusha is rightly considered to be the historical centre of the national musical culture of Azerbaijan. The Armenian musicologist at the start of the century, V. D. Karganov, named Shusha the conservatory of the Transcaucasus. He wrote: "Shusha, this blessed homeland of poetry, music and song, supplies the Transcaucasus with musicians and singers; it serves as a conservatory for the whole of Transcaucasia, providing it for every season and indeed month with new songs and new motifs".[60] It is striking that Uzeir bek Hajibeyli, the founder of the national and in general of the oriental art of opera, received his first musical lessons in precisely this town? In this connection one of the Russian musicologists wrote:

> . . . Shusha has long enjoyed the reputation of a musical centre and is glorified throughout the whole Caucasus as the inextinguishable home of popular musical talents. The musicians of Shusha made the history of Azerbaijani music and represented it not only at home but also in other oriental countries".[61]

---

58. Adolphe Bergé, *Dichtungen transkaukasischer Sänger des XVIII und XIX Jahrhunderts in azerbeidshischer Mundarts* (Leipzig: Metzger & Wittig, 1868).
59. Firidun bek Köchärli, *Azerbaijani literature*, vol. I (Baku: Elm, 1978), 171, in Russian.
60. V. Karganov, *Caucasian music* (1908, Tblisi), 28, in Russian.

Attempts to deny Azerbaijan's connections with Karabakh by manipulating both historical and cultural categories are thus manifest.

The same can be said of Nakhichevan. The withdrawal of the Ani Bagratids to the Nakhichevan area at the end of the eleventh and beginning of the tenth century was the sole attempt to establish Armenian rule here throughout the whole of the Middle Ages. This attempt was suppressed by Yusuf ibn Abu Saj, representative of the Turkic dynasty of the Sajids, which gave, according to the definition of A. E. Krymskij, a line of energetic rulers to Azerbaijan and Armenia. In 915 he seized the Alinj fortress, where Smbat was hiding with his exchequer. The latter was executed in the town of Dvin.[62]

In the state of the Atabeks of Azerbaijan, the town of Nakhichevan was moved into the category of a political centre, becoming in effect the second capital of this state along with Tabriz.

After the establishment of Russian rule in the Nakhichevan province, the latter was incorporated with the town of Ordubad into the composition of the Armenian region, and then in the form of a district (uezd) within the Erevan Guberniate. The fact that the Nakhichevan and Erevan khanates had been seized in the course of a single campaign served as motive in the hands of the Caucasian military administration of Russia. However, the Russian Government apparently attached no great significance to such facts of splitting land belonging to one owner by land belonging to another, for by the will of the very same government part of the lands of today's Armenia with the towns Dilizhan and Ijevan were incorporated right up to 1918 within the composition of the Kazakh district of the Elizavetpol (Ganja) Guberniate – the second largest (after Baku) administrative unit of north Azerbaijan. On this basis, the Azerbaijanis present no views on Dilizhan and Ijevan, and yet talk of Nakhichevan as an ancient region of Armenia does not go away.

The results of the mass settlement of the area at the divide of the 1820s and 1830s transplanted Armenians could appear the most serious. On the eve of this action, according to a Russian source, the native inhabitants (the Muslims) settled here since the sixth and seventh centuries; that is, from the time of the dominion of the caliphs, numbered 2791 households or 86.5 per cent, whereas the Armenians, the ancient inhabitants, as is indicated there too, numbered 434 households or 13.5 per cent. Soon those transplanted from Persia pushed the number of Armenian households up to 2719, as a result of which their population balance was almost comparable

61. V. Vinogradov. *Uzeir Hajibekov and Azerbaijani music in Muzgiz* No. 14 (1938, Moscow), in Russian.
62. See Stepanos Taronskiy (Asogik), *Universal history.* Russian translation by N. Emin (Moscow, 1864), 113; M. Kagankatvatsi, *History of the Albanians.* Russian translation by Patkanov, (St Petersburg, 1861), 273–4.

with that of the Turks, comprising 49.4 per cent.[63] Another source notes pointedly that "[t]he great part of the Armenians of the Nakhichevan district settled here from the Azerbaijan province [southern Azerbaijan] after the conclusion of the Turkmanchai peace with Persia in 1828.[64] However, in proportion to the weakening of the operation of "volitional factors", the demographic situation in the area towards the end of the nineteenth century began to follow a peaceful course. The practice, rightly described by Maître de Maleville as the transformation of the minority into the majority by means of the liquidation of the Muslim population, in this particular case misfired.

With the formation of the independent states of Transcaucasia, an unending struggle went on between Azerbaijan and Armenia over the Nakhichevan and the Sharur–Daralagez districts. The allied powers at one point mooted a project for forming a general guberniate under the protectorate of the USA, after which they inclined to a hand-over of the districts to the government of Armenia. The people themselves made the decisive statement in forming their own Arax republic. Not without the co-operation of the 11th Red Army of Bolshevik Russia, the Nakhichevan Soviet Republic was formed on 28 June 1920, which proclaimed itself to be part of the Azerbaijan SSR. Soon the 11th army transposed its experiment to Armenia, and on 1 December 1920 N. Narimanov, chief of sovietized Azerbaijan, issued an order for the withdrawal of Azerbaijani forces from Zangezur. A day earlier Zangezur, on the decision of the Politburo and Orgbureau of the Central Committee of the Communist Party of Azerbaijan, where everything was being directed by Ordzhonikidze, had been transferred to Armenia, which had only just been sovietized. The decision had a fatal significance for Nakhichevan and for the whole of Azerbaijan. Its territory, comprising $91,300 \, km^2$, was reduced to $86,600 \, km^2$. The republic, whose sovereignty was guaranteed by treaty with the Russian Soviet Federative Socialist Republic, was dismembered – and so skilfully that Nakhichevan found itself in total isolation. One of the problems of the strategy of the Dashnak party was realized. Already in the years of the First World War, as a historian humbly writes in one official report-addendum presented to the state organs of Russia, the following was said: "[t]he Armenian people, who split Tatar[65] Transcaucasia and Azerbaijan from the Turks of Asia Minor, are a wedge driven into the flesh of the Turkic tribes ... We cannot permit this wedge to disappear and in its place the appear-

---

63. Statistical description of the Nakhichevan province. Compiled by V. Grugorev and published with Supreme Approbation (St Petersburg, 1833), 31, in Russian.

64. *Materials for the study of the economic circumstances of the state peasant of Transcaucasia*, vol. I (Tblisi, 1885), 561; also S. Glinka, *Description of the Trans-settlement of the Azerbaijani Armenians within the borders of Russia* (Moscow, 1831), both in Russian.

65. The Armenians call the Azerbaijanis Turks or Tatars, but in the present case, of course, preference is given to an alternative designation, accepted in imperial parlance.

ance of a compact mass of Muslims who are hostile towards us.[66]

The treaty of 20 March 1921 between Russia and Turkey somewhat smoothed over the bitterness of the loss, when it was agreed that the Nakhichevan region was an autonomous territory under the protectorate of Azerbaijan. The said protectorate would not be allowed to surrender "to any third state". Turkey, which acquired a border with the Nakhichevan Republic, became the guarantor of its autonomous status.

On 13 October 1921, representatives of the five republics concerned – Russia, Turkey, Azerbaijan, Armenia and Georgia – signed an agreement by which the current existing borders were created. Both agreements are still valid, especially as those governments that signed the first article of the Kars treaty declared the invalidity of all preceding agreements between them, with the exception of the March treaty of 1921.

The Kars treaty is considered "the charter of diplomatic agreements" concerning Eastern Anatolia and Transcaucasia. Under the authority of the Armenian SSR in this agreement is the signature of the Commissar of Foreign Affairs, A. Mravian, and the Commissar of Internal Affairs, P. Makinzian. From this it follows that, until the Republic of Armenia officially denounces the agreement, all her open and secret acts regarding Karabakh and Nakhichevan must be qualified by the United Nations and other world organizations.

On 15 July 1987, one of the Dashnak leaders, A. Papazian, wrote the following in his party newspaper *Gamk*: "The Armenians have historical claims. The Armenian nation has a historical land situated on the borders of the Caucasus . . . Today we have clearly defined territorial claims". The Dashnaks did not reveal exactly which territory "on the Caucasian border". Here in the USSR, where Communist propaganda is presented in the guise of internationalism, the "taboo" was disturbed in the very same year by the academic A. Aganbekian. Mikael Gorbachev found himself in Paris *en route* to the USA, and said the following; "I would like the Karabakh (situated in the northeast of the republic) to become Armenian. As an economist, I consider that this region is more linked to Armenia than to Azerbaijan". This was given the go-ahead, albeit under an "economic guise". However, the historical camouflage was not forgotten. The account of the publication of the French Communists begins with the passage: "of Karabakh and Nakhichvan – ancient Armenian lands, annexed to the Azerbaijani Republic".

The president of Armenia has revealed on more than one occasion that Erevan does not have any territorial pretensions to Azerbaijan. However, the decision of the Armenian SSR in 1989 regarding the "uniting" of the Nagorno–Karabakh autonomous region to Armenia was not annulled. In

---

66. J. Kirakosyan, *Western Armenia in the years of the First World War* (Erevan: Erevan University Press, 1971), 411, in Russian.

that year, the parliament of the Armenian Republic made a decision that arranged the prohibition of participation in other agreements in which the Karabakh was considered to be a part of Azerbaijan.

The problem of national minorities in a sovereign state was replaced by the Armenians with an artificial absolutist law on the self-determination of the Karabakhian Armenians, and was later treated exclusively as a territorial problem. An election is hopeless, because a similar approach led Armenia to an unavoidable contradiction with the principle of the inviolability of borders, which is recognized by all European states and the world community.

It seems that European and American politicians do not fully acknowledge the fact that the mountainous Karabakh is not the outskirts of Azerbaijan in the literal sense. The region is geographically closer to Armenia, but it has no borders with this country. In this sense, the region is a middle territory of Azerbaijan; that is, between Karabakh and Armenia there lies a stretch of Azerbaijani land equal to the area of half the mountainous part of the Karabakh itself. From this it follows that the idea of the merging of the Karabakh with Armenia or other modifications will inevitably result in the annexing of new Azerbaijani land. It is well known in Armenia that, without this, the existence of the "republics" of the mountainous Karabakh is impossible. Therefore, those who support Armenia's act in the "name of the self-determination" of the Karabakh are encouraging her to open annexation. In this case it is hardly possible to talk of devotion to the Helsinki process. Now it is obvious to every unprejudiced person that at the root of the Karabakh conflict lies an attempt by Armenia to "defend" the interests of Armenians in Azerbaijan by force of arms – with this aim, she unleashed war on the territory of another state.

There is a platform for a redirection of this tragic movement of events. This is the unconditional recognition of the inviolability of existing state borders and the securing of constitutional rights for all people and nationalities, and on these grounds a quick ceasefire. There is no alternative political solution to the Karabakh problem. The problem cannot be solved by having troops march onto the territory of another state and annexing that territory, not only because this is a violation of international law, but because a protracted war inevitably leads to a dreadful politico-economic and moral expenditure for the aggressor.

CHAPTER SEVEN

The geopolitics of Georgia
JOHN F. R. WRIGHT

Discussion of post-Soviet societies has focused upon the nationalist element in determining the reason new states arose with the break-up of
Soviet communism. Among Western policy-makers the nationalist phenomena that appeared (or seemed to have arisen) following adoption of
glasnost were viewed as particularly negative. Following the August 1991
failed coup in Moscow (the Baltic states apart), it was only when Russia
declared itself to be sovereign and independent that the world community
came to recognize the independence and hence sovereignty of the other
republics. The driving force of specifically Western policy that wanted to
preserve the Union, albeit in a looser liberal democratic form, was greeted
with incredulity by those in the republics. After all, they argued, did the
West not want the peoples of the Soviet Union to be free? And surely that
freedom could only come about by being independent. Moreover, being
independent meant having a state. In most cases the new republics, particularly those in the western part of the Union, looked back in history to find
some period when they had been independent before. This was considered to be highly significant in the process of "getting" a state again and
fulfilling independence.

The speed with which the new states emerged threw Western policy-
makers off balance. Suddenly, new political and geographical realities had
to be taken into account. What had been a secure landscape became a mix
of competing groups (ethnic, national, social) over the political and geographical space of the Soviet Union. Previously forgotten areas started to
demand attention, as the troubles that had affected much of Africa and
Asia since the Second World War re-emerged, but now in regions such as
Transneister, Nagorno–Karabakh, and the Fergana Valley.

However, it soon became apparent that few people knew anything of
these regions. Where were the academics, civil servants, business people
and others who could relate and analyze the factors at play in these emergent areas? Who knew and could monitor the languages now being used
as the medium of expression by those in control of the new states? In
essence, policy-makers needed to know what were the parameters for the
supposed new world order, how were these new states going to integrate
themselves into the world family of nations and what were their aspira-

tions, particularly with regard to other states?

The purpose of this chapter is to consider one of these states, namely Georgia, and to examine how Georgians viewed their own position and what the determinants of Georgia's position actually are. In so doing the following will consider the interests of outside states in Georgia and the local geopolitical determinants in play in Georgian political and social life. In the latter case, detailed consideration will be given to the confrontation between different parties based upon the territory of Abkhazia.

Clearly, a definition of geopolitics is required. In his volume published in 1986, Patrick O'Sullivan states geopolitics to be "the study of the geography of relations between wielders of power be they rulers of nations or of transnational bodies". Another category needs to be included into this, namely local non-ruling parties, who aspire to be rulers or at least to hold a share in the ruling process. Thus, when we put "geo" in front of "politics", it is the geographical realities of a given situation (and we mean geography in its widest sense) that are the determinants in any given relationship.

This notion of geopolitics is useful but suggests something static. That is, what is our concern is only those who are rulers, and their spatial interaction with other rulers or transnational entities, for example, companies or international bodies. The danger is that it seems to exclude nations who don't have a state. Unless this caveat or extension is included, we shall fail to understand the geopolitics of Georgia and the wider Caucasus, let alone other conflicts in the world where local facets of ethnicity are to the fore.

Normally, when the word geopolitics is employed, the next word that comes to mind is borders. The geographical reality of something defined as separating one state or geopolitical entity from another is the border. Throughout most of the world, borders were decided not through local mutual agreement by neighbouring state entities, but instead by external imperial powers. The same case may be made concerning the evolution of borders in the geographical area of the former Soviet Union.

The evolution of Georgia's borders

Georgia lies at the heart of the Caucasian region. The whole area is largely geographically self-contained, being bounded by two seas – the Black Sea and the Caspian to west and east – and two mountain ranges – the higher and lower Caucasus to the north and south. However, within the area there is great geographical diversity, ranging from high mountain valleys to fertile plains.

Georgia itself mirrors in microcosm this broader landscape. The northern part of the country is mountainous (the southern slopes of the greater Caucasian range); the south also rises to the west–east lower Caucasian

135

range. The western parts of the country are washed by the eastern shores of the Black Sea, whereas the eastern province of the Kakhetian Plain stretches to the country's border with neighbouring Azerbaijan. The country, however, is divided into western and eastern parts by the Surami mountain range. To the north, there are two main cross-routes to the southern steppes of Russia, through Abkhazia in the northwest of the country and north from the capital Tbilisi through Ossetia by the Georgian military highway.

The country has been prey to successive invasion and occupation throughout history: whether this was Greek, Roman, Mongol or Arab, or the later empires mentioned above. Although Georgia attained unity and extended its geographical extent in the eleventh and twelfth centuries, its history reflected the competition between external invaders, who until the nineteenth century, divided the land between specific spheres of influence. These divisions were based upon local principalities, whose rulers shifted alliance from the sixteenth to the eighteenth century to ensure survival. In this way it would be difficult to distinguish an actual Georgian state. Instead, there were regions that were allied to larger entities; that is, the Ottoman and Persian empires. Western Georgia or Imeretia fell increasingly under Ottoman influence, along with the local adjoining principalities of Mingrelia, Meschia or Samtskhe, Guria, Abkhazia and Suania, whereas the eastern regions of the country Kartli and Kakheti were drawn into the Persian sphere of influence.[1]

In 1783 King Erek'le II signed the treaty of Georgievsk with Russia, believing that the Christian empire to the north afforded Georgia the best protection against the perceived encroaching power of Islam.[2] Georgia fell within the realm of the Russian empire successively as follows: Kartli and Kakheti (effectively Eastern Georgia in 1801), Mingrelia (part of Western Georgia) in 1803, Imeretia to the west of the country in 1804, with Abkhazia following by 1810. Therefore, it was following Russian annexation of the Georgian principalities that the modern nation of Georgia as a defined geographical entity began to take shape.

Along with the rest of the Caucasus region, the area of Georgia was renamed and divided into guberniates or provinces. The guberniates of Tiflis, Kutaisi and Sukhumi, effectively include all of present-day Georgia,

---

1. For a discussion of this period, see Carl Max Kortepeter, *Ottoman Imperialism during the reformation: Europe and the Caucasus* (New York: New York University Press, 1972), ch. 3, and Henry John Armani, *The Russian annexation of the kingdom of Imeretia, 1800–1815: in the light of Russo–Ottoman relations*, 7–25 (Ann Arbor, Michigan: University Microfilms International, 1971).

2. *Georgievscis traktati 1783 tslis kheloshucruleba rusethis mparcelobashi aghmosavleth sakarthvelos shesvlis shesakheb.* (The Treaty of Georgievsk of 1783 between Eastern Georgia and Russia). Georgian and Russian texts with an English summary (Tbilisi: Metzniereba, 1983).

apart from the Ajarian region in the southwest of the country that continued under Ottoman control until its transfer to Russia through the Treaty
of Berlin in 1878.

Following the collapse of the Russian Empire in the wake of the First
World War and the revolution in St Petersburg, Georgia gained its first
brief period of independence from 1918 to 1921. One significant feature for
border codification from this period was a peace-treaty with Russia signed
on 7 May 1920, in Moscow.[3] Articles three and four of the treaty demarcated Georgia's boundaries and specifically the northern border. These
placed Georgia's northern frontier as stretching from the Black Sea in the
west along the River Psou to Mt Akhakhcha and then to Mt Agapeta, and
then along the frontier of the former Black Sea Region, Kutaisi and Tiflis
guberniates to the Zakataly region and along Zakataly's eastern border to
the Armenian frontier of the Russian empire.

Through the treaties of San Stefano and Berlin, the region known as
Ajaria around Batumi transferred from the Ottomans to Russia and upon
independence to Georgia. Thus, it was that Georgia's borders became
defined. However, what we have seen is the way that it was external powers who shaped the borders of Georgia as much as any local national
grouping. This had consequences upon how Georgians view their own
geopolitical position, to which attention is now given.

Georgian geopolitical perceptions

Head of State in Georgia, Eduard Shevardnadze has stated that his country and the Caucasus as a whole is crucial to world peace. Dire scenarios
have been painted, suggesting that those conflicts taking place in the Transcaucasus could grow into major conflicts involving Russia, Turkey, Iran,
and then the whole world. Such statements are not confined to political
leaders. If one discusses with Georgians the conflicts now affecting their
state, there is wide belief that what may have started as local disputes can
draw in other powers.

Georgians will also relate that their country has immense strategic significance, because it remains with its neighbour Armenia a Christian (thus
friendly) state within an encroaching sea of Islam (presumably hostile).
The threat of Islam has widened and been brought closer to the West, with
the collapse of communism. For the West, Georgia must be important

---

3. Peace Treaty, with special supplementary agreement and special secret supplement between
Georgia and the Russian Soviet Federative Socialist Republic, in *Soviet Treaty Series: a collection of bilateral treaties, agreements and conventions etc., concluded between the Soviet Union
and Foreign Powers*, compiled and edited by Leonard Shapiro, vol. 1, 44–6 (Washington DC:
The Georgetown University Press, 1950).

because of its Christian status. Although the Georgians themselves feel surrounded, they believe that they should be particularly assisted because of this perceived Islamic threat. In this regard some Georgian politicians have drawn parallels with Israel about their geopolitical position.

Shevardnadze has taken the argument further. He perceives Georgia (and the Transcaucasus) as a bridging point between north and south and east and west. Georgia, he maintains, can provide the transportation system, to allow the speedy transfer of goods and services from the developed West to the new markets and opportunities in Central Asia and China. Incidentally, he sees for himself a wider role than being merely the ruler of Georgia. Using his perceived stature in the world community, following his role in the ending of the Cold War, he would like to be viewed as the West's man in the Transcaucasian region as a whole.

Since the collapse of the Soviet Union, however, no conflict that has surfaced has extended beyond its particular locale, and no non-Soviet groups or non-Russian republics have been involved, at least overtly. The position at the beginning of the century was different, for example, in Georgia when German and British troops were as noticeable as Russian or local forces. It is widely felt that the factors pertaining in the Caucasus are similar to those of the first two decades of the twentieth century, particularly by local (i.e. Georgian) geopolitical thinkers. By examining the actual geopolitical and geostrategic aspects of Georgia today, particularly the immediate consequence of Soviet collapse, we shall see that the position is qualitatively different, which in turn produces a different set of challenges for local political leaders.

Georgia's geopolitical position

In the age of empires, borders served really to mark military and political extent. In general it was unimportant that a local peasant felt himself to belong to a particular empire. Under the feudal system, taxes and tithes were paid to the local landlord or prince. Whether you were ostensibly part of the Ottoman or Persian empire, it made little difference both to your daily life and to your world outlook.

Even as Georgia and the whole Caucasian area came under Russian control in the nineteenth century, cross-border movements were still common.[4] Such fluidity came to an abrupt halt following the Bolshevik revolution in Russia. Despite a brief flirtation with independence from 1918 to 1921, Georgia, like the rest of the Transcaucasus, came under the control first of the Red Army and then the whole might of the Soviet state apparatus. Until 1936, Georgia was administered through the Transcaucasian fed-

---

4. For a discussion of such cross-border activities bearing upon the Persian Caucasian border, particularly with Azerbaijan, see Cosroe Chaqueri, *La social-democratie en Iran* (Florence: Editions Mazdak, 1979)

eration and afterwards through the mechanism of the Georgian Soviet Socialist Republic.

Geopolitically there were two main consequences of Georgia's incorporation into the Soviet Union. The first concerns borders, the second nationality.

The impact of the Soviet Union brought for the first time in the region a clearly defined border that, through the combined effects of being an ideological barrier and of the Cold War following the Second World War, resulted in an actual closed frontier between the successor empire states of the USSR, Turkey and Iran. The fact of communist collapse has reopened the southern borders and there has been a revival of local trading and commerce. However, to argue that the three countries of Turkey, Iran and Russia will be involved in direct competition and control of the area denies certain other geopolitical realities.

For both Iran and Turkey the imperative of modern state creation and economic development has forced foreign policy and trade to look elsewhere over the past 70 years. Examination of the location of industry in both countries reveals that for Turkey the concentration is in the west and south of the country with its main trade through the Mediterranean basin; for Iran, concentration is in the southwest of the country and the main emphasis of commerce and interest is through the Gulf. It is true that both countries' foreign policy elites have made diplomatic overtures to both the Caucasus and Central Asia and both see possible openings. At the same time they perhaps have larger concerns. For Turkey, access to European markets and entry into the European community remains the overriding concern, whereas for Iran its very economic precariousness mitigates against any large-scale involvement economically or ideologically in the southern successor states.

Concerning Russia, the full consequences of the loss of the larger empire of the Baltic states, the Slavic west and the Transcaucasus and Central Asia, have yet to be fully determined. In the Transcaucasus, however, one factor has become clear and this concerns borders. For almost 200 years, the southern border of Russia was directly with Iran and Turkey. The collapse of the Soviet Union has forced this southern border to retreat northwards to the northern frontiers of Georgia and Azerbaijan.

This retreat has in its wake introduced a vacuum in Transcaucasia, where for the first time it should be up to local groups to determine and codify their fate. This position is completely new to the region. It might be argued that the same position obtained after the First World War, when the three dominant nationalities of the region attained brief independence. This is a mistaken view. First, there was still the notion of active involvement by outside powers: Turkey, Germany, Britain and Russia.[5] Furthermore, the very fact of imminent Red Army invasion attests to a temporary set of circumstances. Without entering into details, it would be naïve to suppose that in 1918 the new Soviet Union had really forsworn intervention in the lands of the former Russian empire. Therefore, in the aftermath of the First World War, Russia's temporary retreat was just that, merely temporary. Today it is different. The Russians face for the first time for 200 years that they no longer have a recognized border with the Middle East. Whether Russia accepts this is another matter and, as will be demonstrated later in this chapter, it is using differing mechanisms and policies to gain or maintain its foothold beyond its defined southern borders.

This leads us to the second legacy of the Soviet Union in the area. If we take Transcaucasia as a whole, the areas where conflict is taking place share a commonality. The three conflict regions – Nagorno–Karabakh, Ossetia and Abkhazia – were all autonomous regions of varying degrees within the USSR. This second factor, therefore, is the codification of a union of territory with a nationality or religion. In Georgia, at the time of Soviet collapse, there were three autonomies: the Abkhaz Autonomous Soviet Socialist Republic, the South Ossetian Autonomous Oblast and the Ajarian Autonomous Soviet Socialist Republic. The first two were created on the basis of ethnicity, the latter on the basis of religion. Whatever the rights and wrongs of these creations, they have fuelled and they continue to fuel conflict inside the country. Why?

When you are in Georgia, most Georgians will explain the current conflicts as being mainly the inheritance from the Soviet Union. These are the conflicts in Abkhazia and South Ossetia. Their argument runs as follows. The Soviet Union created in Georgia three autonomous regions; these areas were created to divide Georgia and prevent it from being a unified entity. During the Soviet period, elites grew up in these regions and gathered certain privileges. Because in Abkhazia and Ossetia things were based upon ethnic descent, Abkhazians, for example, came to dominate all privileged positions, both political and cultural. With the independence of Georgia, these elites wanted to preserve their privilege and have taken the mantle of separatist (nationalist) expression to divide local populations on the basis of ethnicity. The result has been conflict.

There is a half truth in what they are saying, but it misses a deeper level of understanding that I hope to now explain. Before, we were discussing the competition by empires for control. Under what may be termed a balance of power, local rights were maintained. In the modern age there is a vacuum. This vacuum is supposed to be filled by the local states, that is Georgia, Armenia and Azerbaijani. However, all these governments and states are comparatively weak and disorganized.

The Georgian state, however, is particularly weak. Despite this weakness, since at least 1989, there has been the attempt to create a nation-state.

---

5. For a full review of this period see Firuz Kazemzadeh, *The struggle for Transcaucasia*, (Oxford: G. Ronald, 1951).

This process became stronger and, combined with a strong political nationalism, induced conflict. The nation-state as a model demands a fixed territory defining it from other states. This is the norm as a desire in the twentieth century. However, when it becomes combined with strong nationalist pressures, this can be detrimental to minorities. In Georgia, this is a particular dilemma, given the numbers of non-Georgians present. In geopolitical terms, the desired creation of the nation-state, combined with the wish for effective strong central government as the sole interlocutor with the outside, has had the result of attempting to define borders in a strict sense and to cut off local movements.

In the early part of this century, concentration was focused on the southern borders and, once the Soviets took control, the border became fixed and impenetrable. With the Soviet collapse and Russia's retreat, the focus of geopolitics has moved north to the Georgian/Russian Federation frontier. During the Soviet period, the border merely defined administrative units but did not cut local people away from each other. The new situation of independent supposedly nation-states does. When we look at where conflict is occurring, it is around this northern border, that is to say, in Abkhazia and South Ossetia. This new situation, when looked at from Tbilisi, demands that these areas be included as part of the territory of Georgia. Until independence, Georgians could happily consider that Abkhazia and South Ossetia were Georgian lands, Abkhazians and South Ossetians could happily claim that these lands were theirs. It did not matter. No-one could do anything about it. All were part of the Soviet Union and, despite the legal niceties of theoretical nationalities' policies and constitutions, only those in the Politburo in Moscow held the power to do anything.

The perception of being cut off because of borders being defined by nation-states is nowhere more eloquently put than by the Ossetians. The North Ossetian Supreme Soviet passed a resolution not to be excluded from discussions concerning the delineation of the border between the Russian Federation and Georgia. This resolution stated:[6]

Any talks on delimiting the section of the border which divides Ossetia into two parts must take this as their starting point together with the need to establish a special border regime which will take account of the unitary Ossetian people.

Despite protestations from Georgia that, in the case of the Ossetians, those who resided in the southern part in the territory of Georgia were recent settlers, many Ossetians feel as much as the Georgians do about themselves that they are a single people and thus have the right to form

6. SWB February 1st 1993 SU/1601/B4 North Ossetia appeals to Yeltsin over border with Georgia

141

their own state straddling both northern and southern parts of what they term historic Ossetia.

The consequences of the Soviet Union upon Georgia served to localize its main geopolitical dilemmas. Rather than being engaged in its traditional role between competing powers north, south, east and west, it became bogged down in local disputes on the margins of the state's domain.

The Georgian–Abkhazian dispute

Although the conflict in Ossetia proved bloody and resulted in significant loss of life, it was fairly confinable, and once Russia and Georgia sat down and hammered out an agreement for a tripartite troop structure over the area in Dagomys in 1992, the conflict lessened, and from 1992 to 1994 there was little or no fighting, although a political settlement has still to be fully worked through.

However, in the northwest of Georgia, namely Abkhazia, conflict became more protracted, included several outside parties, and it revealed in microcosm Georgia's geopolitical and political difficulties.

The perceptions

When discussing states or groups of people who want to dislocate themselves from states, we tend to imagine that either side of a confrontation is cohesive and unified in both its purpose and action. Transposed into these conflicts it would seem on the face of it that, say, both the Abkhazians and the Georgians were united distinct entities. If both sides met and discussed their mutual grievances and were able to reach some compromise, it would be enforced. Hopes were raised to some extent on 3 September 1992, in Moscow, when the parties to the dispute signed documents on reducing tension in the region. The process did not work and fighting continued. Why?

Shortly after the agreement was reached, there were immediate recriminations on both sides suggesting the other had broken cease-fires or were not observing some of the guidelines agreed. On the Georgian side, although Eduard Shevardnadze had been the signatory of the agreement as Head of the State Council, at that time, he had neither control over the armed forces of the country nor any institutionalized legitimacy. It will be remembered that Shevardnadze was brought back to Georgia earlier in 1992 to head the State Council, pending elections that took place in November 1992. Equal power was held by two men, Tengiz Kitovani and Jaba Ioseliani. These two had been instrumental in ousting the former president Zviad Gamsakhurdia in December 1991 and had built up their own effective private armies. Kitovani's army had the name of the

National Guard, whereas Ioseliani's were called the Mkhedrioni or Horsemen.

Each of these three sent out differing signals to the Abkhazian leaders. Eduard Shevardnadze seemed to sit somewhere between a hard-line approach and conciliation. If one examines Shevardnadze's briefings and statements from September to December 1992, each week there was a different tack. On the one hand he was saying everything should be geared towards stopping the fighting and entering constructive dialogue with Ardzinba, the head of the Abkhazian leadership. On the other hand he was also stating there was no solution and only military victory for the Georgians could be countenanced. Kitovani was the hard-liner who had led his troops into Sukhumi back in August 1992, which had provoked the outbreak of fighting. Ioseliani was clear that he had no real liking for the Moscow agreement and he felt that minority rights were relatively unimportant. He was more interested in a strong centralized state including Abkhazia. He made play of the fact that the Abkhaz were a privileged people and that, anyway, they are a minority in their own land. He did not like the idea of preserving any form of autonomy.[7] At the same time a commission was in existence in Tbilisi, which had one or two Abkhazians sitting on it who were formulating ideas on how to solve the crisis. Speaking to a number of them they seemed to be for a certain autonomy for the region and were looking at examples of federalism around the world to see what would best fit the particular circumstances of Georgia and its relationship with Abkhazia. To the Abkhazian leadership, therefore, there was a variety of signals emanating from Tbilisi, making it unclear whether any agreement that was struck with the Georgian leadership actually had the backing of a majority and would be implemented.

Turning to the other side, how do the Abkhazians look to the Georgians. One thing is clear: the Abkhaz seem far more organized in their methods. This is reflected in their military successes, which must have come as a shock to the Georgians. To the Georgians there were two confusing issues. It remained unclear what the Abkhaz were seeking. Several political options suggested themselves, although none was effectively articulated. These were:
- outright independence
- to join the Russian federation
- some federal structure with Georgia
- federalism with the mountain peoples of the Caucasus
- federalism with both Georgia and the mountain peoples of the Caucasus
- federalism with both Georgia and the mountain peoples of the Caucasus and the Russian Federation.

---

7. Private interview conducted in Tbilisi, September 1992.

Furthermore, to the Georgians the position was further complicated and confused by the presence of troops and volunteers from the Confederation of Mountain Peoples. In essence, this is a voluntary formation of the peoples of the north Caucasus, as distinct from the leaders of the successor autonomous regions of the ex-USSR, apart from the Chechen leadership. The thrust of their endeavours is against Russia, from which they are attempting through a confederate structure to gain independence. The Abkhazians were one of the prime movers in establishing this confederation. To the others in the organization, Abkhazia is a particularly useful member. Quite apart from ethnic links between Abkhazians and other northwest Caucasian peoples, the Kabardians, Adyge, and Cherkess, Abkhazian territory provides all the others with port access to the Black Sea and hence to external trade markets.

Although the confederation sees its main foe as Russia, anything that can be done to destabilize the situation in Georgia is to them an advantage, as this is bound in their mind to lead to conflict between Georgia and Russia. In this prognosis they have had some success. Since the recent conflict started in August 1992, although its genesis goes back further, there have been increasing demands made by Georgian politicians to get rid of all Russian troops from the Republic. The Georgian side therefore was faced with the Abkhazians, who for their own reasons were not prepared to state clearly what they wanted, as well as volunteers from outside the state who on the one hand were supporting the Abkhaz while also pursuing their own agenda, even if this was not being performed in a particularly coherent way.

If one imagines that the relative positions were complex, another factor had to be brought into the equation. This was the position of Russia. On the face of it, the Russian government has been looking at avenues for a peaceful negotiation to the crisis, as exemplified by the 3 September meeting and agreement in Moscow. Clearly, it is in the interests of Russia to have a stable southern frontier. Moreover, agreement with Georgia over the status of the border would help to ensure that the peoples of the north Caucasus would continue to be administered within the Russian Federation.

Neither the Abkhazians nor the Georgians perceived Russia as neutral. Within the Georgian parliament and public at large, Russia was seen to be behind the Abkhazians' efforts to dislocate themselves from the Georgian state. They were accused of trying to subvert Georgian sovereignty by supplying weapons and personnel to the other side. At the same time the Abkhazians believed that the Russians did not really care about their fate. In Abkhazian minds, this became clearer as the conflict continued. They saw in the end that Russia was more likely to work with a state (i.e. Georgia) than a people. Neither side seemed to admit that there was perhaps more than one Russia acting in the Caucasus, as will be seen later.

The foregoing suggests that the differing perceptions of each other based upon confusing and changing positions made resolution to the conflict appear almost impossible.

The positions

If there was to be a solution, it would have to be based upon some understanding of the actual position of each of the players to it. This next section, therefore, attempts to clear away the confusing perceptions and examine the respective positions of the competing parties and their capacity to realize their ambitions.

The Georgians Georgia requires a defined northern border and demands that Abkhazia be included as part of the territory of the Republic of Georgia. It is unclear whether Abkhazia should be governed centrally from Tbilisi or by some form of local government. In the latter case it is unclear what the relationship should be between the local government and the central authority. The Georgian government considers Abkhazia vital as a supply route to Russia. The only rail link from Russia to Georgia is through Abkhazia. Indeed, this requirement provided one of the pretexts for military intervention in August 1992, following the looting of trains in Mingrelia, the neighbouring region to Abkhazia in Georgia.

In essence the Georgians claim that, by virtue of Georgia's being a member of the United Nations, the world community has recognized the borders of the state and within these borders must remain Abkhazia. This was made clear in a letter from Eduard Shevardnadze to Boutros Boutros Ghali, Secretary General of United Nations. In the latter's report to the Security Council, dated 28 January 1993, he points out that "The Government of Georgia would welcome the good offices of the Secretary-General to study the Abkhaz problem and to make recommendations for its peaceful resolution. The Government of Georgia would be willing to commit itself to these recommendations on the understanding they respect the territorial integrity and sovereignty of Georgia as well as the human rights of all citizens of Georgia".[8] The Georgians can point to the Russian–Georgian treaty of 1920 and the Russian–Georgian treaty of 1994, both of which placed Abkhazia within the borders of Georgia.

The Georgians have no military power to enforce their position and have lacked a unified strategy in dealing with Abkhazia. Indeed, such was the ineptness of the Georgian military that in September–October 1993 it effectively lost Abkhazia following the fall of Sukhumi. Since then, Georgia has had to rely upon diplomacy and Russia to maintain even a foothold in determining the region's future status. The country was forced into

---

8. Report of the Secretary General on the situation in Abkhazia, Republic of Georgia. January 28th, 1993 (S/25188).

with Russia, allowing the latter permanent military bases in Georgia. As a consequence of military defeat, it has faced a huge refugee problem, with at least five per cent of the population (mainly from Abkhazia) becoming displaced. Couple this with an almost defunct official economy leaving average wages at under the equivalent of one dollar per month, the Georgian state is in a weak negotiating position.

The Abkhazians   The Abkhazians demand, at the very least, some form of autonomy within Georgia. However, the longer the conflict persisted with Georgia, the more they wanted to dislocate themselves from that state. They also want some linkage with the other members of the Confederation of Mountain Peoples of the Caucasus. Whether the Abkhazians want all-out independence remains unclear. There have been calls for a referendum to be conducted to determine the future status of the region, but this was announced after the departure of most of the Georgians from the territory in October 1993. With perhaps over 40 per cent of the population at the beginning of 1993 unable to vote, it is unlikely that anyone other than the Abkhazian leadership would accept the results of such an initiative.

The Abkhazians are well organized and have scored notable military victories. The disadvantage for the Abkhaz is their size. There are only 90,000 or so of them. There is growing encouragement to émigré communities to join them in their hour of need. This is partially successful. There are for example probably some 500,000 Abkhaz in Turkey. In the short term they see little reason for negotiation, in the long term it is necessary, as economic rather than political imperatives take over.

The Confederation of Mountain Peoples   The Confederation of Mountain Peoples is a part of the conflict in Abkhazia. In the main unelected, it is reasonable to assume that it speaks for the majority of north Caucasian people. Its main strategy is anti-Russian and pro-independence. Memories go back to nineteenth-century fights against the encroaching Russian Empire. Destabilization in Russian–Georgian relations is to its benefit, as it is perceived as a way to gain at the least greater autonomy within the Russian Federation or outright independence. It is against a clearly defined border between Russia and Georgia. It would also like port access to the Black Sea through Abkhazia. The Abkhazians as members of the confederation have seemingly no objection to this.

Being made up of a variety of ethnic groups, the Confederation is prone to internal dissent. This has already manifested itself between the Ingush and the Ossetians over land claims. There is also the danger of one group gaining dominance, for instance the Chechens under their leader Dudayev. Although seemingly a man of real-politick, he is also vehemently anti-Russian. He played host to ex-President of Georgia Gamsakhurdia, which was a source of concern to other members of the

khurdia, which was a source of concern to other members of the Confederation. This fact alone made it difficult for the Georgian government to open negotiations or even recognize the Confederation as anything more than a terrorist organization. Since the fall of Sukhumi in October 1993, the Confederation has lost something of its influence. This was partly a result of disagreements concerning the share of spoils in Abkhazia. It appeared that many volunteers were offered houses on the Black Sea coast for helping in the fighting, but these were not forthcoming. Also, with pressure coming from a variety of different sources to oust the leader of Chechenia during 1994, the Confederation now lacks much of its impetus as specifically local north Caucasian politics have come to the fore.

Russia   The position of Russia looks vastly different from Tbilisi or Baku than it does from London or New York. Throughout the Caucasus, Russia is perceived to be flexing its muscles to bring the troublesome peoples of the area under its own control. One commentator has stated that Russia's intention has been to "install and support pro-Russian governments in the Transcaucasus as a guarantee of stability".[9] Such an argument suggests that Russia was behind both the fall of Gamsakhurdia and Elchibey in Azerbaijan and the introduction of pro-Russian leaders Shevardnadze and Aliev respectively. Such an analysis would go down well in the Caucasus, but it credits Russia with a brilliantly manipulative plan for dominance. Clearly, Russia has foreign policy interests in the region and has concluded agreements with Georgia and Armenia for the stationing of permanent Russian military bases in those countries. Russia is keen that the three Transcaucasian countries do not fall outside its sphere of influence and it adopts policies to ensure that its presence is maintained.

However, it is as much the weakness of the local states themselves and the lack of any other external influence (whether that be Western, Turkish or Iranian) that has enabled Russia to pursue its version of the Monroe doctrine on its southern flank. With respect to Abkhazia, the Russian government above all must want peace and stability on its southern flank. Equally, it will not countenance a reduction in territorial/sovereign control, although it might devolve administrative responsibility. This, quite apart from the Caucasus itself, is attributable to other geopolitical considerations within the Russian Federation, notably concerning Tatarstan. Russia would like to see a clearly defined border between itself and Georgia. The Russian government is unlikely to offer greater power to the Confederation of Mountain Peoples.

The Russian government and state, like all successor states in the area of the former Soviet Union, is prone to instability. It is possible for individ-

9. Elizabeth Fuller, "Russian Strategy in the Transcaucasus since the demise of the USSR", *Berichte des Bundesinstituts für Ostwissenschaftliche und Internationale Studien* **40**, 3, 1994.

uals and groups to destabilize delicate positions. There is also tension between the executive and the legislative. The legislative tends to be more hard line in its approach towards Georgia. There is no guarantee that what is agreed by Yeltsin's government will be passed by parliament.

If these are the respective positions of the parties to the dispute in Abkhazia, the resultant question must be what the chances for a political settlement are.

Political solutions

Following lengthy negotiations and travails, Russian/CIS peace-keeping forces finally arrived in Abkhazia on 24 June 1994. Both the Georgian parliament and Russian Federation Council blocked the troops' presence for over a month. In the latter case the reason for the delay was attributable to a combined coalition of moderates who did not want to see Russian soldiers dying in a "foreign" land along with radical nationalists (the Zhirinovsky faction and the former communists), who had supported to varying degrees the Abkhazians during the conflict, and did not see why any concession should be given to Georgia. Perhaps typically in the Georgian parliament's case, the majority feeling was that the arrival of Russian troops was yet another sign of Georgia's loss of sovereignty and independence. There are some in the parliament who believe that a further storming of Abkhazia is the correct policy, forgetting the actual capabilities of Georgia's armed forces. Head of State Mr Shevardnadze employed brinkmanship techniques to force agreement through his own parliament, threatening to resign again, and he finally convinced enough parliamentarians that an agreement reached on 14 May 1994, in Moscow, for peace-keeping troops was in Georgia's patriotic interest and offered the best chance for the return of refugees.

The main features of the agreement were:

- That both sides fully observe the cease-fire by land, sea and air.
- All heavy equipment (artillery and mortars over 80 mm calibre, tanks and armoured personnel carriers) will be removed from what is termed the security zone. This is an area delimited 12 km either side of the Inguri River.
- The stationing of CIS peace-keeping troops and military observers in the zone with heavy equipment moved into designated areas under UN military surveillance.
- The withdrawal of Georgian troops from the Kodori gorge and their replacement by CIS and UN peace-keepers.
- Voluntary formations made up of people from outside are to be disbanded and withdrawn. (This is a reference to the peoples of the north Caucasus who fought on the side of the Abkhazians.)
- The peace-keeping forces will assist with the return of refugees and displaced people, first to the Gali region.

- Talks will continue on a full-scale political settlement.

Although the first six points are specific to installing peace-keepers and securing immediate military stability, it is with the last factor that we are concerned. Given the foregoing discussion of the relative positions of the parties to the dispute, their strengths and weaknesses and the perceptions of each other, it seems that a political solution appears some way off. Naturally, the possibility of a settlement rests upon the desire of those involved to substitute fighting for diplomacy and compromise. The agreement to introduce peace-keepers is a positive sign that at least the fighting will stop. It is more difficult to create conditions where those peace-keepers are no longer necessary. As matters stand at the time of writing it looks as though these troops will be in Abkhazia for the foreseeable future, unless the focus of a search for solutions changes.

Discussions between the parties to the dispute are focusing on the political: whether Abkhazia should be an autonomous entity within Georgia or be sovereign with treaty-ties to Georgia, or form some other political structure. By concentrating on these sorts of issues, which in the end will have to be addressed, it is unlikely that a mutually beneficial agreement will be reached. At the moment, the Abkhazians will not accept a status that defines them in Georgia as autonomous. The fears that led to the conflict in the first place have been exacerbated and they would not believe Georgian promises of virtual self-government within the Georgian state, however intentioned. On the other hand, it is unlikely that Georgia would ultimately agree to any measures that recognized Abkhazia as distinct or with equal international rights.

Examining the question geopolitically, however, might yield benefits in seeking a mutually acceptable solution. One of the major features of the conflict is that the various parties to the conflict have been looking into Abkhazia rather than out from the territory. The Georgian government sent troops into Abkhazia, as did the Confederation of Mountain Peoples. Russia viewed the territory as of strategic relevance again, concentrating on movements into the region. Given that all parties want some degree of control, a stance that opted to spread out from Abkhazia particularly in the economic domain could prove fruitful. Now that there are peace-keepers stationed in the territory and the process of limited demilitarization has begun, concomitant with the return of refugees on both sides could be the establishment of a free economic zone through the region. This would have the benefit of concentrating all minds on the rebuilding process and allow all outside parties the opportunity to move through without hindrance; ultimately the successes, as and when they occur, could be mirrored in the neighbouring regions. Agreement could be reached to ensure that whatever taxes are collected are kept locally, say for ten years.

Eventually, in five years, discussion could begin on the future sovereignty of the region. It would be hoped that over that period the process of economic building would become the predominant consideration and the mutual suspicions might have dissipated somewhat. The peoples of Abkhazia do not need to look too far for local examples. In Turkey, Trebizond has been established as a free port. This is in recognition that the town now has a significant role to play in the movement of goods and services from the Middle East through the Caucasus and Central Asia. In the north Caucasus, Ingushetia in early 1994 was established as a free economic zone to reduce tension and attract economic regeneration programmes. Similarly, in Kutaisi in the Imeretian region of Georgia, measures have focused on the economic rather than the political to try to make the city a model from which other regions and cities of Georgia can follow. By doing so, it is already receiving external assistance from the European Union and other bodies.

Conclusion

This discussion of Georgia has attempted to highlight that the nature of the country's geopolitics has changed in the modern age. Rather than being a strategic buffer zone, ripe for external intervention from surrounding empires, Georgia's main geopolitical dilemmas are local and internal. It has been the weakness of the state to counter these difficulties, which have allowed external manipulation and intervention, particularly from Russia. Rather than examine the minutiae of the arguments by opposing sides to the disputes and conflicts that have plagued the country since its independence, the objective has been to look at the broad parameters. By doing so, in the case of Abkhazia at least, it is possible to discern areas where there are opportunities for mutual advancement and the reduction of threats. These areas are principally economic. The fact that conflict groups are now prepared to agree to cease-fires, and that they are holding for reasonable periods is an encouraging feature. So too is a discernible shift in priorities, not only in Georgia but in Azerbaijan and Armenia as well, towards the economy and away from sloganeering politics, which leaves one feeling that the Transcaucasus is cautiously starting the long haul away from ethnic and nationalist fratricide, although pockets of that will continue, towards efforts to revive and rebuild its currently defunct economies.

CHAPTER EIGHT
The Georgian/South Ossetian territorial and boundary dispute
JULIAN BIRCH

There is a tendency, when speaking of territorial and border problems of small ethnic groups, to refer to the issue in terms of the titular nationality of the area; thus, in this present case, we frequently hear of the Ossetian problem. And yet, in reality, this begs the issue of how far the eponymous group really is or was the cause of the problem, and how far the problem was created for them by outside forces.

That the Ossetians have a territorial problem there is no doubt, for, despite being a distinct and recognized single people, they now find themselves divided and as citizens of two different sovereign states – those in the north in the Russian federation, and those in the south across the Daryal Pass in Georgia. Moreover, this comes in an age (indeed, a century and a half) that has belied Karl Marx's assertion in the Communist manifesto of 1848 that "National differences and antagonisms between peoples are daily vanishing, owing to the development of the bourgeoisie, to freedom of commerce, to the world market, to uniformity in the mode of production and in the conditions of life".[1]

On most continents the impact of nationalism has been felt as never before, and most ethnic groups with a distinct identity and a coherent territory have come to feel the need to throw off any overarching authority not their own in favour of taking control of their own affairs. In this instance it has resulted in the reduction of the Ossetian capital of Tskhinvali into a mini-Beirut, as Georgians and Ossetians fight for control.

The chapter explores the reasons for the Ossetian dilemma by looking at the patterns of their settlement, the overlordship of their current territorial range, the ethnic identification of the people within this range, the current flare up of the dispute, the external influences on the self-assertion of the Ossetians, and the prospects given this context.

---

1. K. Marx, "The communist manifesto". In *Karl Marx and Fredrick Engels: selected works*, 51 (Moscow: Progress Publishers, 1980).

Patterns of Ossetian settlement

Ossetian claims to a pre-eminent proprietary right to their present territorial range are understandable given the current pressures under which they find themselves, but are certainly not based on a presence there since time immemorial. Fairly long as their settlement there may have been, they are, without much doubt, an incomer group that sought refuge in their present mountain-straddling domain, much as we find in some other parts of the Caucasus and throughout other high ranges such as the Himalayas. The less hospitable, less easily occupied, terrain typically goes to the latecomers to an area, but is chosen in preference to areas where they are under pressure.

Although it is not intended here to get too bogged down in the more obscure and hypothetical aspects of Ossetian history, it is necessary to examine briefly what is presently known of their historical geography for the light it sheds on their own, and rival, claims to their present territory – an important source of the present bloody conflict.

As far as recorded history is concerned, Ossetian origins may be sought in the semi-nomadic Sarmatian people. They were resident to the north of the Caspian Sea, along the River Don and in Ciscaucasia, just prior to the modern era. In the first century BC, some tribes broke away from the main group, settling eventually in the first century AD by the Sea of Azov, between the Kuban and Terek rivers, and elsewhere in Ciscaucasia, according to Roman and Byzantine sources.[2]

Some of these Iranian-language group people were to become known to Byzantine writers as the Alan. From their new home they carried out raids into the Transcaucasian region among others, before being conquered themselves by the Huns in AD 372. Some, however, thereafter moved into the foothills of the north Caucasus, where, by the sixth century, they united with several the tribes already present to create a union known in surviving sources as Alania.[3] The autochthonous peoples of the area appear to have been eastern Circassians, or Kerkete as they were anciently known – ancestors of today's Kabardians.

It was to be from this fusion of Alan–Sarmatians and aboriginal peoples of the north Caucasus that the modern day Ossetians were to emerge, with the Alan element predominating both culturally and linguistically.[4]

Such then was the pattern of movement into present-day North Ossetia. With respect to South Ossetia, as presently constituted, Ossetian settle-

---

2. See the *Great Soviet encyclopaedia*, vol. 23, 395 (New York: Macmillan, 1979).
3. M. I. Isayev, *National languages in the USSR – problems and solutions*, 66 (Moscow: Progress Publishers, 1977).
4. V. I. Abayev, *Ossetinskiy yazyk i fol'klor* (*Ossetian language and folklore*), 75 (Leningrad & Moscow: Academy of Sciences, 1949).

ment came more recently. Following the thirteenth-century Mongol invasion and the fourteenth-century incursion of Tamerlane, which drove many of them farther into the mountainous gorges of the upper Terek and the north-central Caucasus (somewhat breaking up their cohesion as a people), many small groups also crossed the summits into the territory of Georgia.[5] There they initially settled on the southern slopes of the Glavnyi range, becoming known as the Tualläg linguistic/cultural subgroup.

In the course of the seventeenth and eighteenth centuries, these high mountain Ossetians began to spread out from the southern slopes to the foothills and plains to the south. There they cultivated the land rather than raising livestock, as in their more mountainous abode.[6] Varied as their agricultural base now was, they were recovering their common identity again by this period, distinct as it was from their Georgian neighbours.

Although the size of the Ossetian population at this juncture is not easy to estimate, but possibly around 100,000 or less, that of Georgia was itself quite small. It has in fact been estimated that, as a result of internal conflicts and clashes with the Turkish-backed Lezghians, at the end of the eighteenth century the Georgian population had probably dropped to less than half a million.[7] Thus, the potential for conflict was limited at this stage, and land was available for both groups.

Since the eighteenth century, the pattern of settlement of Georgians and Ossetians has remained largely the same, with some trickle of both groups into the area from the south and north respectively. They lived alongside each other in larger settlements such as the regional capital of Tskhinvali (population circa 45,000 in the 1980s), or in distinct villages scattered about and interspersed.

Of course, as in any other such case, the question arises as to how long a people has to be resident in any particular area before it becomes accepted as the indigenous population with an unassailable right to that territory and control of its affairs? Crude a measure as it may be, it is to a large degree the measure of property rights within many territories – the prescriptive right, or "possession is nine-tenths of the law". But what of prior claims to that territory that may have been swept aside *de facto*? What of claims of a later incursor group who became the majority? There are matters resolvable only by *force majeure*, by negotiation, or by outside adjudication.

---

5. *Great Soviet encyclopaedia*, vol. 30, 459 (1982).
6. Ibid.
7. D. M. Lang, *A modern history of Georgia* (London: Weidenfeld & Nicolson, 1962), 36.

Patterns of overlordship and control in South Ossetia

Occupation of a territory is one thing. *De facto* political and military control of that territory is quite another. And so it has been with what we now know as South Ossetia.

The Alan–Ossetian nation to the north of the Caucasus prevailed from the ninth to the thirteenth centuries, reaching its apogée as an independent entity between the tenth and twelfth centuries.[8] The end of this phase of control over their own affairs came with the Mongol–Tatar invasion of their new area of settlement in 1222–39, a period of subordination that lasted until the fifteenth century.[9]

With the withdrawal from direct control by the Mongols, the Ossetians, in the late fifteenth and early sixteenth centuries, steadily re-emerged as a distinct entity, but with a fragmented and partial feudal system of their own, coupled with elements of a clan society. At this time however, far from being autonomous, they came under the influence of the neighbouring Kabardinian princes, themselves still subject in turn to the Crimean Tatar Khans.[10]

In the middle of the sixteenth century, as the Kabardians came under Russian protection (in place of the old Tatar overlordship), they brought many of the Ossetians with them into this new relationship – even affording them now some protection against more bellicose neighbours also living to the north of the mountains. Along with Kabardia, this northern part of what was to become Ossetia was however the only part formally annexed by Russia after the Russo–Turkish war of 1768–74, under the terms of the Treaty of Kuchuk Kainarji.[11] Ossetians, thus having become part of Russia, began to spread back in the second half of the eighteenth and the first half of the nineteenth centuries, into the Mozdok region and the Vladikavkaz plain to the north.[12]

Those Ossetians (the Tuallӓg) who, under the same pressure of Mongol invasion, crossed the main mountain range to the south, were there to become subjects of Georgian feudal lords[13] who had established a feudal structure in the area in the thirteenth century.[14] This territory had become part of the Iberian state as far back as the second half of the first millennium BC,[15] and most of the newcomers were to settle in its Kartli Kingdom suc-

---

8. *Great Soviet encyclopaedia* 1982, vol. 30, 459 and (1979) vol. 23, 395.
9. Ibid. 1979, vol. 23, 395.
10. Ibid., 394.
11. Ibid., 395. It was fully incorporated in 1806. On Russian/Ossetian relations in this period see M. M. Biiev, *Russko–Osetinskie otnosheniya (Russian–Ossetian relations)* (Ordzhonikidze, 1970).
12. Ibid., 395 and (1978) vol. 18, 590.
13. Ibid. 1978, vol. 18, 590.
14. Ibid. 1982, vol. 30, 459.

cessor, although some extended the range of Ossetian settlement westwards into the other Georgian kingdom of Imeretia.[16] Here they were reduced to being serfs, although retaining aspects of their old clan structure.[17]

With Russia's absorption of Georgia in 1801, these southern Ossetians too became subjects of the empire in addition to their more local Georgian feudal overlords. Thus, by the early nineteenth century, both North and South Ossetians lay within the same political entity, although subject to differing local overlords. This situation (in essence) was to prevail until the revolutions of 1917.

Soviet sources always stressed the way in which this incorporation into Russia was advantageous to the Ossetians, in the first instance, in the north, by associating them with a more advanced culture and economy, and secondly by affording them protection against enemies. In the case of the later incorporation of the South Ossetians, it brought them into close association with their confrères in the north, as well as affording them the same cultural and economic advantages. In some ways also, the Christian South Ossetians were better equipped to adapt to the values of their new Russian overlords than their Muslim neighbours incorporated in the eighteenth and nineteenth centuries.[18]

Under Russian dominion, northern Ossetia became part of Terek Oblast (created in 1861) as the Ossetian Military Okrug, centred on Vladikavkaz, whereas southern Ossetia formed part of Tbilisi Oblast.[19]

However, as with many of the other mountain peoples, their new situation was far from uniformly beneficial, nor was it met entirely with equanimity. Indeed, Ossetians played a major part in the mass uprising of 1804 against brutal use of their, and other peoples', forced labour along the Georgian military highway – the supply line for the then Russian bridgehead in Georgia. In the process, a Don Cossack regiment sent against them was defeated before they were brought to heel by a combination of changing weather and Russian reinforcements. Harsh, if understandable, reprisals were then taken against the mountaineers.[20] Further Ossetian peasant uprisings occurred in South Ossetia in 1810, 1830, 1840 and 1850.[21] With no ownership of their land until 1864,[22] no written language, and little freedom, they were one of the poorest people in the region, their national poet Khetagurov perceiving them as on the verge of extinction.

---

15. Ibid.
16. Ibid.
17. Ibid.
18. R. Pipes, *The formation of the Soviet Union – communism and nationalism 1917–23* (Cambridge, Mass.: Harvard University Press, 1964), 95.
19. *Great Soviet encyclopaedia* 1979, vol. 23, 395.
20. Lang 1962, 49.
21. *Great Soviet encyclopaedia* 1982, vol. 30, 459.
22. Ibid.

The presence of Ossetians in both Russia and in Russia's colony, the former Georgia, came to take on a renewed significance with the fall of the Russian empire in 1917–18, and the beginnings of Georgia's prolonged process of separation from Russia, a process only to be completed in 1990–1.

Whatever advantages there had been for Georgia in agreeing to the Treaty of Georgievskin July 1783, whereby she became a favoured protectorate of Russia, these had begun to pall quickly as a result of the full annexation of 1801. As the nineteenth century wore on, these negative aspects of the relationship became ever more evident, variously in the shape of corruption, repression, Russification, and reduction to the status of a mere administrative province. The land too was increasingly taken out of the hands of the Georgian feudal holders, some of whom were replaced by Russians.[23] Early revolts had failed, only to be followed by the common colonial experience of reluctant acquiescence. By the early twentieth century, however, a revival of Georgian national consciousness and assertiveness eventually began through the medium of the church, the Society for the Spread of Literacy among the Georgians, educationalists, and the Menshevik wing of the Social Democratic Party, with its call for national fulfilment through international co-operation among the working class.[24]

It was eventually the action of this latter group, the Mensheviks, seizing power, following the breakdown of the Tsarist order and its provisional successor, which was to impact significantly on the modern-day Ossetians. This seizure of control brought for the Ossetians a fear of Georgian intentions during the process of nation-state building, almost mirroring Georgian fears of Russia.

Initially, in 1917–18 in the form of membership of a Transcaucasian federation (together with Armenia and Azerbaijan), the Georgians declared themselves independent on 22 April 1918. However, this was not to last and the Georgian Mensheviks formed a new and purely Georgian government which, in a Deed of Independence, declared its separation from Russia on 26 May 1918. Significantly, the Deed guaranteed equal political and social rights, as well as free development, for all the ethnic minorities within Georgia. With them into this new situation went the South Ossetians, now cut off again from their compatriots in the north, in the Russian republic – variously in the Terek Oblast (until 1920),[25] then in the Ossetian Okrug of the Gortsyi (Gorskaya) Autonomous Republic (17 November 1920 to 7 July 1924).[26]

---

23. Lang 1962, 43, 45, 54, 65–7, 103, 132.
24. Pipes 1964, 17.
25. In which a Terek People's Soviet Socialist Republic was briefly declared in 1918 before acknowledging the sovereignty of the Russian republic.
26. Its formation was actually confirmed by the All-Russian Central Executive Committee on 20 January 1921.

In the south, in Georgia, in the words of Richard Pipes, "[i]n its endeavour to create a homogeneous national state, the Tbilisi government showed little sympathy for the attempts of [its] minority groups to secure political and cultural autonomy.[27]

In fact, the Bolshevik-dominated South Ossetian National Soviet was outlawed by the Tbilisi government in 1919 and national self-determination was denied to the South Ossetians.[28] Ossetians certainly participated in revolts against the newly independent Georgian regime in March 1918, October 1919 and April–June 1920,[29] although these were by no means exclusively or essentially nationalist in orientation, being peasant-based or backed by Bolsheviks in North Ossetia.[30] These uprisings were, however, bloodily suppressed by the Georgians, especially that of 1920 when 5,000 are said to have died and some 20,000 Ossetians fled into Russia.[31] The Georgian Peoples Guard also took particularly stern action to ensure that the Ossetians understood the new reality – by burning villages and destroying crops.[32] Inevitably this would have short-term success only, with the grievances being harboured by those who survived. Indeed, the 1920 case was to be something of a foretaste of what was to recur in the 1980s and 1990s.[33]

The Georgian Menshevik government's overlordship of South Ossetia was to last only until February 1921, when the Red Army, assisted by local Georgian Bolsheviks, invaded and seized control of the whole of Georgia. In this way, it was again reduced to being part of a larger entity, the Transcaucasian Socialist Federal Soviet Republic, in 1922.[34] As a Union republic, it was to be but a part of the even larger Soviet Union from later in 1922 up to 1936. Seen by many Georgians as a renewal of the Russian empire by other means and under a different name, it appeared that the day of Georgian independence had been postponed, but hardly abandoned.

For the Ossetians, the new arrangement was potentially quite desirable, in that it kept North and South Ossetia within the same state. However, fateful problems quickly appeared. The first of these took the form of the

27. Pipes (1964: 212).
28. Lang (1962: 228).
29. *Great Soviet encyclopaedia*, vol. 30 (1982: 459).
30. Pipes (1964: 218), Lang (1962: 228).
31. *Great Soviet encyclopaedia*, vol. 30 (1982: 459); Lang (1962: 228–9).
32. Lang (1962: 228–9).
33. See for example, the statement of the chairman of the South Ossetian regional council, Zanaur N. Gassiev, in October 1991: "In the early twenties the Georgians burned South Ossetian villages. Now seventy years later, they are doing it again". Interview in the *International Herald Tribune*, 4 October 1991.
34. See S. V. Kharmandaryan, *Lenin i stanovlenie zakavkazskoy federatsii 1921–23 (Lenin and the formation of the Transcaucasian federation)*, especially 35–114 (Erevan: Academy of Sciences, 1969).

creation on 20 April 1922 of the South Ossetian Autonomous Oblast of some 3,900km^2 within Georgia, centred upon Tskhinvali.[35] Although the Bolsheviks at the time may have been trying to protect the Ossetians, the decision was to be interpreted later as an instance of divide and rule. Either way, it was a somewhat artificial creation, including, as it did, many Georgians.

This was followed by the creation within the Russian republic of a similar North Ossetian Autonomous Oblast (eventually of some 8,000km^2) on 7 July 1924,[36] embracing what Bennigsen and Wimbush have called, generally ... the most pro-Russian among the north Caucasus mountaineers.[37]

That these decisions were far from welcome among the Ossetians is indicated by the presence in Moscow in May 1925 of representatives of both the new territories to discuss their reunification with the central authorities.[38] The outcome was negative from their point of view, since it could be achieved only at the expense of the Russian Republic, the Georgian Republic, or both. For such a small group, it may well have appeared to the central authorities to be potentially too disruptive.

In 1936, the Transcaucasian Union Republic was broken up into its three constituent parts, with Georgia now becoming a Union republic in its own right. Thus, the division of the Ossetias was perpetuated, the northern part within the Russian Republic, the south within Georgia. However, at this same time in 1936, the situation was further complicated by a distinction being introduced between the two Ossetian territories. That part in Russia was reorganized as an Autonomous Republic on 5 December 1936, whereas the southern part remained merely an Autonomous Oblast within Georgia. What then was the nature of the distinction between these two latter-day systems of overlordship, and why was it applied in this case, where it was to have the effect of further complicating Ossetian aspirations towards unity?

Both types of territory were essentially administrative subdivisions of a Union republic, as created by the 1936 constitution. In the case of the Autonomous Republic, "on its territory [lived] a majority of the members of one of the nationalities inhabiting the respective Union Republic, and the Autonomous Republic [was] named after that nationality". As a part of a Union republic, such an autonomous republic did not have the right to secede. North Ossetia was but one of 16 such units within the Russian Republic. In contrast, an Autonomous Oblast was "inhabited chiefly by the members of one nationality, after which it [was] named", although they similarly had no unilateral right of secession. South Ossetia was the

35. *Great Soviet encyclopaedia* 1982, vol. 30, 459.
36. Ibid. 1979, vol. 23, 394.
37. A. Bennigsen & S. E. Wimbush, *Muslims of the Soviet empire*, 206 (London: Hurst, 1985).
38. J. V. Stalin, *Works*, vol. 7, 427 (Moscow: Foreign Languages Publishing House, 1954).

only such unit created in Georgia (which did however possess two of the autonomous republics in the shape of Abkhazia and Adzharia).

What then were the motivations and consequences of these essentially externally taken decisions? The motivations have long been contested and may indeed have been varied at the time. Three in particular have gained currency.

- It was the consequence of a genuine desire to give expression to legitimate Ossetian aspirations, as an emergent nation, seeking some control over their own affairs and destiny – at least as far as was compatible with their numbers and dispersal among other peoples.
- It was an attempt to win the support of Ossetians living elsewhere in neighbouring territories and thereby undermine the basis for any further territorial demands that could not readily be met – making the best of a difficult job.
- It was an attempt by the Soviet, largely Russian-dominated, centre to undermine the particularly virulent nationalism of the Georgians by a process of divide and rule.

To each of these cases objections can be raised. With respect to the first a single uniform territory could probably have been created to attract in Ossetian immigrants, since few ethnic groups in the area were neatly distributed and Georgia's interests were no longer paramount after the invasion of 1921 and the crushing of the 1924 revolt. In the second case, the number of Ossetians outside their new territories was not great, and there was nothing really unique about the way their case was handled (cf. the Buryat Mongols or the Lezghians). With the third case, it could be objected that if this was the goal, then a territory could well have been created for the 300,000 Mingrelians.[39]

If the motivations are still not entirely clear, the consequences at least are more apparent. The Ossetians were divided in their subordination to a higher power, but also made more vulnerable should those two Union republics ever go their separate ways. The changes of 1922, 1936 and 1944 (when North Ossetia gained some territory from the deported Ingush)[40] cumulatively meant that North Ossetia was destined to become more Russified, whereas South Ossetia was likely to come under increasing Georgian influence.

Ossetian opposition to the new situation seems, at the time, to have been fairly muted and largely confined to some resistance to suppression of customs and traditions (as found throughout the USSR) and to the imposition of collectivization (again nothing unique).[41] With Georgia under the

39. A case made in R. Wixman, *Language aspects of ethnic patterns and processes in the north Caucasus*, Research Paper 191 (p. 130), Department of Geography, University of Chicago, 1980.
40. See W. Kolarz, *Russia and her colonies* (New York: Archon, 1967), 192.

firm central control of avowedly internationalist Georgians and Mingreli-ans (Stalin and Beria), and their nomenclature successors, an uneasy truce, and acceptance of a *fait accompli*, settled over the area until the late 1980s.

Ethnic identification and loyalties in South Ossetia

Small as their numbers may be in global terms (604,000 in 1990),[42] locally the Ossetians are relatively numerous. After the deportation of the Chechens in 1944, they became numerically "the largest of the mountain peoples of the north Caucasus".[43] Certainly to this day, they have been far more numerous in North Ossetia and the Russian republic (440,000 in 1989), than in South Ossetia and Georgia (164,055 in 1989).[44] Approxi-mately two thirds of Ossetians actually lived within their two national ter-ritories at the start of the current troubles in 1989. This helped them to retain a strong cultural and linguistic identity.[45] In the more specific, and immediately pertinent, case of South Ossetia, where 10.8 per cent of all Ossetians were living in 1989, several other items of statistical evidence throw important light on the nature of the clash of interests so evident there:

- Of Georgia's overall population of 5,443,000 in 1989, 164,055 or circa 3 per cent were Ossetians.
- Of Georgia's overall population, 98,527 lived in South Ossetia.
- Of South Ossetia's population, 66.2 per cent were Ossetian and 29 per cent Georgian.
- Only 65,000 of the 164,000 Ossetians in Georgia as a whole in fact lived in South Ossetia. 98,000 thus lived elsewhere in Georgia.
- Around 90 per cent of the population in South Ossetia lived in the centre and south of the Oblast, thus bringing the South Ossetians into close contact with the Georgians. Indeed, the South Ossetian capital, Tskhinvali, was not only surrounded by Georgian villages, it lay a mere 120km^2 from the Georgian capital of Tbilisi.
- In Tskhinvali, with its population of 45,000 at the beginning of the recent conflict, Ossetians outnumbered Georgians by at least 2 to 1.[46]

What emerges from this statistical portrait is the comparatively small

41. Ibid., 192.
42. *The Georgian Messenger*, Tbilisi, 11 October – 8 November 1990, and the *International Her-ald Tribune*, 4 October 1991.
43. Kolarz 1967, 191.
44. *The Georgian Messenger* and the *International Herald Tribune*, 4 October 1991.
45. In post-Second World War censuses this maintenance of the Ossetian language has remained at over 98 per cent among those in the north and south combined.
46. Zaria Vostoka, Tbilisi, 23 March 1990; *The Georgian Messenger*, Tbilisi, 11 October – 8 November 1990; and *Great Soviet encyclopaedia* 1982, vol. 30, 459.

scale of any conflict that might arise in South Ossetia when set alongside many of the ethnic clashes of interest of our time – small, that is, as long as it remained confined to South Ossetia. Should the two "overlords" of Georgia and the Russian Republic become involved – as inevitably they would – then the issue took on a wholly new, larger and more dangerous complexion.

This statistical portrait of ethnic identification and self-identification is however incomplete without some reference to the impact of external cultural pressures on the South Ossetians well before the flare up in inter-ethnic relations in 1989. These Tualläg Ossetians, eastern orthodox Christians unlike the many Muslims among their confrères in the north, had already had both their culture and language significantly influenced by their Georgian neighbours. From the eighteenth to the mid-nineteenth centuries, their literary language was in fact written in the Georgian script.[47] After a subsequent Cyrillic phase (and a brief experiment with a Latin script, 1923–38), there was a return to a Georgian script from 1938–54.[48] However, towards the end of this period, from the late 1940s to 1953, Ossetian language schools were all closed,[49] and a Cyrillic script was readopted/reimposed for both parts of Ossetia from 1954 onwards.[50] The impact of these policies has, however, divided observers and commentators. Hewitt has spoken of the Ossetians as being reluctant to be Georgianized, much in the way that Georgians were reluctant to be Russified.[51] Reluctant or not, in 1984 Wixman referred to South Ossetians as in the process of being "assimilated" by the Georgians.[52] Like other republics, it appeared that Georgia was already showing signs of a desire for firm control over the minorities living within its territory.[53]

The present conflict – origins and causes

The outbreak of the present conflict between the Ossetians and the Georgians can be traced back to 1988–9, although the physical destruction and the killing only began in 1989. What reactivated the clash of interests rather depends upon which side is recounting the story. For the Ossetians, the straw that broke the camel's back was probably the November 1988

47. R. Wixman, *The peoples of the USSR*, 51 (Armonk, NY: Sharp, 1984).
48. S. Akiner, *Islamic peoples of the Soviet Union*, 189 (London: Kegan Paul International, 1986).
49. B. G. Hewitt, "Aspects of language planning in Georgia". In *Language planning in the Soviet Union*, M. Kirkwood, 139 (London: Macmillan, 1989).
50. Akiner 1986, 189.
51. Hewitt 1989, 141.
52. Wixman 1984, 151 & 196.
53. See for example, an observer's account in the *Sunday Times*, London, 3 April 1988.

publication of a law strengthening the position of the Georgian language in the republic as a whole.[54] For the Georgians, it was the support offered in a newspaper letter in March 1989 by an Ossetian college lecturer, Alan Chochiev, to the Abkhazian people (with whom the Georgians were already in often violent conflict) and his call for the administrative status of the South Ossetian Oblast to be upgraded and transferred to the Russian republic to protect its separateness.[55] From that point onwards, a spiral of open hostility set in. However, these were, in a sense, only the catalysts that triggered the violent phase of conflict. There were clearly more substantial matters involved, and grievances of a broader character, which led to the horrendous pattern of slaughter and homelessness that was to emerge – intensely felt grievances exploitable by Ossetian and Georgian leaders in South Ossetia, and by external forces outside the Oblast. By no means all of the extensive range of factors which provoked ethnic conflicts between the Russians and the ethnic minorities of their empire were present in this more localized clash between minorities. Nevertheless, at least six factors played their part in producing this clash – and then sustaining it once in progress:

- the heritage of antagonism
- economic grievances
- Georgian moves to independence from Russia
- Georgian insensitivity to Ossetian needs
- the emergence of an Ossetian nationalist movement
- external manipulation of the issue.

We can now consider each of these in turn.

The heritage of antagonism

Although the idea that inexorably hanging over everyone is a fixed national identity just waiting to be prompted into defensive or offensive action on behalf of that group is not really sustainable over millennia, it is fairly apparent, from what has been said above, that a strong tribal/communal/group memory of conflict earlier in this century at least did hover over the minds of Georgians and Ossetians, and informed and shaped their attitudes towards each other into the 1980s. This was especially so in the case of the Ossetians, among whom it was sustained and passed down by word of mouth as a folk memory, however ill documented it may have been. There were many alive able to recall the bitter events and carnage of the early 1920s – an Ossetian holocaust was earnestly kept alive, much as

---

54. See *Kommunisti*, Tbilisi, 3 November 1988; and E. Fuller, Draft "State program" on Georgian language published, Radio Liberty research paper, RL 559/88, 12 December 1988.
55. This letter to an Abkhaz district newspaper was later reprinted in a Georgian newspaper (*Literaturuli Sakartvelo*, 5 May 1989) whereupon it evoked broader protests from Georgian, including violent acts over the summer (see Zaria Vostoka, 23 July 1989).

in the case of the Armenian holocaust at the hands of the Turks. For their part, nationalist Georgians could recall the way so many Ossetians, for whatever reasons, sided with the Russians and Bolsheviks during and after the revolutions of 1917 – forces seen as highly detrimental to Georgian interests and aspirations. These memories were easily and quickly to colour the war of words.

Economic grievances

Exploitation by the central planners and ministries in Moscow, albeit not always to the exclusive advantage of the Russians, had long been an issue of concern to nationalists in other parts of the USSR. Elements of such a case were also to be seen in the South Ossetian position, although here it was not so much the Russians as the Georgians who were perceived as the immediate architects of a growing poverty, and failure on the part of the old order to provide the quality of life it had so long promised.

In this instance, an unusual dimension was added to the feeling of impending economic failure and collapse of the social infrastructure by the outbreak of typhoid in the South Ossetian capital, Tskhinvali, in April 1988.[56] This provoked three days of demonstrations and resulted in the dismissal of the party leader, Feliks Sanakoyev, after 14 years in power.[57] Such concessions were taken by many now to be a sign of weakness, and were being followed up by renewed demands for further changes in a number of a minority areas of the USSR.

In late 1990, South Ossetian nationalists went on to claim that their economy was not only stagnating, but that the standard of living there was well below that of the rest of Georgia.[58]

Georgian moves to secure independence

Although a Georgian action in the field of language policy was to be a catalyst for the sudden upsurge in South Ossetian separatism, cultural grievances and claims of discrimination generally seem to have played a much less significant part in the build-up to this dispute than in many others across the USSR.[59] Indeed, a considerable range of Ossetian cultural facilities existed within Georgia, including the Tskhinvali Pedagogical Institute where separatist leader Alan Chochiev taught – establishments where nationalist values traditionally have taken root and attained articulate expression.[60] Georgians have actually claimed they have done much for

---

56. *Komsomolskaya Pravda*, Moscow, 26 April 1988.
57. Ibid.
58. *Moscow News* **46**, 8–9, 1990.
59. See D. Slider, "The politics of Georgia's independence". In *Problems of communism*, vol. XL, (November–December 1991), 75–6.
60. Ibid., 75.

the Ossetians and that, by way of comparison, there are no exclusively Ossetian language schools in North Ossetia where Russian holds sway.[61] Moreover, Georgian leaders throughout the conflict have insisted that, although there can be no question of going back to *political* autonomy for South Ossetia, cultural autonomy remained distinctly possible.[62] Similarly, in relation to positions of power within their own area, the South Ossetians were in a relatively strong situation.[63]

What threatened this relatively stable cultural and gubernatorial context was Georgia's increasing alienation from the USSR and the growing opportunities she had, with Gorbachev as Soviet leader, to do something about her aspirations. This process began to take shape in 1987–8,[64] with the emergence of informal groups and then outright political parties with varying degrees of commitment to greater autonomy, or even outright independence, for Georgia) in place of its existing relationship with Russia via the USSR.[65] No matter that these groups quickly divided into moderates and radicals, respectively willing to work for these ends within the existing system or rejecting co-operation with the system, the implications for the South Ossetians were quickly clear – the prospect of a heightened emphasis on loyalty to Georgia and the probability of eventual severance of political links with North Ossetia.

Under the leadership of Zviad Gamsakhurdia, the drive towards the restructuring of the Soviet Union gathered pace in November 1988 with the Georgian parliament's granting to itself the right to veto all Union laws, declaring natural resources to be republican property, and rejecting measures designed by the centre to revamp the federal constitution.[66] Although the three Baltic republics made a good deal of the opposition front-running, they were closely followed by Georgia and Moldova throughout 1989. The Tbilisi massacre of 9 April 1989 came to mark a point of no return in the process, to be followed by the founding congress of the Georgian Popular Front umbrella opposition organization,[67] the new draft

---

61. See *The Guardian*, London, 14 February 1991.
62. See the Georgian Foreign Minister's statement of February 1991. *TASS*, 16 February 1991; or the offer made by Georgian President Zviad Gamsakhurdia the following month. *TASS*, 6 March 1991.
63. Slider 1991, 75.
64. See particularly J. Aves, *Paths to national independence in Georgia 1987–90* (Occasional Paper 15, School of Slavonic and East European Studies, University of London, 1991).
65. See E. Fuller, *Georgia edges towards secession*, Radio Liberty research paper, RL243/90, 28 May 1990. In *Report on the USSR*, 1 June 1990, 15–16.
66. *The Independent*, London, 25 November 1988.
67. See E. Fuller, *Towards Georgian independence – Georgian formal and informal groups and their programmes*, Radio Liberty research paper, RL280/89, 7 June 1989; J. Aves, "Opposition political organizations in Georgia", *Slovo – a Journal of Contemporary Soviet and East European Affairs* 3 (1990), especially 29; and J. Aves, "Paths to national independence in Georgia 1987–90", op. cit., 16–18.

programme on the increased use of the Georgian language in all spheres of public life in August 1989,[68] and the formation of the radical Main Committee for National Salvation a little later.[69]

By this time, the conflict within South Ossetia was becoming severe. Georgia nevertheless pressed ahead in its drive for independence. In early 1990, a joint conference of nationalist groups gathered to discuss the further path of that process,[70] to be followed by the 9 March denunciation by the Georgian parliament of Georgia's forcible incorporation into the USSR and its approval of measures on the defence of state sovereignty – effectively a declaration of sovereignty.[71] There was, by 1990, widespread support in Georgia for the abolition of the autonomous Oblast status of South Ossetia, it being argued that this too had been imposed upon Georgia following the Soviet invasion of 1921 and the creation of a new state structure.[72]

March 1990 witnessed the emergence of the National Forum seeking to create an alternative parliament and form a transitional government,[73] whereas the more formal institutional arrangements brought victory in October 1990 elections to the Round Table / Free Georgia coalition group of nationalist parties.[74] Under the impact of this new situation, the Georgian Communist Party declared its independence from the CPSU in December 1990;[75] the KGB went over to the new government in Tbilisi;[76] the parliament refused to participate in Gorbachev's new Union treaty referendum in February 1991;[77] Georgia held its own referendum on independence in March[78] and the Georgian parliament declared independence on the 9 April.[79] After that, the breaking of links with Moscow on 6 September 1991, after the failed coup and counter-coup there, was to be almost a formality – a recognition of a *fait accompli*.

Georgia's seemingly unstoppable move towards this break with *her* overload had thus provided a cause of the clash with the Ossetians; but, once the conflict had been rekindled, her continued pursuit of her legitimate goal served to sustain that smaller source of vexation.

---

68. E. Fuller, "Georgia edges towards secession", op. cit., 15–16.

69. Aves, "Paths to national independence", op. cit., 31.

70. Ibid., 40.

71. *Zaria Vostoka*, 10 March 1990.

72. See for example, *Akhalgazrda Iverieli*, 5 April 1990.

73. Aves, "Opposition political organizations in Georgia", op. cit., 22–3; and Aves, "Paths to national independence", op. cit., 43.

74. *Associated Press* (AP), 28 October 1990; and Aves, "Paths to national independence, op. cit., 44–52.

75. *TASS*, 8 December 1990.

76. *The Independent*, 8 February 1991.

77. *TASS*, 28 February 1991.

78. *TASS* and AP, 1 April 1991.

79. AP, 9 April 1991.

Georgian insensitivity to Ossetian needs

It has to be admitted that a parallel downside to Georgia's pursuit of *her* interest was a marked degree of Georgian insensitivity to *Ossetian* needs – particularly those of certainty about their future and the borders of their territory. This was no uniquely Georgian phenomenon. Larger nations have a long track record of looking after their own majority interests first, with their minorities coming a poor second. This is most evidently so at crucial points in their history where their very fate is in the balance, and the process of gaining independence can be just such a point. How many times was the cry heard from Africa and elsewhere in the 1950s and 1960s that at such a point in dealing with the old imperial overload, and in the immediate aftermath of independence, "unity is all, united we stand, divided we fall". And how often was that unity enforced until the deed was done. The problem was always how to cope with minority views in the independence process, and then in the post-independence settlement. At what point was the voice of the minority to be heard again and how?

In the case of Georgia, with some 30 per cent of its population composed of ethnic minorities, there was undoubtedly a legitimate fear of the debilitating effect this could have in undermining Georgian claims to independence and the way in which it could result in a fragmented state entity. After the Abkhazian, Adzhars, and the Ossetians, could not the Mingrelians and Svan follow suit?

Some of the Georgian leaders, in their pursuit of a unified front in dealing with the USSR and Russia, did seem almost to go out of their way to be offensive to the minorities in the republic, including the South Ossetians. For example, Gamsakhurdia in June 1990 declared mixed marriages a threat to the survival of the Georgian nation:[80] he went on, in October that same year, to guarantee the safety of non-Georgians in the republic, as long as they did not "violate the interest of the Georgian people or commit any crime".[81]

He pulled no punches either when he declared of the Ossetians that "They have no right to a state here in Georgia. They are a national minority. Their homeland is North Ossetian . . Here they are newcomers".[82] Subsequently, in March 1991, he threatened to withhold Georgian citizenship – and hence ownership of land – from the whole population of districts where the majority of the population voted against Georgian independence in the referendum on that issue.[83] More broadly, the Georgian Supreme Soviet adopted an election law in August 1990 that debarred the participation of groups and parties concerned only with a specific area of

---

80. *Literaturuli sakartvelo*, 8 June 1990.
81. Ibid., 5 October 1990.
82. Cited in *The Guardian*, 14 February 1991.
83. *Vestnik Gruzii*, 9 March 1991.

the republic, and so it was that Ossetian groups were unable to compete the following October.[84]

As far as the question of Ossetian political autonomy and territory was concerned, Gamsakhurdia's own promises in September and November 1990,[85] as well as that of the Round Table coalition's election manifesto of October 1990,[86] were quickly reneged upon, with merely cultural autonomy being on offer after the elections. And yet, whether the Georgians liked it or not, Ossetians did actually exist within Georgia and they had to be taken into some account, however slightly.

As a result of decisions they opposed from the beginning – witness the 1925 deputation to Moscow – the Ossetians had already been split between two republics of the USSR with their two centres of power. The one Ossetian people was, it now seemed, to be torn asunder still more decisively than ever before in the interests of Georgia, with little or no consultation, nor much prospect of any future ability to control their own affairs. Some parallels could be drawn with the position of the Catholic/Republican Irish in Northern Ireland.

The Georgians, in pursuit of their own nation-state interests, effectively placed the Ossetian issue on the political back-burner, if not totally out of sight of the cooker, while the problems with Moscow were resolved. There seemed to be little willingness to compromise with the Ossetians, and certainly not over the question of what had long been a formidable (although certainly not an impenetrable) mountain frontier with Georgia's northern neighbour, Russia.

It might be objected here, from the Georgian side, that Russia herself was not offering any comparable compromise territorial settlement to North Ossetia, allowing the creation of a buffer-zone state (incorporating perhaps some at least of South Ossetia) between herself and Georgia, in an era where mountains have largely ceased to provide secure frontiers. In fact, in most of their public statements, the Ossetian leaders seemed quite willing to come under the protective umbrella of Russia (for the time being at least), rather than attain a state entirely of their own. Moscow, they doubtless reasoned, was still quite powerful as a potential protector, but had the advantage of being far away and with enough problems of its own.

Thus, while Georgia was in the freedom fighting, then nation-state building, phase of her own development, it gave the Ossetians the distinct impression of their being second-rate citizens whose position could only worsen. Perhaps some sympathy for the Georgians could have been

---

84. *AP*, 28 October 1990; see also E. Fuller, "Round table coalition wins resounding victory in Georgian Supreme Soviet elections". In Radio Liberty report on the USSR, 16 November 1990, 13.

85. See *Zaria Vostoka*, 21 September and 16 November 1990.

86. See text in *Kommunisti*, 19 October 1990.

shown by the Ossetians, but this too would probably have weakened their position still further. That, for Gamsakhurdia, the South Ossetian issue became something of a convenient form of distraction as his Georgian enemies closed in on him in August–September 1991, could not detract from its intractability. No more change of leadership was going to make it easy to achieve compromise. This required more tolerance than most Georgians were prepared to show to the Ossetians.

The emergence of the Ossetian Popular Front

A probably crucial factor in stiffening the resolve of many ethnic minorities in the USSR in taking on their more powerful overlords was the emergence among them of the umbrella organizations called Popular Fronts.[87] These embraced a wide range of often disparate and dispersed informal groups, and frequently small incipient parties with some autonomist or nationalist aspiration in their programmes – groupings that gained strength through linking up with other like-minded groups around their native regions. Their purpose was to produce a concentration of effort around the one cause that united them, carrying the process of greater political separation through to its successful conclusion. Although some seemed to expect that, out of such an umbrella-like structure, a harmonious coalition government could then be formed to carry the new state through its early years, it seemed to others just as likely that, once its initial goal of change had been achieved, it would fragment, in the manner of Solidarnosc in Poland, and there would be a return to the pre-independence divisive politics.

While the three Baltic republics led the way in this type of development in the course of 1988, other Union republics were quick to follow. Autonomous republics tended to be a little way behind in this process. However, in the case of South Ossetia, where the number of informal groups reflected the small population, just such a Front was founded in January 1989 – Ademon Nykhas (or Popular Shrine),[88] under the chairmanship of Alan Chochiev.[89] The leadership, including people such as Zara Abayeva and Kshar Djigkaev, as well as their supporters, feared an independent Georgia as much as, if not more than, a communist USSR, in terms of upholding their rights. Although the supposedly "internationalist" Moscow centre seemed increasingly less dependable for ensuring their very survival, there was still a strong residual feeling that it was better than the only obvious alternative. Even the Ossetian communists felt able to co-operate with Ademon

---

87. See P. Goble, "Ethnic politics in the USSR", *Problems of Communism* **38**, (July/August 1989), 9–10.
88. See E. Fuller, "The South Ossetian campaign for unification", *Report on the USSR* **49** (1989), 17–20; and Aves, "Opposition political organizations in Georgia", op. cit., 27.
89. See above.

Nykhas, which, in its early days, pledged to act in accord with the Soviet constitution and offered continued fealty to the CPSU.[90] Once on its feet, Ademon Nykhas carried out a good deal of protective and promotional campaigning on behalf of the South Ossetian, and general Ossetian, causes through appeals to the USSR Council of Ministers, the USSR Supreme Soviet, the CPSU Central Committee and the Georgian Supreme Soviet.[91] In this way, it sought central, or Russian, protection from the Georgians, and promoted the idea of transfer of the South Ossetian Oblast to the Russian republic. It was then not only in practically at the beginning of the present era of conflict, but it helped sustain Ossetian solidarity on the various issues involved once conflict had in fact occurred. In its turn, it caused, among Georgians in the Oblast, the feeling that they too were to become second-class citizens if the Ossetians had their way – the more so as the clashes grew more bitter. Indeed, by February 1990, many Georgians there had fled into Georgia, camping out at public buildings in Tbilisi, and calling for enforcement of their rights and an annulment of Ossetia's already modest separate status as an autonomous Oblast.[92]

External manipulation of the issue

There is little doubt now that although there were entirely indigenous factors that set South Ossetian Ossetians and South Ossetian Georgians at one another's throats, the issue owed something in its origins to external involvement, and even more in its persistence. These "external" forces were primarily Georgia, Russia and the USSR. In the case of two of them, of course, they were only external in a limited way. South Ossetia was technically part of Georgia at the start of the present dispute, but the ethnic Ossetians no longer wished it to be. Both were also part of the USSR, but that political organization disappeared during the dispute. Only Russia was technically an outside party and even then it had an Ossetian population sub-unit of its own. Nevertheless, in this context we shall consider the role of Georgia and of Russia in both the *origins* and *continued development* of the present dispute.

So far this chapter has examined, under the question of overlordship, some of the attitudes and motivations of all three external parties that originally formed the heart of the problem, and which shaped the institutional framework in the 1920s and 1930s. What were the external influences at work then?

---

90. See the Front's charter in *Sovetskaya Ossetiya*, 23 August 1990.
91. See E. Fuller, "Georgian Parliament votes to abolish Ossetian autonomy", Radio Liberty research report, RL512/90, 11 December 1990, in *Report on the USSR*, 21 December 1990; and E. Fuller, "The South Ossetian campaign for unification", in *Report on the USSR* 49 (1989), 17–20.
92. *The Independent*, 7 February 1990.

Soviet (including North Ossetian) and Russian Bolsheviks played a major part in trying to stir up revolutionary activity among the inhabitants of northern parts of the Georgian Republic, including the peasants of South Ossetia.[93] Indeed, in the spring of 1920 a South Ossetian Revolutionary Committee was formed by the Caucasian Bureau of the All Russian Communist Party, with the purpose of heading an armed rebellion against the new Georgian Menshevik regime in Tbilisi. To this end, a Russian-backed force crossed the border into Georgia to engage the Georgian Army and People's Guard.[94] As mentioned above, the Georgians not only defeated this force but retaliated with vigour against the Ossetian villages in the areas of support for the rebellion.[95]

The very creation of South Ossetia in 1922, after the successful Bolshevik intervention in Georgia, can be interpreted variously as having been designed by the Soviet and Russian Bolsheviks as a reward to the Ossetians for their support of the Bolshevik cause against the Georgian Mensheviks, as an attempt to protect the Ossetians from the Georgians, or as an attempt to divide and rule more effectively over two parties now set at loggerheads.

For its part, the briefly independent Georgian regime of 1918–21 was more intent on its own national consolidation to be overly concerned with making many concessions to the Ossetians or to draw fine distinctions between fellow-Christian South Ossetians and Bolshevik North Ossetians. It turned quite ruthlessly upon what was perceived as an expendable fifth column.

In the case of the present hostilities, there are reflections of these earlier interventions and involvement by all three external parties – the USSR, Russia and Georgia – but, as in the past, the waters are muddied. There are problems, first of separation of perceptions and assertions from reality and evidence, and a secondary problem lies in separating wilful central governmental involvement from collusion carried out ad hoc at local level. Let us turn then to the accusations and some of the available evidence, both central and local, in each case.

USSR *involvement*

From the Georgian side, the accusing finger was quickly pointed not so much at the small Ossetian population in the South Ossetian Republic as the real source of the conflict as at the government of the USSR and President Gorbachev. In general they perceived the Soviet centre as continuing to pursue its increasingly abstract notion of a unified Soviet people and an inherently united proletariat working towards a common goal. This was a

---

93. Pipes 1964, 218.
94. Lang 1962, 228–9.
95. Ibid.

friendship among the peoples that was being imposed at a time when their interests most definitely were not in common.[96]

More specifically, the Georgian leadership went on to make a wide range of accusations about Soviet governmental involvement and collusion with the Ossetians. Thus, at the level of general intervention, Gamsakhurdia declared, in January 1991, that the Ossetian nationalists "are agents of Gorbachev, who is applying pressure on us through this war".[97] The following month he claimed that, in a telephone call, Gorbachev threatened to detach South Ossetia from Georgia, unless the latter signed the new Union Treaty the centre was proposing, a change later rejected by a Gorbachev spokesman, who denied knowledge of such a call.[98] Later that same month, Gamsakhurdia claimed that Gorbachev was "drafting a decree to take over Ossetia".[99] Then again, in replying to a telegram from Gorbachev, the Georgian President declared in March 1991, "Gorbachev is the main reason for the bloodshed. It is the Kremlin's war against Georgia because we are fighting for independence".[100] In Georgian eyes, then, the Ossetians had forfeited the right to moral support and sympathy by willingly allowing themselves to be used as a pawn by the Soviet government.

At the more local level of collaboration on the ground between the Ossetians and Soviet federal forces stationed there, Georgian accusations flew equally thick and fast. Gamsakhurdia again was prominent in making these charges, as when, in December 1990, he accused the Soviet Ministry of Internal Affairs investigators and troops of siding with the Ossetian separatists, and sent a statement to that effect to the USSR Congress of Deputies in Moscow.[101] In an interview in March 1991 he went further, declaring that "[t]he Soviet army is fighting against us, together with the Ossetian extremists. They give the Ossetians new technology, rockets, weapons".[102] Further still, in a telegram to Gorbachev in April 1991, Gamsakhurdia threatened a general strike unless Soviet Army and Interior Ministry troops were withdrawn from South Ossetia, where, he claimed, they were abetting the Ossetians in attacks on Georgian villages.[103]

How far were such accusations mere hyperbole and rhetoric in the heat of war from a leader worn down by a lifetime of struggle with Moscow, so near to his goal, and yet moving steadily towards becoming seen as a

---

96. A clear and concise exposition of these views is given by Giorgi Gachechiladze in *The Georgian Messenger*, Tbilisi, 11 October to 8 November 1990, 3.
97. Cited in *The Independent*, 25 January 1991, and repeated in an interview with *El Mundo*, Madrid, 18 February 1991.
98. *Reuters*, 27 February 1991.
99. *Financial Times*, 27 February 1991.
100. *Daily Telegraph*, 1 April 1991.
101. *TASS*, 19 December 1990.
102. *Washington Post* interview in the *International Herald Tribune*, 22 March 1991.
103. Radio Liberty *Report on the USSR*, 19 April 1991, 23.

somewhat dangerous fanatic by his own side? In the early stages of the conflict, Russia's direct interference was far from proven, as was admitted by a Georgian observer in the newspaper Zaria Vostoka.[104] Gamsakhurdia's initial claims that the KGB had supplied arms to the South Ossetian Popular Front was also denied by the KGB.[105] The coincidence of the upsurges of minority activism in several Union republics that were seeking independence could well have been that in several instances. Indeed, the conflict in another part of Georgia, in Abkhazia, had been in existence for some time and did not especially need Soviet central involvement to stimulate it.[106] What motives then could have brought about Soviet federal involvement? Several possibilities were suggested by the Georgians, varying in form with the passage of time.

In the first instance, in Georgia's eyes, the Soviet Government would have been prompted to intervene on the side of the Ossetians by a desire to slow down and undermine Georgia's drive towards independence by weakening her internal cohesion, her "national wholeness" as it became known in the republic. As one Georgian commentator declared "[i]t should be understood by every ethnic group living in Georgia that the fate of each of them depends upon the fate of the Georgian nation. Only the revival of an independent Georgia can guarantee their future. Any ethnic group continuing to let itself be used as a blind weapon is signing its own suicide".[107]

Parallels could indeed be drawn with the sudden emergence of previously little known ethnic demands in several other republics in the process of seeking independence, as with the Poles in Lithuania or the Gagauz in Moldova. Were some of these at least partly the work of Soviet security agencies? This was certainly a pattern found with other retreating colonial powers: dividing the nationalists, backing minorities, and then abandoning them to their fate. Georgians were also quick to note the initial absence of any comparable separatism in North Ossetia, within the Russian republic. This suggested motive was to be updated later with the suggestion that Soviet behaviour in keeping the conflict going, once it had started, was intended to focus attention on Georgia's intransigence and inflexibility, and thereby continue to discredit its secession drive before the eyes of the outside world, which would eventually be asked to recognize it.[108]

A second, and more developed, version of this interpretation of the Soviet Union's possible motives in interfering, however furtively, saw the

---

104. *Zaria Vostoka*, 6 September 1989.

105. *Sovetskaya Latviya*, Riga, 7 February 1990.

106. See for example, D. Slider, "Crisis and response in Soviet nationality policy – the case of Abkhazia", *Central Asian Survey* **4** (1985), 51–68.

107. *The Georgian Messenger*, 11 October to 8 November, 1990.

108. Jonathan Steele in *The Guardian*, 13 February 1991.

centre as seeking to create a sufficiently unstable situation to provide a pretext for intervening directly, perhaps even to maintain a foothold of power and influence south of the main Caucasus chain; even if most of Georgia did succeed in breaking away from the USSR, South Ossetia would remain as a wedge in the heart of Georgia.[109] Some 120,000 Soviet-control-led troops were in fact already in Georgia in 1990,[110] and South Ossetia would have been a useful point to which to withdraw them. Similarly, the Georgian military highway ran through the mountain heart of Ossetia from Russia, while the new road tunnel linking the two Ossetias made matters even more convenient. Awareness of this may well have provoked the explosion that blocked the road to the tunnel in February 1991.[111] This view was particularly prevalent following Gorbachev's order of 7 January 1991 for the removal of Georgian forces from South Ossetia, and Moscow's decision of 11 February to send tanks to the area.[112] The Georgian Supreme Soviet declared such a call "outright interference in the internal affairs of a sovereign republic"[113] and stated that enforcement of the order would be regarded as an act of war.[114] Gamsakhurdia proclaimed that Moscow was "consciously trying to create anarchy so it can restore order".[115]

Other possible Soviet motives for intervention were to be suggested later, when the conflict was fully under way. In particular there was a widespread belief, especially in Georgia again, that continued interference by the centre was designed to pressure Georgia into signing Gorbachev's new Union treaty by displaying the kind of chaos that would follow should Georgia actually gain some form of independence. Not only would there be an Abkhazian problem, but also an Ossetian problem, and possi-bly an Adzharian problem. In the same way the pressure could have been intended to get Georgia to participate in the 1991, referendum on main-taining the Union. Indeed, on 28 February 1991 the Georgian Supreme Soviet accused the USSR of fomenting trouble for precisely this end.[116]

A final possible motive for Soviet involvement was said to be to allow Gorbachev a pretext to assert and impose his recently acquired presiden-tial powers. A display of his powers was thought by many at this stage to be necessary if he was to retain control over what already appeared to be a fragmenting federal edifice.

In fact, of course, neither the display of presidential power nor the direct intervention possibilities ever came to fruition, and were thus con-

---

109. *Financial Times*, 19 February 1991.
110. *The Independent*, 23 January 1991.
111. *The Guardian*, 13 February 1991.
112. *Radio Moscow*, 11 January 1991, and *The Times*, 11 January 1991.
113. *Daily Telegraph*, 10 January 1991.
114. *International Herald Tribune* and *Financial Times*, 10 January 1991.
115. Interview cited in the *Financial Times*, 23 January 1991.
116. *Report on the USSR*, 8 March 1991, 31.

fined to being hypothetical motives. Perhaps Ossetia was just too minor a problem among the many confronting Gorbachev. Indeed, Gamsakhurdia's own extremism as President of Georgia became such that opponents such as Giorgi Chanturia claimed that it was Gamsakhurdia who was a tool of Moscow aimed at discrediting the Georgian independence movement.[117]

What then of the evidence of Soviet interference at a general open, political level, and at the more furtive level of collusion with the Ossetians locally? Much probably remains a closed book for the moment, but some open indicators are available of both types of action.

At the level of political manipulation, the actions were often overt, and, in some instances, legitimate acts of interference within the framework of the Soviet constitution. Among these we may include Gorbachev's decree of 7 January 1991[118] ordering the Georgian Ministry of the Interior and KGB units out of South Ossetia (which the Georgian parliament actually rejected on the grounds of unwarranted interference);[119] the USSR Supreme Soviet's February 1991 threat to impose a state of emergency on South Ossetia without consent if the Georgian Government did not extend their own state of emergency;[120] and the USSR Council of the Federation's June 1991 condemnation of Georgia's alleged driving out of Ossetians as being not only against the USSR's constitution but also against international human rights agreements.[121] Other instances of pressure on Georgia and consequent support for the Ossetians coming from the USSR would have to include a letter Gamsakhurdia claimed to have received on 10 January 1991 from the Soviet Chief of Staff, General Mikhail Moiseyev, declaring that the Soviet army could not remain passive in the face of anti-army activities and threats to soldiers in Georgia;[122] the help that Soviet Interior Ministry forces gave to enable the South Ossetians to vote in Gorbachev's referendum on preserving the USSR;[123] and perhaps the tacit support given to the formation of a national salvation committee in South Ossetia, about which the Georgian Minister of the Interior complained in a letter in April 1991 to the Soviet Minister of the Interior, on the grounds that it subverted Georgian authority.[124]

Interestingly, the Ossetians were reported as being disappointed by the Soviet Union's failure to intervene directly and forcefully to enforce Gorbachev's above-mentioned decree of 7 January 1991.[125] Nevertheless, some

117. See *International Herald Tribune*, 22 March 1991.
118. *TASS*, 7 January 1991.
119. *Reuters*, 9 January 1991.
120. *TASS* and *Reuters*, 20 February 1991.
121. *TASS*, 4 June 1991.
122. *The Times*, 11 January 1991.
123. The *Independent on Sunday*, London, 14 April 1991.
124. *Radio Tbilisi*, 23 April 1991.

confirmation that Moscow had indeed exploited the situation (essentially to get at Georgia) up to the August 1991 coup did indeed come from the South Ossetian spokesman Stanislav Kochiev in September 1991.[126]

Soviet collusion with the Ossetians on the ground at local level did also seem to be the case in some instances, although how far it was a consistent policy and how far the action of local officials representing the centre there is not always clear. Although the Georgians made many sweeping changes in this connection.[127] Some were more specific, and were occasionally backed by outside observers. Four aspects of collusion do seem to have had substance on some occasions. In the first instance there was the matter of Soviet Interior Ministry troops standing by while Georgians were forced to flee from their homes in what was still part of their own republic,[128] and then subsequently refusing to allow some of them to return to homes in South Ossetia.[129] Secondly, although Gorbachev had called on Georgian forces to leave the area in January 1991, he took no immediate reciprocal steps to disarm the Ossetian volunteer forces, then said to be numbering 50,000.[130] In Georgian eyes this indicated connivance. Indeed, the third aspect of the collusion case entails the supply of weapons to the Ossetians. The Georgians have claimed that these weapons were variously stolen by the Ossetians, hired out to them, or even sold by Soviet Army or Interior Ministry troops.[131] And substantial and heavy weapons there were in action, for all to see, in the hands of the Ossetian volunteers – mortars, anti-tank rockets, landmines and automatic rifles.[132] They certainly did not

---

125. *The Independent*, 25 January 1991. The remaining 6000 Soviet/CIS MVD troops were eventually withdrawn on 26 April 1992 – *Le Monde*, 30 April 1992.

126. *Financial Times*, 13 September 1991.

127. For example, Gamsakhurdia accused Gorbachev directly of "supporting terrorism in South Ossetia". *The Times*, 11 January 1991; the Georgian parliament, in a letter to the commander of the Soviet Transcaucasian Military District, charged the troops with actually encouraging the violence. Radio Tbilisi, 15 February 1991.

128. Ibid.

129. The *Independent on Sunday*, 14 April 1991.

130. *The Times*, 11 January 1991. Indeed Soviet MVD officials were reported as drinking with Ossetian Front leaders in February 1991. *Financial Times*, 19 February 1991.

131. Gamsakhurdia claimed to have proof that the weapons came from Red Army bases in an interview cited in the *Financial Times*, 23 January 1991, a charge he repeated in an interview with AP, 6 February 1991. Georgian Interior Minister, Dilari Khabuliani, similarly claimed there was evidence to this effect – *The Independent*, 25 January 1991. Nikolai Shubitidze an official in Kareli, claimed that the cost of hiring an automatic rifle was 300 roubles – the *Independent on Sunday*, 14 April 1991. See also the interview with the commander of the remaining 300 CIS army troops in Tskhinvali in May 1992, in Le Monde 30 May 1992.

132. *The Independent*, 30 January 1991; and *International Herald Tribune*, 22 March 1991. That the weapons did not come from Soviet sources was somewhat unconvincingly claimed by the chairman of the South Ossetian Soviet, Thorez Kulumbekov – *Financial Times*, 25 January 1991.

grow on trees locally. Finally, the collusion amounted to Soviet troop-assisted breaking of the blockade imposed by the Georgians to bring the Ossetians to heel.[133] To these instances could probably be added the involvement of Spetsnaz troops of Soviet Military Intelligence (GRU) based at Lagadek in Georgia, although this can only be inferred from their recent emergence in Azerbaijan's conflicts.[134]

As underdogs, the Ossetians could well have gained some sympathy from non-Georgian Soviet forces locally deployed: but as part of a matter of obvious political concern to the centre, the Ossetians were just as likely to have been seen as a means to an end by the Soviet Government in its clash with Georgia.

Russian Republic involvement

At the outset of the conflict it is not entirely easy to separate USSR involvement from that of the Russian Republic. The two were often seen as synonymous in the Georgian Republic by virtue of the enormous size of the Russian Republic, the overlap of institutions between the USSR and the RSFSR, and the longstanding pre-eminence of Russians in bodies such as the decision-making Party Politburo. However, with the Russian Republic's declaration of sovereignty on 11 June 1990, Yeltsin's break with the Communist Party in July 1990, and his election to power as President of the Russian Republic in June 1991, the situation shifted significantly. Yeltsin and the Russian Government had in effect made the first steps in taking on the Soviet Government, and thus cleared the way for other republics to do likewise. The Georgian nationalist leadership had, it seemed, every reason to look upon him, and thus the Russian Republic, as something of an ally with a shared anti-communist, anti-federalist cause. Indeed, President Gamsakhurdia of Georgia and Yeltsin, as chairman of the Russian parliament, met at Kazbegi in Georgia on 23 March 1991, where they agreed a joint policing force to disarm ethnic militias, called for the withdrawal of USSR Ministry of Defence units, agreed on compensation for and return of refugees, and sought a restoration of legal authority.[135]

On the contrary, the South Ossetians had, at first glance, rather less reason for optimism on the question of whether Yeltsin's Russia would take up their cause in the place of the USSR. Apart from some friendly noises about Russia's own federal form, many of Russia's reformers seemed increasingly nationalist in orientation – much like those in Georgia – concerned with their own affairs. Despite their pro-Bolshevik past, modern Ossetians had been attracted less by the USSR's communism than by the

---

133. *Radio Tbilisi*, 8 April 1991, and *Izvestiya*, Moscow, 9 April 1991.
134. See *The Guardian*, 20 May 1992.
135. *Interfax*, 24 March 1991; *The Times*, 25 March 1991; *Le Monde*, 26 March 1991; and *Sakartvelos Respublika*, 26 March 1991.

protection the USSR could offer against the Georgians. Would an inward-looking Russia be interested any more?

What motives would the Russian Republic in fact have for intervening in the South Ossetian/Georgian conflict under this new order? Obviously the Russian Republic had some interest in the matter from the outset, in so far as the majority of the Ossetian population actually lived there and the North Ossetian Autonomous Republic was a constituent part of it. Sooner or later, there would doubtless be same spillover of the problem. Indeed, it came very quickly in the shape of South Ossetian calls for their linkage with North Ossetia as part of the Russian Republic, and in the form of South Ossetian refugees fleeing into North Ossetia.

Beyond that, Russia's motives inevitably underwent some change during the present crisis: first, with the coming to power of many reformers and democrats in the elections of March 1989 and Yeltsin's own election as Russian president; secondly, with the collapse of the Communist Party regime in August–September 1991; and thirdly, with the collapse of the USSR in December 1991.

In fact some confusing messages emerge about the independent Russia's position under Yeltsin. After the Moscow coup and its reversal in August 1991, Gamsakhurdia claimed that Yeltsin was actually in agreement with him on the handling of the Ossetian issue.[136] Similarly, by his handling of the Chechen problem in October-November 1991, Yeltsin also gave out signals that he was not inclined to allow any effective further fragmentation of his own republic by the actions of autonomous units within it.[137] Nevertheless, an Ossetian delegation returned from a meeting with Yeltsin in September 1991 apparently reassured by what they too had been told.[138]

The positions of Yeltsin and Russia were undoubtedly made easier with Gamsakhurdia's growing heavy-handedness and unpopularity at home, but Russian intervention was increasingly problematical as Georgia's independence took on an ever-more secure form. It was not only no longer a USSR matter, it was not even a Commonwealth of Independent States (CIS) issue, as Georgia chose not to participate in the latter. Remaining CIS forces in the area had to be used with discretion until their withdrawal was brought about.

As long as the South Ossetians seek unification with their brothers in the north, Russia will retain an active interest in the issue. Should the Ossetians not get her support, and be tempted to seek an independent state straddling the mountains, that interest may become a matter of much greater concern.

---

136. *Le Monde*, 18 September 1991.
137. See A. Sheehy, *Power struggle in Checheno–Ingushetia*, Radio Liberty research paper, RL398/91, 8 November 1991. In *Report on the USSR* 3 (15 November 1991), 20–26.
138. *Le Monde*, 18 September 1991.

What evidence then has there been of Russian interference or collusion in the conflict to date? At the level of interference, some of its involvement has of course come through the governing agencies in North Ossetia, such as the latter's protest of December 1990 against the revocation of South Ossetian autonomy by the Georgians (who rejected this as crude interference in their internal affairs), and the cutting of gas supplies to Georgia in May 1992.[139]

It was indeed Yeltsin's above-mentioned meeting with Gamsakhurdia on 23 March 1991 that provided one of the first indications that the chairman of the Russian Parliament was indeed seeking to take over the handling of the issue from the still-reigning Soviet president. Thereafter, several Russian interventions were apparent, the more so as Yeltsin and Gamsakhurdia grew apart. At the end of March 1991, soon after the meeting of the two leaders, the Russian Republic's Congress of Deputies called upon Georgia to restore to South Ossetia the status of an Autonomous Oblast,[140] which had been abolished by the Georgian parliament on 11 December 1990.[141] The Russian parliament, at the same time, called for a lifting of the Georgian blockade of Tskhinvali and for the Georgians to allow the return of refugees (as well as seeking urgent action from Gorbachev).[142] Notably, on 2 April 1991, the Georgian parliament rejected all this as gross interference, and went on to claim that the Russian Republic now shared responsibility for any Soviet action taken against Georgia.[143] Later in that same year, after the revolution, it was announced that the Russian Supreme Soviet might impose economic sanctions on Georgia as a whole, if that republic's government did not attempt to end the conflict.[144] After this threat came a vote, on 27 October, to allow President Yeltsin to introduce them as a part of the campaign to get South Ossetia transferred to the RSFSR.[145] A further threat of sanctions was made on 6 November 1991.[146]

Such then has been the kind of action Russia has applied quite openly. At more local level, Russian collusion with the Ossetians has included such actions as an appeal from army officers' wives and Russian mothers in Tskhinvali, to the United Nations and Western governments, for help in halting what they alleged was the genocidal policy of the Georgian Gov-

139. *Zaria Vostoka*, 27 December 1990, and *Le Monde*, 27 May 1992.

140. *TASS*, 31 March 1991.

141. *TASS*, *Reuters* and *Agence France Presse* (AFP), 11 December 1990. See also E. Fuller, *Georgian Parliament votes to abolish Ossetian autonomy*, Radio Liberty research paper, RL512/90, 11 December 1990, in *Report on the USSR*, 21 December 1990, 8–9.

142. *TASS*, 31 March 1991.

143. *TASS*, 2 April 1991.

144. *Interfax*, 22 October 1991.

145. *TASS*, 27 October 1991.

146. *Rossiskaya Gazeta*, Moscow, 7 November 1991. A Russian parliamentary delegation visited the area on 26 May 1992 – *Le Monde*, 30 May 1992.

ernment.[147] How far collusion by the armed forces has changed since the collapse of the USSR is less clear, but Georgian suspicions that it continues receives some backing from the actions of the 14th Army in helping the Trans-Dniestrians against Moldova, even after its transfer to Russian juris-diction in April 1992.[148]

Georgian involvement

The accusing fingers of the South Ossetians, the Soviet Government and, more recently, the Russian parliament have all been pointing at Georgia as both the initiator of the present wave of disorder in South Ossetia, and as the force that has chiefly sustained the violence that has continued now into its fourth year. The Ossetians particularly have seen their actions as ones of self-defence against an aggressively rampant Georgian national-ism, which prevails even beyond the departure of its leader Gamsakhur-dia. This view of Georgia as an external threat was made apparent in several notable statements by Ossetian leaders. The deputy chairman of Tskhinvali soviet declared, in February 1991, "we are the only nation which wants Gorbachev to declare emergency rule".[149] Another Ossetian leader, Gerasim Khugaev, declared the following month that "[w]e are much more worried by Georgian imperialism than Russian imperialism. It is closer to us and we feel it all the time. The Georgians are conducting a chauvinist–nationalist policy against us".[150] Optimists declared that "[a]s long as Gamsakhurdia remains in power, nothing will change for us".[151] Ossetian realists now know that the problem is more than one of changing the Georgian captain.

And yet, of course, Georgian involvement in the issue in many respects is not that of an outside force. South Ossetia, at the outset of the present troubles, was squarely, if not necessarily fairly, situated within the bound-aries of the Georgian Republic. Indeed, with the Georgian parliament's abolition of the Ossetians' status as an autonomous oblast in December 1990, and incorporation of its capital into Gori raion (district) in Georgia in April 1991,[152] the area was theoretically brought even more fully into the Georgian fold. However, against that were the countervailing pressures from the Ossetians to take themselves outside Georgian jurisdiction alto-gether. Already by late August 1989, Ademon Nykhas had sent an appeal to Moscow calling for the unification of North and South Ossetia;[153] in

---

147. *TASS*, 24 October 1991.
148. See for example, *International Herald Tribune*, 21 May 1992.
149. Cited in *The Guardian*, 13 February 1991.
150. *Washington Post* report in *International Herald Tribune*, 22 March 1991.
151. A South Ossetian cited by *Le Monde*, 18 September 1991.
152. *TASS*, 11 December 1990 and *Radio Tbilisi*, 27 April 1991.
153. See E. Fuller, *South Ossetia – analysis of a permanent crisis*, Radio Liberty research report RL82/91, 12 February 1991, in *Report on the USSR*, 15 February 1991, 21.

November some members of the oblast soviet and of the Popular Front had called on the Georgian parliament to upgrade their status to that of an autonomous republic;[154] and on 14 August 1990 the oblast soviet drafted a resolution on sovereignty, calling for local control over land and natural resources, as well as over foreign and domestic policies.[155] Matters were taken further with an actual declaration of independence by Ossetian members of the oblast soviet on 20 September 1990, seeking recognition of a South Ossetian Soviet Democratic Republic as part of the Russian federation,[156] and a vote by the Supreme Soviet of this would be new republic, on 11 December 1990, to subordinate itself directly to the USSR.[157] Undaunted by lack of success in gaining support, the Ossetians voted overwhelmingly in favour of Gorbachev's referendum of 17 March 1991 on the issue of continuation of a union of republics[158] – a referendum boycotted by the rest of Georgia, which held its own referendum on independence on 31 March 1991. They took a step back in May 1991 by voting to abolish their new republic, restoring it to an autonomous oblast, but now under RSFSR jurisdiction.[159] Some North Ossetians by this stage were also campaigning for a reversal of the division of the Ossetian territories in the 1920s.[160] A second attempt was made on 28 November 1991 by the South Ossetian Oblast soviet to declare the area a republic and part of the RSFSR,[161] and, on declaring its independence on 22 December, an attempt was made, in the new circumstances of a collapsing USSR, to gain recognition from all the former Union republics.[162] A referendum among most South Ossetians, on 19 January 1992, produced a result of some 97 per cent in favour of unification with the RSFSR,[163] while on 8 February the oblast soviet went ahead to impose its own state of emergency and approve a decree on South Ossetian citizenship.[164] On 11 February it even sought to lay down the conditions for peace talks with Georgia.[165]

---

154. *Samizdat Press Agency*, cited in *The Times*, 27 November 1989. See also E. Fuller, "The South Ossetian campaign for unification", in *Report on the USSR* 49 (1989), 17–20.

155. *Sabchota Oseti*, 14 August 1990.

156. *TASS*, 20 September 1990; and *Zaria Vostoka*, 22 September 1990. This was rejected by Moscow – see *Zaria Vostoka*, 25 October 1990.

157. *Izvestiya*, 15 December 1990. Moscow rejected this proposal as well – ibid.

158. *Reuters*, 17 March 1991. See E. Fuller, *The All-Union referendum in the Transcaucasus*, Radio Liberty research paper, RL136/91, 21 March 1991. In *Report on the USSR*, 29 March 1991, 3–5.

159. *TASS* and *Radio Tbilisi*, 8 May 1991.

160. *TASS* and *Radio Moscow*, 3 October 1991. Nevertheless, the North Ossetian Supreme Soviet dismissed the appeal of its southern counterpart that it raise the question of unification within the RSFSR with the latter's Supreme Soviet – *TASS*, 22 October 1991.

161. *Radio Moscow* and *TASS*, 28 November 1991.

162. *TASS*, 23 December 1991.

163. *TASS*, 19 and 21 January 1992, and *Express Chronicle*, Moscow, 29 January 1992, 1.

164. *RFE/RL research report*, 21 February 1992, 70.

The impact of all this was that, for the South Ossetians, the Georgians had indeed become an outside force, even if the Georgians themselves were not prepared to accept it. Indeed, Georgians naturally rejected or revoked practically all these measures almost immediately they were taken.[166] The Georgian motivation for its stark and rapid responses lay in the firm conviction that they had a longstanding claim to the territory they called Kartli. Ossetians were but tolerated newcomers who had to play the game by a set of rules already devised by the club. They could not simply come in as a small minority and change those rules, particularly when the club was in difficulties on a broader financial and administrative front. The only factor that really divided the new nationalist leaders of Georgia was whether to go actively to the defence of Georgians living in the oblast or whether to stand back a little from this distraction from the main event.[167]

Evidence of Georgian intervention and collusion with Georgians in Ossetia came in ways other than formal rejection of South Ossetian declarations of intent. Among the many instances of intervention, however legitimate, were the removal of Communist Party officials in the oblast for having allowed the situation to get out of control,[168] the wholesale abolition of its political autonomy in December 1990,[169] the April 1991 incorporation of raions formerly in Ossetia into neighbouring parts of Georgia,[170] the attempts to maintain Georgian MVD policing of the area in December 1990 to January 1991 – understandable as they were in the light of killings of Georgian officials[171] but which produced a spate of attacks on Ossetian property such as the ransacking of the national theatre, damage to a statue of the national poet and destruction of war memorials,[172] the January 1991 cutting of electricity and subsequently gas supplies to the area,[173] and possibly the spread of rumours, in December 1991, of an imminent attack on Ossetian-held positions.[174]

---

165. *ITAR/TASS*, 11 February 1992.
166. For example, in September 1990, the Georgian Supreme Soviet's Presidium proclaimed South Ossetia's declaration of independence a violation of the Georgian constitution, and thus unlawful and invalid – *Zaria Vostoka*, 22 September 1990. Similarly, in December 1990, the Georgians rejected South Ossetia's attempt to subordinate itself directly to the USSR – *Izvestiya*, 15 December 1990. The second attempt at declaring a republic within the RSFSR was also rejected by the Georgian parliament in December 1991 – TASS, 6 December 1991.
167. Aves, "Paths to national independence", op. cit., 33.
168. For example, the removal of Oblast First Secretary in November 1989 – see E. Fuller, "The South Ossetian campaign for unification", in *Report on the USSR* 49 (1989), 17–20.
169. *TASS*, 11 December 1990.
170. *Radio Tbilisi*, 27 April 1990.
171. *The Times*, 14 December 1990.
172. *International Herald Tribune*, 22 March 1991.
173. Allegedly done at the behest of Georgian power workers – *Reuters*, 4 January 1991 and *TASS*, 7 June and 12 December 1991.

As far as collusion with the Georgian paramilitaries at local level in Ossetia is concerned, the evidence of direct Georgian governmental involvement is limited, although abundant in the case of non-governmental actors from Georgia. It was nationalists from the Society of St Ilya the Righteous, among others, who, after meetings in Tbilisi, led the mass and intimidatory march on Tskhinvali on 23 November 1989 to impress on the Ossetians the opposition of Georgians to the separation of South Ossetia from Georgia.[175] Set up in January 1990, the Merab Kostava Society had as a primary goal the provision of material aid to Georgians in areas where they were threatened by minorities, or discriminated against. Ossetia was perceived as just such an instance. The society declared itself prepared to use legal or illegal methods to this end.[176] Armed bands did in fact appear attached to some of these political groups, such as the Legionaries (Legionerebi) and the Society of the White George (Giorgis Sazogadoeba).[177] These, and even Georgian criminal gangs,[178] reputedly sent gunmen to support the Georgians living in and around Tskhinvali, where they took part in street fighting and blockades that, according to the Ossetians, even prevented humanitarian aid from getting through to the capital.[179] On 11 April 1991, the Soviet news agency TASS claimed that some 15,000 armed Georgians were surrounding the capital.

Overall then, on the question of external influences on the conflict, the centre in Moscow, particularly in its manifestation as the USSR, almost certainly used minority against minority in order to sustain the status quo. South Ossetians have nevertheless looked to the centre for support, and been given some, but not without strings attached. The Georgians, closer to the problem than Moscow, were naturally more intimately and extensively involved, although often heavy-handedly as a consequence of the natural and understandable intensity of their feelings on the matter.

Solutions and prospects

Clearly, this issue has brought together both longstanding ethnic grievances and newly arisen complications; it has muddied the distinction between oppressors and oppressed; and it has incorporated highly subjective matters of rights and wrongs.

174. Such rumours led to the creation of a Committee for Self-Defence and the mobilization of Ossetian men and women aged 18 to 60 – *TASS*, 23 December 1991.
175. Samizdat Press Agency, in *The Times*, 18 December 1989.
176. See E. Fuller, "Round table coalition wins resounding victory in Georgian Supreme Soviet elections". In *Report on the USSR*, 16 November 1990, 13.
177. Aves, "Paths to national independence", op. cit., 32–3.
178. *Financial Times*, 19 February 1991.
179. See for example, *TASS*, 12 December 1991.

As in most such crises, the participants have a tendency to resort to hyperbole, which is not always helpful. For example, the Ossetian Front spokesman Kshar Djigkaev was quoted in January 1991 as saying "Georgians want to separate from the Union and we do not. For us it is a matter of national survival".[180] Similarly, Zara Abayeva, of the Ossetian Popular Front, declared that "First they destroyed our autonomy, then they will destroy us as a people".[181] Such statements overlooked the existence of North Ossetia. The Georgians, and not only Gamsakhurdia and his supporters, have been no less prone to divorce matters from reality.

The result has been the creation, at first sight, of yet another seemingly intractable ethnic problem, amenable only to short-term solutions designed to contain it by bringing about a temporary calm, yet essentially putting off the day of reckoning. So what then of the future of the issue? Does an acceptable level of violence simply have to be tolerated and managed, or is there what Gamsakhurdia, apparently inadvertently, called a final solution to the Ossetian problem? And if the latter is the case, what possible solutions are there, and what are the chances of their being implemented? Several possibilities do indeed suggest themselves if the matter is actually to be resolved rather than merely contained indefinitely at the present quite unacceptably high level of mortality, now into several hundred dead.[182] Three main possibilities will be considered here:

- internationally guaranteed Ossetian autonomy within Georgia
- concentration of the Ossetians in North Ossetia
- creation of an independent Ossetian state.

Solution 1 – autonomy within Georgia

The first solution in essence requires a firming up on the status quo by creating conditions for some measure of political autonomy to be restored to that part of Ossetian-occupied territory within Georgia. National cultural

---

180. *The Independent*, 25 January 1991.

181. Cited in *Daily Telegraph*, 7 February 1991.

182. As in most such conflicts, casualty figures are difficult to come by and are of dubious accuracy given their propaganda value. Some idea of the general scale may well be found in the following. According to the chairman of the South Ossetian Soviet in early October 1991, since the previous January, 80 Ossetian villages had been burned, 214 Ossetians killed, 740 wounded, and 106 had disappeared. The Georgian deputy foreign minister claimed these figures were exaggerated, and the Georgians put their own casualties at 35 dead and 10,000 refugees – *International Herald Tribune*, 4 October 1991.

The Democratic Youth League of South Ossetia put Ossetian deaths over the period January 1991 to January 1992 at 380 killed, 150 of them actually outside South Ossetia itself. Nearly 60 were said to be missing (*The Express Chronicle*, 4(234), 29 January 1992.

AFP reported casualties in the area, from November 1989 to April 1992, at some 500 killed – *AFP*, 28 April 1992.

Particularly violent clashes in May 1992 could have added another 50–100 to the total killed. See *ITAR/TASS*, 21 May 1992.

autonomy as the Georgians have offered is no longer enough to guarantee Ossetian rights to exist distinctly from Georgia. Pursuit of outright independence for such small territory and population, although not impossible in the light of some of the oddities already represented in the United Nations, seems fairly pointless, given the existence of the larger Ossetian entity to the north. Indeed, the act of declaring it a republic for the first time was said by the chairman of the Ossetian Committee of People's Deputies to have been just a matter of "self-defence".[183] The independence option is similarly not acceptable to Georgians. Even Gamsakhurdia's chief opponent in 1990–1, Giorgi Chanturia, although a critic of the persecution of minorities[184] declared, in September 1991, that he too was against the re-establishment of political autonomy for South Ossetia,[185] a view shared by former Prime Minister Tengiz Sigua.[186] Regardless of the views of the leadership, and indeed the return to power of Shevardnadze, the Georgian militias have in any event shown no willingness to compromise on this issue in their actions in massacring would-be Ossetian refugees[187] in 1992. Indeed, they have shown little or no willingness to allow Ossetian refugees to return to the area. If this were to be adopted as a solution, the territory would probably have to be redefined or reduced in the light of Ossetian refugee flight and Georgian settlement in recent times. Since the spring of 1991, and despite the Ossetian flight north, the capital, Tskhinvali, has been firmly in Ossetian hands with most of the Georgians gone.[188] This restructuring of population could provide an opportunity for redrawing frontiers in some places. Any new autonomy for a redefined area such as this would however require more than a guarantee from the Georgian government for its security. The United Nations, weak as it was in the past, has shown signs of being able to develop some teeth in this area.

Solution 2 – concentration of Ossetians in North Ossetia

Idealism about the family of man has frequently had to be tempered by the reality that not all of the family wishes to live under the same roof. Europe alone has already witnessed massive movements and separations of peoples for this very reason. Variously whole populations have been pressed into consolidated territories (as in the case of the Germans from eastern Europe and the Sudetenland, or the Greeks of Turkey and the USSR, or the Turks in Bulgaria), divided into distinct parts of the same territory (as with the Greeks and Turks in Cyprus), or polled in referenda to decide their ter-

---

183. *The Independent*, 25 January 1991.
184. See for example, *International Herald Tribune*, 22 March 1991.
185. *Le Monde*, 18 September 1991.
186. Ibid., 20 September 1991.
187. *ITAR/TASS*, 21 May 1991; *The Times*, and the *Morning Star*, London, 21 May 1992; *International Herald Tribune*, 21 May 1992 and *The Independent*, 22 May 1992.
188. See for example, *Le Monde*, 18 September 1991.

ritorial identity. Nor has the practice been confined to Europe or even just to ethnic identity, as witnessed by the creation of India and Pakistan. It may amount to what Mik Magnusson, the chief UN spokesman in Croatia in May 1992, called "ethnic cleansing",[189] and thus be unpleasant to the liberal one-world conscience, but it has plenty of actual precedents and contemporary parallels. It has also proved to be as effective as most alternative measures in such situations.

In the present instance, many South Ossetians certainly believe that it is already a quite consciously applied Georgian policy to drive them out of Georgia, and have them concentrate in North Ossetia, where they have their epicentre in a longer established national homeland. For example, an Ossetian leader, Gerasim Khugaev, was quoted in March 1991 as saying "[t]hey [the Georgians] want to drive us out of here completely",[190] whereas Valentina Slanova, in a similar vein, declared in April 1991, "[t]hey [the Georgians] are driving us from our houses. Entire villages have been burned down".[191] A further report, in October 1991, had another Ossetian claiming that the only reason for the Georgians continued bombardment of Tskhinvali was to drive out the Ossetians.[192]

This viewpoint was also how other interested parties began to interpret the situation. In June 1991, the USSR Council of the Federation criticized the Georgians for driving the Ossetians from the oblast,[193] while the previously mentioned appeal from Soviet and Russian army wives and mothers of October 1991 sought outside help against what they called genocidal policies.[194]

Georgians too, by their words and actions, have given credence to the idea that driving out the Ossetians has indeed been their goal. It was an option seemingly favoured by Gamsakhurdia,[195] who saw the Ossetians as occupiers of Georgian territory. If not willing to play by Georgian rules, they should, in his words "return to their homelands".[196] This was a view he repeated in a February 1991 interview, where he declared that "in the end I think they will all be forced to leave Georgia. It is not my wish but I cannot control this process".[197] Later that same year, a Georgian police colonel was quoted as saying of the Ossetians "[w]hen there are shortages around the republic, why waste commodities on them?"[198]

---

189. *Financial Times*, 26 May 1992.
190. *Washington Post* report in *International Herald Tribune*, 22 March 1991.
191. *Reuters*, in *Daily Telegraph*, 10 April 1991.
192. *International Herald Tribune*, 4 October 1991.
193. TASS, 4 June 1991.
194. TASS, 24 October 1991.
195. See interview of 10 January 1991 in *The Times*, 11 January 1991.
196. Ibid.
197. Interview with Jonathan Steele in *The Guardian*, 14 February 1991.
198. *International Herald Tribune*, 4 October 1991.

Actions spoke as loudly as words, and the draft Georgian law on citizenship of the republic, published in June 1991, sounded some warnings with its provision that it was open to all who knew the Georgian language.[199] Many Ossetians effectively had only Russian as their second language. Gamsakhurdia's call in August 1991 that North Ossetia should rename itself simply Ossetia was clearly another move in the same direction.[200]

Evidence in support of the view that this kind of policy was actually being implemented on the ground came in the shape of the refugee influx into North Ossetia. By October 1991, the Ossetian refugee organization in the north claimed that 83,000 had already fled, and the figure was expected to rise over the winter.[201] Indeed, the 36 victims of the massacre of bus passengers in May 1992 – the worst single incident to date – were *en route* to refuge in the north.[202] The refugees were moreover drawn from parts outside Ossetia as well as from the Oblast itself. The solution was thus well *en route* to implementation.

Although North Ossetia may now have become the safest place for Ossetians; although (to follow a line often used by the Soviet Government *vis-à-vis* the Crimean Tatars) they may be closer to their "traditional" homeland; and although Russia may find it convenient to have a series of anti-Georgian buffer territories between herself and that republic – the situation is not without its own difficulties. Any dramatic increase in the population of North Ossetia, especially around its capital, Vladikavkaz, is likely to exacerbate the Ossetian conflict with the neighbouring Ingush people. This clash – which relates to land given to North Ossetia when the Ingush were deported in 1944 but which, having returned, they now wish to recover as part of their own autonomous oblast – flared up again in April 1991.[203] Indeed, a north Ingush republic was declared in October 1991 as part of the Russian Republic[204] and, the following month, North Ossetia announced the formation of a republican guard and defence committee because of the Ingush problem.[205]

Solution 3 – creation of a unified Ossetian territory

Ostensibly most Ossetians probably want a unification of the territory of the existing North and South Ossetias into a single entity, however difficult that might be straddling such a mountain barrier. Modern communications networks, it can be argued in support, have effectively overcome

199. *TASS*, 25 June 1991.
200. For the rejection of this by the chairman of the North Ossetian Supreme Soviet see *TASS*, 10 August 1991.
201. *International Herald Tribune*, 4 October 1991.
202. *ITAR/TASS*, and *Iprinda*, Tbilisi, 21 May 1992.
203. *TASS*, 20 and 22 April 1992.
204. *Novosti*, 16 October 1991.
205. *Pravda*, 18 November 1991.

that barrier in any event. However, this approach still leaves open the whole question of the position of such a unified territory. Three principal options would seem to exist at present:

- unity within the Russian federation
- unity within the Confederative Union of Mountain Peoples
- unity as an independent state

UNITY WITHIN THE RUSSIAN FEDERATION

At present, many (perhaps most) Ossetians would settle for this. Certainly, it could have been brought about long ago. There is no doubt that territorial boundaries within the old USSR could be changed; they were changed many times.[206] However, this case was seemingly set in stone in the 1920s by the Georgian Stalin, whose hometown, Gori, was so near to Ossetia. Even in more recent times, under Gorbachev, it was difficult to bring about such change, as the number of such contested frontiers mushroomed, and had to be put on ice. Since the collapse of the Soviet Union, over 160 such cases have emerged, and Vladimir Kolossov of the Institute of Geography in Moscow has declared that "only 30 per cent of boundaries of the new territories which formerly made up the USSR are demarcated by the norms of international law.[207]

North Ossetia, the larger and more populous part, is of course already a part of the Russian Republic and it acts as a natural magnet for those in the south. Indeed, many of the actions of the southerners in pursuing separation from Georgia had, as a rider, the request, or even demand, that they also be allowed to join the old Russian Union Republic or the new Russian Federation. This was true of their vote in May 1991 to drop their demand for republican status and return to that of an autonomous oblast,[208] and of their second attempt to declare a republic in November 1991.[209] It was also pursued in other ways, such as the October 1991 appeal from the South Ossetian Oblast soviet to the North Ossetian Supreme Soviet that it should raise the question of unification with the RSFSR Supreme Soviet,[210] and the January 1992 referendum in South Ossetia (and cities in Russia with communities of over 200 Ossetians) in which 97 per cent voted for unification with North Ossetia within Russia.[211] Most starkly, the case was put by the chairman of the South Ossetian Oblast Executive Committee Znaur Gassiev when, in October 1991, he declared that his people would fight to the last man to break with Georgia and join with Russia.[212]

206. See P. Goble, *Can republican borders be changed?*, Radio Liberty research paper, RL405/90. In *Report on the USSR*, 28 September 1990, 20–1.
207. Private correspondence with the author.
208. *TASS* and *Radio Tbilisi*, 8 May 1991.
209. *Radio Moscow* and *TASS*, 28 November 1991.
210. *TASS*, 22 October 1991.
211. *The Express Chronicle*, 4 (234), 29 January 1992, 1.

Support for the cause also came from within North Ossetia as, for example, when the political organization Ademon Tsadis appealed to RSFSR President Yeltsin to reverse the division of the 1920s,[213] while the Russian Supreme Soviet itself voted, in October 1991, to allow Yeltsin to introduce economic sanctions against Georgia as part of the pressure on that republic to relax its hold.[214]

The essential problem with this proposal is that it has now become an issue between two independent sovereign states, and although Georgia's Shevardnadze has shown some inclination to negotiate with the Ossetians,[215] the matter of Georgian sovereignty over South Ossetia is considered a closed book.

UNITY WITHIN THE CONFEDERATIVE UNION OF MOUNTAIN PEOPLES
The option of unity within the context of a Confederation of Mountain Peoples, within or outside the USSR, might have seemed fanciful a few years ago, but with the break-up of the USSR it was inevitable that some similar pressures would develop within the equally multinational Russian Republic. Not only has this pressure taken shape in individual autonomous republics such as Tatarstan, but some seven groupings or confederations of smaller ethnic groups have appeared to represent their causes and possibly move towards some kind of independence. One such grouping was the Assembly of Mountain Peoples of the Caucasus. In March 1990, representatives of informal groups in both North and South Ossetia applied to join the Assembly (AGNK) and were admitted. At its Third Congress in November 1991, the 14 member peoples ratified a treaty on a Confederative Union of the Mountain Peoples, and drew up a statute on its leading organs.[216] The new confederation quickly took up cudgels on behalf of the South Ossetians, when, at its meeting in Tskhinvali on 27 April 1992, it threatened to intervene militarily if there was not an end to the genocide against them by the Georgians.[217]

Significant as this new grouping is, it is far from being an independent entity as yet. Indeed, although the Chechens and Tatars seemed to be willing to take on Moscow, all the other autonomous republics have been brought to heel, voluntarily or otherwise, to sign a new federal treaty with Russia in March 1992, including Kabardino Balkar, Daghestan and North Ossetia among the mountain peoples of the Caucasus.[218]

212. *Report on the USSR*, 8 November 1991, 28.
213. *TASS* and *Radio Moscow*, 3 October 1991.
214. *TASS*, 27 October 1991.
215. On 13 May 1992 he achieved a ceasefire agreement with Ossetian leaders – see *Le Monde*, 16 May 1992.
216. *Vesti* (Russian Television), 4 November 1991.
217. *Le Monde*, 29 April 1991.

UNITY AS AN INDEPENDENT STATE

The prospect of an independent Ossetian state is the third option, but seemingly the least likely prospect at the moment. Even with the better transport links between the two parts, which now exist, this would be an unusual mini-state straddling such a high mountain range. Certainly not unique (one can point to Peru or Ecuador), it meets with the same fundamental objections from Georgia as Solution 3a, suggesting unity within the Russian federation. Georgian territory is non-negotiable, certainly in the case of territory containing such a small and dwindling "outsider" population. If the Ossetians wish for an Ossetian state, and few declare this openly at present, then it will have to be created on the basis of North Ossetia in the Georgian view.

Conclusion

Although many ethnic disputes appear so entrenched as to be intractable, this one does offer some leeway for actual solution. However, this essentially requires concessions by the South Ossetians, who are, in any event, having a solution imposed upon them slowly but surely by the superior force of independent Georgia. With the steady demise of the CIS, and the withdrawal of its remaining forces from the area, only economic and political sanctions remain open to Russia to prevent what seems likely to be a steady withdrawal of the South Ossetians to the safety of the north.

---

218. The treaty was signed on 31 March 1992 – see *The Guardian, International Herald Tribune, Financial Times, Christian Science Monitor, The Independent* and *The Times*, 1 April 1992. It was approved by the Russian Republic's Congress of People's Deputies on 10 April 1992 – see *The Guardian* and the *International Herald Tribune*, 11 April 1992.

CHAPTER NINE

Abkhazia: a problem of identity and ownership[1]

B. G. HEWITT

Introduction

Following the announcement that Mingrelian-born Zviad Gamsakhurdia had succeeded in becoming its first elected president, the Republic of Georgia declared itself independent from the USSR on 9 April 1991. On 25 August 1990 Georgia's hitherto Autonomous Soviet Socialist Republic of Abkhazia had declared itself to be a full Soviet Socialist Republic, independent of Georgia. Though this declaration was promptly rescinded by the authorities in Georgia's capital, Tbilisi, Vladislav Ardzinba was appointed President of Abkhazia on 4 December 1990. At the time of writing (June 1991), although no formal announcement has yet appeared, recognition of Abkhazia's republican status may be imminent.[2] Thus, tension in this and other regions of Transcaucasia seems certain to remain high.

In order better to understand the context of the territorial dispute it is necessary to begin with a consideration of the ethnic affiliations of the peoples concerned. The Abkhazians[3] are related most closely to the Abazinians,[4] who live across the Klukhor Pass in the foothills of the northwest

---

1. This title belongs to three separate versions of my main contribution to the elucidation of the issue of Abkhazia. The first version was prepared for The Nationalities Journal and is to appear in late 1995. The present version was updated in 1992 for presentation at the SOAS conference on Transcaucasian boundaries (and with subsequent additions for this publication). The final version was again updated to the end of 1992 and it appeared in *Central Asia Survey* **12**(3), 267–323, 1993. The historical background is common to all three and, as much ignorance still surrounds discussions of Abkhazia in Western circles, publication of an adapted version two is justifiable for bringing the factual context of the Georgian–Abkhazian dispute to a wider audience. For further information, see my "Demographic manipulation in the Caucasus", *Journal of Refugee Studies*, 1995, and "Yet a third consideration of *Völker, Sprachen und Kulturen des südlichen Kaukasus*", *Central Asia Survey*, **14**, 2, 1995.
2. The author's recently issued visa for Abkhazia already describes it as an SSR.
3. The Abkhazians' self-designation is *aps-wa* and their country is *a-ps-ni*, whereas the Georgians call the people *apxaz-i* and the country *apxaz-et-i*.
4. Self-designation *abaza*.

190

Caucasus, and more distantly to both the Circassians (Cherkess) and the Ubykhs, who lived around Sochi between the rivers Hamish and either Bu or Vardan.[5] The Ubykhs in their entirety, along with many Circassians, Abkhazians and other north Caucasian peoples, migrated to the Ottoman Empire (principally modern-day Turkey) following Russia's conquest of the north Caucasus in 1864. The small language family to which Abkhaz/ Abaza, Circassian and the all but extinct Ubykh belong is called northwest Caucasian. The Georgians,[6] on the other hand, are a south Caucasian people, though there are problems about determining precisely who is correctly describable as "Georgian".

The south Caucasian (or Kartvelian) language family consists of Georgian, Mingrelian, Laz and Svan. Apart from the Laz, whose traditional homeland, Lazistan, lies within Turkey, and the Imerkhevian Georgians, who also reside in Turkey, the bulk of the Georgians, Mingrelians and Svans live within the Republic of Georgia. Georgian is the only literary language of the three – indeed it has been a written language with a distinguished literary culture for 15 centuries – and thus has served as the language of tuition for all Svans as well as most Mingrelians (and Georgians, of course) since the establishment of universal schooling by the Soviets. Although the Georgian language has a generic term *kart-v-el-ur-i* to refer to the Kartvelian language family, it lacks the equivalent human adjective *kart-v-el-el-i* and thus utilizes the adjective *kart-v-el-i* "Georgian" to refer generically to any of these four peoples. From about 1930 up to the census of 1989, the Mingrelians, Svans and the very few Laz resident in Georgia were deprived of the right they had previously enjoyed of designating themselves as Mingrelian, Svan or Laz on their census returns – they were required officially to register as "Georgians". The majority of these peoples do today seem happy with this arrangement, although there is no reason to carry this terminological inaccuracy over into English, where "Kartvelian" should be employed as the generic term.

Below I shall write "Georgian" (within quotation marks) whenever rendering the terms *kart-v-el-i/kart-ul-i* (sc. other than in quotations) in what I regard as their illegitimate sense. It is of course important to stress that the deliberate obfuscation just described applies not only to ethnicity, however fundamental this may be; it also allows the Georgians unceremoniously to appropriate as their own any thing, event or territory that would more properly carry the epithet Mingrelian, Svan or Laz.[7]

The 1989 Soviet census reveals the following demographic picture for Georgia and Abkhazia when compared with the 1979 data.

---

5. Bell (1840: 53, 447).
6. Self-designation = *kart-v-el-i* (cf. *kart-ul-i* "Georgian (thing)"), whereas "Georgia" = *sa-kart-v-el-o* (literally "place designated for the *Kartvels*").

Table 9.1 The population of Georgia.

	1979	1989	1979 (%)	1989 (%)
Whole population	4,993,182	5,400,841	100.0	100.0
"Georgians"	3,433,011	3,787,393	68.8	70.1
Armenians	448,000	437,211	9.0	8.1
Russians	371,608	341,172	7.4	6.3
Azerbaijanis	255,678	307,556	5.1	5.7
Ossetians	160,497	164,055	3.2	3.0
Greeks	95,105	100,324	1.9	1.8
Abkhazians	85,285	95,853	1.7	1.8
Ukrainians	45,036	52,443	0.9	1.0
Kurds	25,688	33,331	0.5	0.6
Georgian Jews	7,974	14,314	0.2	0.3
Jews	20,107	10,312	0.4	0.2
Belorussians	5,702	8,595	0.1	0.2
Assyrians	5,286	6,206	0.1	0.1
Tatars	5,098	4,099	0.1	0.1
Others	29,116	37,977	0.6	0.7

Table 9.2 The population of Abkhazia.

	1979	1989	1979 (%)	1989 (%)
Whole population	486,082	525,061	100.0	100.0
Abkhazians	83,097	93,267	17.1	17.8
"Georgians"	213,322	239,872	43.9	45.7
Armenians	73,350	76,541	15.1	14.6
Russians	79,730	74,913	16.4	14.2
Greeks	13,642	14,664	2.8	2.8
Ukrainians	10,257	11,655	2.1	2.2
Belorussians	1,311	2,084	0.3	0.4
Jews	1,976	1,426	0.4	0.3
Ossetians	952	1,165	0.2	0.2
Tatars	1,485	1,099	0.3	0.2
Others	6,960	8,374	1.4	1.6

Historical survey

For all their curiosity, the ancient Greeks were peculiarly uninterested in the diversity of languages attested among the many peoples with whom their travels brought them into contact, all of whom were classified as barbarians. Specifically, they have left us no evidence of the languages spoken by those tribes their writers named as residing along the east coast of the

---

7. For example, in the legend of the Golden Fleece, Jason visits Colchis, land of King Æetes. Indefinite though the term "Colchians" is, the Georgians conventionally identify them with the ancestors of the Laz–Mingrelians, and since they subsume anything Laz–Mingrelian under the term "Georgian", "Georgia" and a "Georgian" king are thus conjured into one of the most celebrated Greek myths.

Black Sea, which they loosely termed Colchis, described by the Mingrelian scholar Dzhanashia (1988: 295) as "more a geographical than political term, and even then with uncertain boundaries", though for Strabo (first century BC) it extended roughly from Pitsunda in northern Abkhazia to Trebizond (Turkey).

In the general area of Abkhazia, a fragment of Hekataios (c. 500 BC) mentions the *Hēní okhoi* "Charioteers".[8] Skylax of Karyanda (c. 500 BC) also mentions *Akhaioí*, Achaeans, placed by Melikishvili (1970: 400) around Sochi, to the north and yet further north the *Kerkétai*, Circassians/ Cherkess, though Kuipers (1960: 7) queries any link between these ancient and modern ethnonyms. Strabo places the *Zugoí* between the Charioteers and the Achaeans, and these have been identified with the Circassians too.[9] The Apsilians (*gens Absilae*) are first mentioned by Pliny Secundus in the first century AD, whereas Arrian a century later introduces the term *Abasgoí*, "Abazgians", whom he locates to the north of the Apsilians (*Apsí lai*), and to their north he places the *Saní gai* "in whose territory lies Sebastopolis" (K'ech'aghmadze 1961: 43), which is conventionally identi- fied as Abkhazia's modern capital Sukhum.[10] Thus the Apsilians are to be located around Ochamchira (Greek Guē nós). In the sixth century Agathias introduces the *Misimianoí*, who are separated from the Apsilians by the fort at Tibélos (modern Tsebelda).

According to Arrian, the Apsilians and Abazgians were subjects of the Laz. At the start of the 6th century, with its southern border at the River Ghalidzga, Apsilia plus Abazgia, Misimiania and the southern part of the territory of the Sanigai were still dependants of the Laz kingdom (Anchabadze 1959: 6–7) or Lazika, better known in Georgian sources as the Kingdom of Egrisi, the older name of Mingrelia, which itself was in a state of formal vassalage to Byzantium. Christianity was introduced by Justin- ian (AD 543–6). The medieval Georgian Chronicles (*kartlis tskhovreba*) already speak of the Abkhazians (*apxaz-eb-i*). With Byzantium's power on the wane in the late eighth century, Leon II, potentate of the Abkhazians, took his opportunity and "seized Abkhazia and Egrisi as far as the Likhi

---

8. The etymology of this word is clearly Greek, viz. *he:nia* "reins" + *okʰos* "bearer" from *ekʰo:* "I have/hold".
9. cf. Georgian *Dzhik-i* Abkhaz *a-zax°a*.
10. In Abkhaz Aq°'a – see Hewitt (1992b). Moving along the coast from Trebizond, Arrian mentions the following tribes: Trapezuntines, Colchians, Drils, *Sánnoi/Tzánnoi* "(?)Zan"s (NB the Laz self-designation is *ch'an-i*, the Svan term for a Mingrelian is *mi- zän*, and the parent-language of Mingrelian and Laz is known as Zan), Macrones (NB the Mingrelian self-designation is *ma-rg-al-i*), "Charioteers" [sic], Zydreitai, Laz, and then the Apsilians. Procopius of Caesarea (fl. c. 550) mentions a tribe *Broûkhoi* to the north of the Abazgians who have been identified with the Ubykhs (cf. Dumézil 1965: 15), whose self-designation is *tix* (although this has been challenged by Christol 1987: 219). All references in the classical authors to tribes in the region have been gathered and translated into Russian by Gulia (1986: 215–55).

[mountains] and took the title King of the Abkhazians".[11] The resulting kingdom of Abkhazia, comprising the whole of today's western Georgia, lasted for roughly 200 years until the accession of Bagrat III in 975 produced the first king of a united Georgia. From between 780 to 975 the term "Abkhazia" was generally used to refer to the whole of western Georgia. While Georgia remained united (up to approximately 1245), this term became synonymous with *sa-kart-v-el-o* or Georgia, after which time it resumed its original, restricted sense.

Central power in Georgia collapsed with the appearance of the Mongols in the thirteenth century, who caused the country to split into two kingdoms, which "in their turn fragmented into smaller political units, constituting sovereign princedoms (Georgian *samtavroebi*). At the close of the thirteenth century, Georgia as a whole represented a conglomeration of such princedoms" (Anchabadze 1959: 234). In the fourteenth century the Mingrelian prince Giorgi Dadiani acquired the southern half of Abkhazia, restricting the Abkhazian rulers, the Shervashidzes (in Abkhazian *Chachba*), to the north of their domains. Around this period a portion of the population crossed over the Klukhor Pass to become today's Abazinians in the north Caucasus (*Georgian Encyclopædia*, vol. 1: 11). Eventually at the close of the fourteenth century the whole of Abkhazia became vassal of the princedom called Sabediano (essentially Mingrelia), even if "Shervashidze did not obey all the Dadiani commandments".[12] From the early sixteenth century Abkhazia begins to be mentioned as an independent entity; during this century the Ottoman Turks introduced Islam. The Italian missionary, Lamberti, who lived in Mingrelia from 1633 to 1653, puts its border with Abkhazia at the River Kodor (1938: 5).

Taking advantage of a weakening Mingrelia in the 1680s, the Shervashidzes extended their southern border to the River Ingur and strengthened their hold over the territory by increasing the Abkhazian population there. In 1705, three Shervashidze brothers divided up the territory, one taking the north (from Gagra to the Kodor), the second the central Abzhwa region (from the Kodor to the Ghalidzga), and the third, Murzaq'an, the southern part (from the Ghalidzga to the Ingur), and so this province, which is slightly larger than the modern Gali district, became known as Samurzaqano.

In 1810 Abkhazia came under the protection of Tsarist Russia – eastern Georgia had been annexed in 1801, Mingrelia followed in 1803 and the western province of Imeretia in 1804. Both Abkhazia and Mingrelia contin-

---

11. Chronicles I, p. 251 of Q'aukhchishvili's 1955 edition.F
12. The chronicler is Egnatashvili. All references to Abkhazians and Abkhazia in medieval Georgian sources have been gathered and put into Russian by G. Amichba either without Georgian original (1986) or including it (1988). See the latter (pp. 112–3) for this quote.

ued to administer their own provinces until they were taken under full Russian control in 1864 and 1857 respectively, when the war in the north Caucasus ended in Russia's favour.[13] Administrative regions were established in 1810 and altered in various ways thereafter. From 1864 to the 1866, because of Abkhazian rebellion against land reform, Abkhazia was styled the Sukhum Military Department, consisting of the Bzyp, Sukhum and Abzhwa districts plus the prefectorates of Tsebelda and Samurzaqano, all under the control of the Governor General of Kutaisi (capital of Imeretia in western Georgia). In 1866 these prefectorates were abolished, and four new districts were created within the Sukhum Military Department. Another reform was introduced in 1868 when this department was split into the regions of Pitsunda (from Gagra to the Kodor) and Ochamchira (from the Kodor to the Ingur). In 1883 the military department was downgraded and renamed a military district, which from 1903 to 1906 was made directly subservient to the Russian authorities responsible for the Caucasus and based in Tbilisi. From 1904 to 1917 Gagra and its environs were reassigned to the Sochi district of the Black Sea province. During the first eight decades of the nineteenth century it is estimated that over 120,000 Abkhazians migrated or were expelled to the Ottoman Empire, especially in 1864 and 1877–8 in the wake of the Russo–Turkish war.[14]

A Soviet commune was established in Abkhazia in 1918 but lasted for only 40 days, when the Mensheviks, who had come to power in Tbilisi, brought Abkhazia under their control. Soviet power was re-established on 4 March 1921, and the Abkhazian Soviet Socialist Republic was recognized by Georgia's revolutionary committee on 21 May 1921. On 16 December a special contract of alliance was signed between Abkhazia and Georgia. On 13 December 1922 Abkhazia (along with Georgia) entered the Transcaucasian Federation. In February 1931 Abkhazia lost its status of a treaty republic *associated with* Georgia to become a mere autonomous republic *within* Georgia, the position it still officially holds.

The argument

The Georgian position is quite simple, not to say simplistic. Any territory included within the current borders of (Soviet) Georgia is declared indisputably to be Georgian land, so that virtually all articles that have dealt

---

13. Samurzaqano was taken under Russian control in 1845 because of Abkhaz–Mingrelian quarrelling over rights to the area (Saxok'ia 1985: 390).

14. If one includes Abazinians and the whole Ubykh nation, the figure reaches 180,000 (Lakoba 1990: 40, quoting Dzidzaria 1982). Numerous descendants of those who suffered this *Maxadzhirstvo* "exile" live today all over what was then the Ottoman Empire, principally though in Turkey, where, apart from the Ubykhs, they have with a greater or lesser degree of success retained their language(s) and culture(s).

with the problem of Abkhazia since the latest troubles erupted in 1989 have ritualistically described Abkhazia as either "an indivisible part of Georgia"[15] or as "Georgian territory from earliest times".[16] The Abkhazian position is that, while they have lived as neighbours to the Kartvelians (specifically the Mingrelians and Svans) for millennia, they have at times joined forces with their neighbours (specifically the Mingrelians) in the face of common external threats (e.g. Arabs, Turks, . . .). They admit they share with the Kartvelians aspects of what might be called general Caucasian culture; nevertheless they remain a distinct northwest Caucasian people, occupying the southern reaches of what was once (up to 1864) a common northwest Caucasian homeland. They resent Kartvelian encroachment on their land, which has been accompanied by repeated attempts to Georgianize or Kartvelianize their people. They perceive the main threat to the continuing viability of their language and culture as coming from Tbilisi (not Moscow), which leads them to the conclusion that their territorial independence has to be re-established either as a separate and full republic within a newly structured USSR or as a constituent of some Mountain Caucasian Republic, where they would share their fate with other north Caucasian peoples.[17]

The historical settlement of Abkhazia

The Abkhazians, not unreasonably, see the classical ethnonym Apsilian as a Graeco/Roman attempt to render their self-designation *aps-wa*, whereas the classical Abazgians are conventionally viewed as the ancestors of today's Abazinians, whose self-designation is *abaza* and who lived somewhere in Abkhazia prior to their fourteenth century migration northeastwards. The classical Sanigai are identified with the tribe/people called in Abkhazian *a-saj* (plural *a-saj-kwa*), who once lived around the north of the territory. The Turkish traveller Evliya Çelebi visited the region in the 1640s and has left us a sample of the language he ascribed to the Sadzian Abazas – it is clearly Ubykh (located around modern Sochi). As for the Misimians, they have been connected with the Abkhazian clan Marshania, whose ancestral fiefdom incorporated Tsebelda. Stress is laid on the fact that it

---

15. Georgian *sakartvelos ganuq'opeli nac'ili*.
16. Geo. *jirjveli kartuli t'erit'oria*. Indeed, there are indications that Georgia would like to extend its borders into Turkey, Armenia, Azerbaijan and Russia as evidenced by a map that was included in the publicity material for the Rustaveli Symposium held in Finland (11–12 April 1991, Tarku). This showed wedges of the above states falling within this vision of "Greater Georgia" and was no doubt the one shown by Zviad Gamsakhurdia to a visiting foreign correspondent from Moscow in July 1989 (personal communication).
17. Not necessarily *Muslim* peoples. It has been part of the Kartvelian campaign to try to tar the Abkhazians with the brush of Islamic fundamentalism, though, as the "Father of Abkhaz Literature" D. Gulia wrote in his autobiography: "We Abkhazians are equally cool to both Islam and Christianity".

was only after the tragedy of the mass migrations in the nineteenth century that non-Abkhazians began to settle in any significant numbers in Abkhazia and, even so, Abkhazians remained in a majority until at the earliest the 1926 census. As late as 1886 the breakdown of the permanent population was recorded as Abkhazian 58,961, Mingrelian 3,474, Georgian 515, Russian 972, Armenian 1,337, Estonian 637, Greek 2,056, other 1,460.[18] Subsequent censuses (before 1979) present the following picture for the three largest ethnic groups (Table 9.3).

Table 9.3 Demographic changes in Abkhazia, 1897–1970.

	1897	1926	1939	1959	1970
Abkhazians	58,697	55,918	56,147	61,197	77,276
Kartvelians	25,875	67,494	91,067	158,221	199,595
Russians	5,135	20,456	60,201	86,715	92,889

At least two strategies have been adopted by the Kartvelians when advancing arguments in support of their contention that the land belongs to them. The first strategy and the least objectionable, accepts that, whereas Abkhazians may have age-old rights in Abkhazia, Kartvelians possess not only the status of co-aboriginals but have always formed the majority population, although the latter assertion is immediately faced with the problematic evidence contained in the population figures. The wilder stance denies the Abkhazians any presence in Abkhazia until at most 500 years ago. Strategy (a) would perhaps grudgingly allow the correlations Abazgians = Abazinians, Apsilians = Abkhazians but would follow Eusebius of Caesarea (c. 260–340) in seeing an equation between the Sanigai and the Sannoi (Dzhanashia 1959: 9–11), which latter people everyone accepts were Kartvelians, despite the geographical distance separating these two tribes according to the classical authors, and then conclude that "the coastal strip of western Georgia was entirely inhabited by Georgian tribes" (K'ech'aghmadze 1961: 12; quoted by Gunba 1989: 6). As for the Misimians, classicist Simon Q'auxchishvili had suggested as early as 1936 (p. 174) that they were a Svan tribe – the Svans' self-designation is *mu-shwän*. However, Q'auxchishvili's over-enthusiasm for detecting Kartvelian roots is illustrated by his 1965 statement (p. 28) that the Greek *Hēní okhoi* was Kartvelian in its etymology (cf. *n.* 7).

The second strategy denies Abkhazians any presence in Abkhazia until at most 500 years ago. This line of thinking received its first exposé in the late 1940s by Pavle Ingoroq'va in the journal *mnatobi* (*Luminary*), who then went on to publish his argument in chapter 4 of his monumental *giorgi merchule* in 1954. In short, he argued that the Abkhazians referred to in medi-

18. The source is *Svod statisticheskix dannyx o naselenii Zakavkazskogo kraja, izvlechennyx iz posemejnyx spiskov 1886*, Tbilisi 1893.

eval Georgian sources had been a Kartvelian tribe who had no genetic affiliation to the Abkhazians of today. These last, he claimed, migrated from the north Caucasus only in the seventeenth century, displacing the Kartvelians resident there and adopting the ethnonym of the dislodged population. In partial support of this extraordinary theory he adduced the testimony of Evliya Çelebi to the effect that the Abkhazians of his day were speakers of Mingrelian.[19] Ingoroq'va's theory was favourably received by (among others) Q'auxchishvili and phonetician Giorgi Axvlediani.[20] Though Ingoroq'va was discredited when the anti-Abkhazian policy of 1933–53 was reversed, it is essential to mention this distortion of history here, because his ideas are being enthusiastically redisseminated by certain individuals. In the April 1989 issue of *lit'erat'uruli sakartvelo* (*Literary Georgia*), for example, critic Rost'om Chxeidze published an article lavishing praise of Ingoroq'va, urging his academic rehabilitation for his "contribution to the study of the history of western Georgia". Similarly, in 1989, in the unofficial *Letopis' 4* (*Chronicle 4*), a pamphlet instructing the Mingrelians how to conduct anti-Abkhazian agitation, Gamsakhurdia urged them to read Ingoroq'va to learn how they are the true inheritors of the territory of Abkhazia. Again in the paper *kartuli pilmi* (*Georgian film*) Gamsakhurdia sought to lecture the late A. Sakharov on how the Abkhazians had come to Abkhazia only "2–3 centuries ago". In a two-part article published over the 1989–90 New Year in the paper *saxalxo ganatleba* (*Popular education*) the Svan linguist, Aleksandre Oniani, strove to buttress the Ingoroq'va hypothesis, even though his date for the Abkhazians' arrival on Georgian soil was 400–500 years ago, presumably because he knew that Çelebi's text when correctly translated does not support a seventeenth-century influx.[21] Historian Miriam Lortkipanidze in the February 1990 issue of *Literary Georgia* dignifies Ingoroq'va further by describing him as the author of one of three "scholarly" theories on the ethnogenesis of the Abkhazians. Although Lortkipanidze makes it clear that she herself does not subscribe to the Ingoroq'va view, she still states: "It is precisely from the 17th century that there appear the first reports of the existence of a spoken language different from Georgian (Mingrelian) to the north of the River Kodor". Perhaps Lortkipanidze is ignorant of the existence of the travel diary of Johannes de Galonifontibus, who passed through the Caucasus in 1404 and wrote:

---

19. Those Southern Abkhazians living alongside Mingrelians have tended to be bilingual in this language, and Çelebi's text actually supports an identical state of affairs for his day too, when he says that the Southern Abkhazians *also* spoke Mingrelian. Ingoroq'va's mistranslation is ascribed by Anchabadze (1959: 295) to Çelebi's Russian translator, F. Brun.
20. A variant has now been proposed by Academician Tamaz Gamq'relidze in the journal *Macne* (2, 1991: 7–16). For a detailed rebuttal see Hewitt (1992a).
21. For a full discussion with counter-arguments see Hewitt (1992b, 1993).

Beyond these [Circassians] is Abkhazia, a small hilly country . . .
They have their own language . . . To the east of them, in the direction
of Georgia, lies the country called Mingrelia . . . They have their own
language . . . Georgia is to the east of this country. Georgia is not an
integral whole . . . They have their own language.

However that may be, Lortkipanidze most certainly was and is aware
that the great Georgian queen Tamar (1184–1213) gave the nickname
"Lasha" to her son Giorgi, a term the *Georgian chronicles* interpret as
"enlightener of the world in the language of the Apsars". In Abkhazian the
word for bright is *a-laṣa*, which surely suggests that "Apsar" is an
attempted rendition of *aps-wa*.[22]

Samurzaqano

Given Abkhazia's historically fluctuating southern border, it might have
been expected that a border issue would have developed over the possession of Samurzaqano (largely today's Gali district). Perhaps because the
question of Abkhazia is an all or nothing struggle, no particular arguments
currently centre around this southern province. This has not always been
the case, and the one-time debate over the Abkhazian versus Mingrelian
occupation of Samurzaqano (and of Abkhazia in general) is a convenient
bridge between the problems of history and Georgianization.

In 1877 the Georgian educationalist and writer Iak'ob Gogebashvili
wrote a series of newspaper articles on the theme "Who should be settled
in Abkhazia?". The last wave of Abkhazian migration to Turkey had just
occurred, and Gogebashvili was moved, in view of the fact that "Abkhazia
will never again be able to see its own children", to ask who should be sent
in as "colonizers".[23] Because of the extent of malarial marshes (since
drained) "to which the Abkhazians had become acclimatized over many
centuries in their own region", Gogebashvili argued that the obvious colonizers should consist of Mingrelians, since the climate in their territory
was most similar to that prevailing in Abkhazia. In addition, they were the
most adept of the Kartvelians at adapting to new conditions; there was a
shortage of land in Mingrelia; already in Sukhum and Ochamchira they

22. Q'auxch'ishvili, however, on p. 636 of volume II of his edition of these Chronicles (1959)
    glosses the term "Apsars" as "one of the Georgian tribes in western Georgia". It should
    perhaps be also noted that the street on which the Linguistics Institute of the Georgian
    Academy of Sciences stands has now been renamed "Ingoroq'va Street" from its former
    designation as "Dzerzhinski Street".
23. The 1952 editors felt it necessary to gloss this term on p. 93, thus: "Gogebashvili here and
    below uses the word "colonizer" not in its modern sense but to mean the persons settled
    there". Obviously they sensed some discomfort over one of the leading Georgians of the
    1870s describing Kartvelian settlers on territory that had been by 1952 long and strenu-
    ously argued to be Georgian soil as "colonizers"!

had gained control of commerce; and finally, "the Mingrelians by them-selves would rush to Abkhazia, when in order to settle other nationalities there the use of artificial means is necessary".[24] Tedo Saxok'ia, a leading Mingrelian intellectual, confirmed this when writing in 1903 and referring to Abkhazia's central region, spoke of an increase in local commercial activity "especially after the Mingrelians began to flood into the district . . . following the [Russo–Turkish] war". However, in the course of his discus-sion, Gogebashvili appends a revealing comment to his mention of the res-idents of Samurzaqano:

> From a political viewpoint the Mingrelians are just as Russian as the Muscovites, and in this way they can exercise influence over those tribes with whom they happen to have a relationship. A striking proof of this is given by the fact . . . that, thanks to Mingrelian influ-ence, the Samurzaqanoans – *a branch of the Abkhazian race* – who have permanent intercourse with the Mingrelians, have become entirely faithful subjects of Russia.

This observation is significant in view of the fact that in his well known school textbook *bunebis k'ari* (*Nature's door*) Gogebashvili subsequently wrote that "the Mingrelians and the Samurzaqanoans are one people".[25]

In 1899 a debate took place over the ethnic status of the Samurza-qanoans in the pages of the *Chernomorskij Vestnik* (*Black Sea Herald*) between Kartvelians K. Mach'avariani and, it is believed, Tedo Saxok'ia, who employed the pseudonym "Samurzaqan", the latter arguing for their Mingrelian ethnicity, the former that they were Abkhazians. On 8 May the following conversation between Mach'avariani and the Samurzaqanoan peasant Uru Gua was reported:

UG – Why are you putting these questions to me?

KM – Some people maintain that the Samurzaqanoans are Mingreli-ans, that they spoke and speak Mingrelian, and that the whole of Samurzaqano formed part of the princedom of Mingrelia.

---

24. The 1952 editors note: "Gogebashvili's ideas on the settlement of Abkhazia's empty ter-ritory by Georgians achieved their actual realisation under the conditions of Soviet power" (p. 93). This unequivocally confirms the Abkhazian complaint, discussed below, about the manipulation of local demography in the 1930–40s.
25. It is not known when or why Gogebashvili changed his mind. The 1868 edition of this work does not contain the relevant section, but it is included in the 7th edition of 1892, which is the earliest version at my disposal, and I thank Michael Daly of the Bodleian Library (who died after the first variant of this paper was completed) for making it accessible to me.

UG – What's that you say? I'll tell you this. I well recall my father and grandfather. They never spoke Mingrelian. Everyone conversed in Abkhaz. Take the communities of Bedia, Chxortoli, Okumi, Gali, Tsarche – everywhere you'll hear Abkhaz among adults. If in Saberio, Ot'obaia, Dixazurgi they speak Mingrelian, this is thanks to the residents of these villages having close contacts with the Mingrelians. Don't our names, surnames, manners, customs and even our superstitions prove we are Abkhazians and not Mingrelians? In the [18]50s you'd almost never hear Mingrelian anywhere in Samurzaqano.[26] Up to then a Mingrelian was a curiosity. May I ask you who *you* are?

KM – A Georgian.

UG – Where did you learn Mingrelian and Abkhaz?

KM – I was born in Mingrelia but grew up in Samurzaqano and Abkhazia.

In 1913 Mach'avariani put the number of Abkhazians in Samurzaqano at 33,639. The charge is made by Abkhazians today that by fiat of the Menshevik authorities in 1919 30,000 or so Samurzaqanoan Abkhazians were arbitrarily reclassified as "Georgian", a practice they claim that was continued for the census of 1926. For this reason, they say, the accuracy of this census in Abkhazia must remain open to severe doubt. And indeed a glance at the figures for the Abkhazian and Kartvelian populations of Abkhazia and their relative balances between 1897 and 1926 does suggest that something odd was happening. Lezhava speaks of "natural assimilation". Whatever the truth may be, all agree that today the Gali district has to all intents and purposes been fully Mingrelianized.

In a pamphlet published by the Rustaveli Society in 1990 entitled *Georgia – a little empire?* (designed to answer this charge made by A. Sakharov in his article in *Ogonyok* in July 1989) I. Antelava not only queries the ethnicity of those residing between Sukhum [sic!] and the Ingur but asks how

---

26. Bell's observation in 1840 (p. 53) that Abkhaz was spoken down to the Mingrelian frontier (at the Ingur) would seem to support this, though G. Rosen, writing *Über das Mingrelische, Suanische und Abchasische* in 1844, challenges it by stating that the linguistic frontier between Abkhaz and Mingrelian was the "Erti-c'q'ali" (p. 431), somewhat to the north. Bell includes in his Appendix xiv the Abkhaz word *agrua* "slave". This is clearly the same as today's ethnonym *a-gir-wa* "Mingrelian" and tends to support the often-heard boast that the first Mingrelians brought in to Abkhazia were unskilled peasants to do the manual work disdained by the Abkhazians. Saxok'ia (1985: 399) talks of the Abkhazians having been spoiled by nature and possessed of such a dislike of physical labour that they have to summon a carpenter from elsewhere just to fit a plank of wood!

the Abkhazian leaders can lay claim to Sukhum itself "the majority population of which always was and remains Georgian" – in the associated footnote he observes that in 1886 Sukhum had only three Abkhazian residents! This is a good illustration of the misuse to which statistics lend themselves, for there was a simple explanation. It is stated by Saxok'ia (1985: 381) that "the former indigenous Abkhazians were deprived of the right to take up residence near the town of Sukhum (for a distance of 20km), on the grounds they were untrustworthy elements" (pro-Turkish in their sympathies). Needless to say, Antelava did not deign to impart this additional piece of information to his readers.

Georgianization

The *Abkhazian letter* is an 87-page document signed by 60 leading Abkhazians completed on 17 June 1988 for transmission to Gorbachev. The hope was that the Abkhazians too could take advantage of *perestroika* and finally resolve the problems of Abkhazia that were ascribed to their having been dominated by Tbilisi for so long. The letter defends the historical distinctness (i.e. non-Kartvelian status) of the Abkhazians and presents a list of the grievances held against the Kartvelians. It dates the start of Georgianization to the first influx of Kartvelians in the latter half of the last century. In a sense this is beyond dispute, but it is not necessary to impute any hostile intent at this stage – after all, why should someone not have the benefit of land where, as one Abkhazian once put it "all you have to do is throw seeds out of your window, and Nature does the rest to bestow a vegetable plot upon you?" But the situation had certainly altered by the time of the acquisition of power in Tbilisi by the Mensheviks in 1918, who "used fire and sword in their passage through South Ossetia, bent on the cause of the violent Georgianization of these peoples ... Zhordania took the route of aggression, deciding to employ all force to capture the whole Sochi District as far as Tuapse ... lands which had no links with Georgia proper". Furthermore, "ignoring the specifics of Abkhazia, where the majority population spoke Russian, the Mensheviks in pursuance of realizing a programme for the 'nationalization' of the region forced upon schools 'the obligatory teaching of the Georgian (state) language'".

To jump for a moment to modern times, the draft of a state programme for the Georgian language, which appeared in the autumn of 1988 and was promulgated into law in August 1989 with its clauses about the obligatory teaching of Georgian in all schools within the republic and tests in Georgian language and literature as prerequisites for entry into higher education, rekindled the old worries of 1918–21 (and not only among Georgia's Abkhazian minority) about being saddled with a language they regard as totally unnecessary. It may seem odd that Georgian was not always an obligatory subject in the republic's schools,[27] but, to concentrate on Abkhazia, the reason for this is clear – although Kartvelians constitute around

45 per cent of the population, these are almost wholly Mingrelians, who tend to speak among themselves in Mingrelian, even if they also know Georgian from their schooling. And so, Georgian is actually very sparsely heard in Abkhazia. Abkhazians are either bilingual in Abkhaz and Russian or trilingual in these two tongues plus Mingrelian. Not unnaturally, they regard the imposition of yet another language, which, while Abkhazia was part of the USSR where Russian was unavoidable, will benefit them little, as a threat to the numerically least strong of their languages, namely Abkhaz. Were Georgia, including Abkhazia, to break all ties with the Russian-speaking world, then a natural process of evolution would eventually replace Russian with Georgian among Georgia's minorities. But to have tried to force Georgian on unwilling recipients in the conditions prevailing in 1988–9 was to invite trouble and lend credence to the widespread belief that an independent Georgia would see the completion of the Georgianization strategy of 1918–21 (and 1933–53).

"The establishment of Soviet power on 4 March 1921 was received by the peoples of Abkhazia as liberation from occupation by the Georgian Democratic Republic and the repressive regime of the ruling Menshevik Party". But the undermining of the subsequently declared Soviet Socialist Republic of Abkhazia on 31 March 1921 by its demotion first to a treaty republic on 16 December 1921 and finally to an autonomous republic within Georgia in February 1931 is credited to Stalin (who was responsible for nationalities at the time), Sergo Ordzhonik'idze, his fellow countryman and chief lieutenant in the Caucasus as secretary of the Caucasian bureau and in general, to the manoeuvrings of the authorities in Tbilisi in alliance with Stalin at the centre.

Mingrelian Lavrent'i Beria was appointed head of the Georgian party in 1931 and chairman of the Transcaucasian party committee in 1932. From 1933 he instituted an anti-Abkhazian policy that was maintained and strengthened until the deaths of both himself and Stalin in 1953. Quite independently of "The Terror", which affected all Soviet republics (including Georgia's Kartvelian residents) in 1936–8, Abkhazia experienced a forced importation of various nationalities, especially Mingrelians and Georgians from such western provinces as Mingrelia, Rach'a and Lechkhumi – Abkhazians recall truckloads of these, often unwilling, immigrants being dumped with nowhere to live and thus having to be given temporary refuge by the locals themselves. The effect of this was to reduce the Abkhazian part of the population to below 20 per cent. In 1938, when Cyrillic was introduced as a base for the writing systems of all the "young written languages" (such as Abkhaz) that had been awarded the status of "literary languages" early in the Soviet period as part of the drive to eradicate illiteracy,[28] Abkhaz (along with Ossetic in Georgia's autonomous

---

27. Language-planning in Georgia is discussed in Hewitt (1989).

region of South Ossetia) was forced to adopt the Georgian script (until 1953). From the mid-1940s, under K'andid Chark'viani's stewardship of the Georgian party with Ak'ak'i Mgeladze in control in Sukhum, teaching in and of Abkhaz was abolished, and Abkhaz language schools were turned into Georgian language schools. At this time the publishing of materials in Abkhaz was stopped. The belief is widespread that there was a plan to transport the Abkhazians in their entirety to central Asia, and that the theory of Ingoroq'va, discussed above, was made to order as a kind of scholarly justification for their removal from territory to which, it would have been said, they have no justifiable claim. One Abkhazian, prominent in the 1940s, is reported to have revealed prior to his death that the authorities had wished to avoid the upheaval that had accompanied the transportation eastwards during the war years of all the other peoples whose cases are now so well documented. They were convinced that after both Beria's artificial merging of Kartvelian elements with the native residents, who were now swamped in their own republic, as well as Chark'viani-Mgeladze's closure of the Abkhaz language schools and local publishing, that enough had probably been done to effect the Georgianization (Mingrelianization) within a couple of generations of all remaining Abkhazians.

Information for the period 1953–79 is most readily accessible in the study made by American Sovietologist Darrell Slider. He shows that, although the extremes of the discriminatory policy towards the Abkhazians, their language and culture were halted and to a degree reversed by the reopening of schools, re-entry of Abkhazians into local politics and the re-emergence of radio broadcasting and publishing in Abkhaz, all was not well *in comparison with the other regions of Soviet Georgia* in the spheres of access to higher education, backwardness in industrialization, and deprivation to the tune of 40 per cent by the Tbilisi authorities in terms of the local budget as measured on a per capita basis. Matters came to head in 1977–8[29] in connection with the Union-wide deliberations over the shape of the new Brezhnevite constitutions. Just as the Kartvelians took the opportunity to demonstrate in Tbilisi in defence of the rights of the Georgian language in the republican constitution, so 130 prominent Abkhazians had despatched a letter to the Kremlin listing their continued complaints against what they saw as the continuing Georgianization of their country. They even sought secession from Georgia, and union with

28. The absence of any development of a literary Abkhaz language during the Abkhazian Kingdom and its reliance on (first Greek and then) Georgian as state- and church-language is used by the Kartvelians as a further argument that, historically, Abkhazia must have seen itself as an ordinary part of Georgia. Examples of the use of Latin in medieval European liturgy or of Greek, Aramaic etc., as state languages in non-Greek or non-Aramaic countries are ignored.

29. In fact there had been protests also in 1957 and 1967.

the Russian federation, an extremely bold step at the time. There were public disturbances in 1978, and troops were sent in, as then reported in the Western media.[30] In response, a commission arrived from Moscow, and a variety of measures were recommended as a way of ameliorating the situation. In Slider's words: "In essence, the Georgian leadership was forced to admit that many of the complaints made by Abkhaz nationalists were legitimate". The changes included an increase in the general budget, the upgrading of Sukhum's Pedagogical Institute into a university (only the second in Georgia), reservation of places at Tbilisi University for students from Abkhazia,[31] introduction of Abkhazian television broadcasts, increase in publishing, and development of local enterprises. However, Moscow refused to countenance any secession from Georgia or to allow the withdrawal of constitutional recognition of the Georgian language in Abkhazia.

And yet the changes of 1978–9 brought no long-lasting fundamental improvement. The final eight pages of the Abkhazian letter address the problems of today (i.e. 1988). In essence, the charge is that Abkhazia's autonomy is a total fiction; although Abkhazians may hold figurehead positions in government, all crucial decisions are taken in Tbilisi by, and for the advantage of, Kartvelians. The Kartvelian hold on power takes a more covert and subtle form than in the past, but in the critical question of land tenure, policy in 1988 was a simple continuation of what the Mensheviks had begun and what Beria and his successors later reactivated. The suggested solution was a radical shift of status, namely the recreation of the original Abkhazian SSR, so that Abkhazia could henceforth meaningfully control its own destiny.

It is unclear when knowledge of the Abkhazian letter first filtered through to the general public in central Georgia, but, when its aspirations received emphatic endorsement at a huge public meeting on 18 March 1989 in the village of Lykhny in the form of the Lykhny Declaration, signed by 37,000 locals (Kartvelians as well as other non-Abkhazians significantly among them), this immediately became headline news in Tbilisi. The consequences were dire. An intense anti-Abkhazian campaign was started by leaders of the various (then) unofficial parties,[32] among virtually all of whom it became common practice to refer to the Abkhazians as

---

30. The Kartvelian *samizdat*-reports about Abkhazians attacking Kartvelians, taken at their face-value by Slider, should be treated with caution in view of the role played by their author, Boris K'ak'ubava, in various anti-Abkhazian gatherings organized in Abkhazia by such dangerous demagogues as the late Merab K'ost'ava in early 1989, for example on 1 April in Lykhny. It is true, however, that road-signs in Georgian were defaced.
31. It is unclear whether this was for the exclusive benefit of ethnic Abkhazians.
32. The dissidents Zviad Gamsakhurdia and Merab K'ost'ava had for some years already been producing underground documents complaining about what they regarded as the repression of the Georgian language and the Kartvelian population in Abkhazia.

"Apswas", thereby implying that the "true" Abkhazians were in fact some other people; indeed, the then leader of the Rustaveli Society, Ak'ak'i Bakradze, is reported to have told a meeting of Mingrelians in Sukhum that *they* were the descendants of the original Abkhazian residents of the Black Sea littoral! A whole series of distasteful articles, denigrating both Abkhazian history as well as individuals, was run by the Georgian press in all of its outlets, which suggests that the campaign must have had the approval of the republican authorities, as the Party's grip on power had not at that stage been shattered. Students and staff in the Georgian sector of the Abkhaz State University were encouraged to agitate for protection against the encroachment of Russian in the university (a charge the Abkhazians say is completely bogus). This demand was seized upon, and the Georgian Ministry of Higher Education announced that it was opening a branch of Tbilisi University in Sukhum to be based on the Georgian sector of the existing university. Recognizing the threat to the continuing viability of their own higher educational establishment, the Abkhazians strenuously but legally campaigned against it. They succeeded in having an official commission appointed in Moscow, which backed them by condemning Tbilisi's action as illegal. Nevertheless, plans to hold entrance exams went ahead, and the result was the series of ethnic clashes in Sukhum on 15 July and in Ochamchira on 16 July 1989. The still unpublished personal investigation into these events, carried out on the spot as they were unfolding, by Russian journalist, Viktor Popkov, clearly reveals that the premeditation behind these clashes lay on the Kartvelian side.[33]

The situation, not surprisingly, remains tense. Under the guidance of Ardzinba and *Aydgilara* (Unity), the National Forum of Abkhazia, whose first chairman was writer Aleksei Gogua and which is now headed by archaeologist Sergei Shamba, the Abkhazians continue to pursue their cause with moderation and dignity. In an interview with two Kartvelian journalists, published in a June 1991 issue of *Literary Georgia*, Shamba observes:

> This year it is possible that they [the new government in Tbilisi] will be sending us Prefects, which again contravenes our constitution . . . But of late, when the signing of the new union treaty has come on the agenda and a real danger has been created of Abkhazia departing from Georgia, one regularly hears entreaties for us not to sign and that we should settle our differences. Right now, look, a delegation has come and is telling us to have no fears because we shall have real autonomy. But this is just an extension of the old dialogue. What is

---

33. Popkov's work takes the form of a book on the ethnic problems facing the USSR, one section of which deals with Abkhazia. These two chapters were translated into English and distributed to every American senator by an activist in the USA in 1990.

autonomy? . . . The right to autonomy is already enshrined in the constitutions of both Abkhazia and Georgia. We are no longer satisfied with this.

It is unlikely that a single Abkhazian in Abkhazia would object to a word of this, for the events leading up to, during, and following the clashes of 1989 have produced a unique and impressive solidarity among the entire nation from its humblest to its most eminent representative – there is, however, a regrettable if understandable tiny band of exceptions among certain Abkhazians who have made careers for themselves in Tbilisi!

The three-part attempted rebuttal of the Abkhazian letter by a group of academics published in *Dawn of the East* (28–30 July 1989) was unfortunately not available to me during the composition of the first version of this paper in June 1991.

In specific response to the Abkhazian letter is the 119 page *simartle apxazetze (Truth about Abkhazia)*,[34] which was rushed out by literary critic Roman Miminoshvili and writer Guram Pandzhik'idze in 1990 (Pandzhik'idze became chairman of the Georgian Writers' Union in the wake of the overthrow of Gamsakhurdia). In style and content it can all too sadly serve as a typical example of Kartvelian works of the genre, with its admixture of arrogance, irony, aprioristic argumentation, avoidance of issues, and the inevitable downright abuse.[35] Many of the Kartvelian lines of defence/attack already outlined are repeated in this pamphlet; some of the others will now be discussed.

Complaints about attempts to Georgianize Abkhazia are dismissed on the grounds that, since Abkhazia is an integral part of Georgia, talk of Georgianizing Georgia is a contradiction in terms. Equally the use of force during the Menshevik period cannot be held against the Georgians, who were merely defending their own territory from Bolsheviks and/or White Russians under Denikin. However, the authors do try to distance the Mensheviks from responsibility, pointing out "the fact should be noted that the Bolshevik revolt in the spring of 1918 was put down not by 'Menshevik Georgia' but by the Transcaucasian *Sejm* [parliament]". Six pages later, with regrettable self-contradiction, they do nevertheless, state that "the Menshevik Government of the Georgian Democratic Republic . . . was putting down Bolshevik demonstrations". To prove that pro-Kartvelian

---

34. Also available in a Russian version. An Abkhazian reply to this was published in numbers 6 and 7 of *Edinenie* "Unity" (Sukhum, Dec. 1990) by Vitalij Sharia and Guram Gumba.

35. Donald Rayfield (forthcoming) has compared the language employed in the modern Georgian press in reference to Abkhazia with that used for ritual denunciations in the Georgian press at the time of The Purges (1936–8).

sentiment was not foreign to the Abkhazians as recently as the early years of this century, they quote from Menteshashvili & Surguladze (1989) to the effect that an Abkhazian delegation visited the Tsarist Transcaucasian Viceroy in Tbilisi in 1916 to urge that Abkhazia not be assigned to the (Russian) Black Sea district, and that, if it could not become an administrative district in its own right, it should be part of the (west Georgian) Kutaisi district. Allusion is also made to speeches delivered throughout the 1920s by Nestor Lakoba,[36] head of the Abkhazian Bolsheviks (until murdered by Beria in 1936), wherein he states that the proclamation of a full Abkhazian Soviet republic in 1921 was a temporary necessity, because of the ill-feeling created among the Abkhazians by the actions of the Mensheviks;[37] any attempt immediately to subordinate Abkhazia to Georgia would have been unacceptable, even though Lakoba (and colleagues) seemingly felt that this was the only practical solution. Thus, Abkhazia's downgrading to an autonomous republic in 1931 cannot, they argue, be blamed on the dirty deeds of Stalin, Ordzhonik'idze and the Kartvelians in general. If such were the views of Abkhazian representatives in 1916 and throughout the 1920s, who, they ask, has engineered this ethnic division in the 1980s? The answer, of course, is not necessarily the one that is rhetorically implied!

Any people will choose its allies according to the circumstances prevailing at the time.[38] In 1916 the choice was association with fellow Caucasians or linkage with a part of the empire once inhabited by close relatives but now inhabited and ruled by the very Russians whose actions had denuded of its indigenous population as well as that of much of Abkhazia. Shamba makes the point thus in his interview of 21 June 1991:

> If 100 years ago we were warring against the Russians, and Georgia supported us, today somehow the position is reversed. Vested interests define everything, and we would be idiots if we allowed ourselves to be governed not by interests but by such emotions as the supposed thought that the Kartvelians are our brothers, whereas 100 years ago it was the Russians who were fighting us . . .

Much the same point was made in her letter to *Index on censorship*[39] by

---

36. The source is *N. A. Lakoba: Stat'i i rechi* (*N. A. Lakoba: articles and speeches*) (1987 Sukhum: Alashara).
37. By not challenging this motive, the authors implicitly acknowledge that the Mensheviks *were* guilty of excesses in Abkhazia!
38. Just as in the late eighteenth century Georgia itself sought the protection of Holy Russia, which in turn led to its (i.e. East Georgia's) incorporation into the Empire in 1801.
39. "An Abkhazian's response" (sc. to letters from two Georgians attacking an earlier, anonymous article on the Abkhaz–Kartvelian dispute in the same journal of January 1990), pp. 30–1 of the May 1990 issue.

Zaira Khiba when she remarked: "Only when Georgia acquires worthy
leaders who are reasonable in word and deed will there be harmony with
the ethnic minorities" for in that case "... the country could now have
been proceeding towards peaceful independence with the full support of
all those living within its current boundaries". As regards Lakoba, the
sheer idealism that fired the early supporters of the revolution before it
was perverted by Stalin should not be overlooked. It is quite likely, however naïve we may judge it with the benefit of hindsight, that Lakoba
firmly believed that, with the dawning of a new age, any existing local
enmities would disappear as workers came together in a new spirit of co-
operation. If such was the case, why should not Caucasian Abkhazia work
closely with (even within) Caucasian Georgia? At the time of his writing
in the 1920s, Lakoba, like most others, had no inkling that Stalin would
become the bloodthirsty tyrant now universally recognized. So possible
innocence on the part of Lakoba (and colleagues) in no way rules out possible skulduggery on the part of Stalin and (certain of) his fellow countrymen in this matter also.

The pamphleteers skirt over the rather important period 1933–53,[40] and
Beria is named just once in the whole booklet: "they [the Abkhazians] will
say that in the years 1937–59 Beria and his heirs settled up to 100,000 people in Abkhazia". The authors go on to argue that Abkhazia's cosmopoli-
tan structure is the result of Tsarist measures or the importation of outside
labour by the Abkhazian authorities themselves. It is acknowledged that
"at a certain period Abkhaz schools were closed", which is "an unforgiv-
able crime". On the following page, however, they proceed to make the
quite extraordinary assertion: "The only 'crime' which can be imputed to
the Georgian people is that, starting from the 19th century, at the wish of
those who inspired the Georgian national liberation movement ... there
began and continues to this day, unfortunately without any result, not the
Georgianization of the Abkhazians but rather our defending them from
being Russified and our preservation of them as Abkhazians". A similar
boast was made by linguist Nani Ch'anishvili in the middle of 1990 during
a *Voice of America* radio-link between Tbilisi and some Kartvelologists in
America.[41]

The Abkhazians stand accused of being an ungrateful and hugely privileged minority. What other people of less than 100,000 population has its
own university, television channel and so many of its own citizens in
prominent positions when it constitutes only 18 per cent of its province's
population? Kartvelians making these debating points never inform their

---

40. When pressed to account for what happened in Abkhazia at this time, the usual
    response is that everything was done on orders from the Kremlin. But who was then dic-
    tating Kremlin policy?!
41. The dialogue was reprinted in *Popular Education* (5 July 1990: 14–16).

audience that the Abkhaz sector of the Abkhaz State University was always the smallest of the three (*viz.* Abkhaz, Russian, Georgian), as, despite its name, the university was always designed to cater for the needs of the whole of western Georgia.[42] When television broadcasting in Abkhaz began, there were only two 30-minute programmes each week; in 1989, programming increased to three one-hour slots; such broadcasts now no longer mask Georgian transmissions from Tbilisi, about which local Kartvelians were formerly right to feel aggrieved. Allusion has already been made to Abkhazian over-representation in party positions. Interestingly, though, over-representation is not foreign to Kartvelians either – John Russell[43] compares the figures whereby Kartvelians form 1.4 per cent of the USSR population, whereas they filled 3.2 per cent of places at the Congress of People's Deputies and 3.7 per cent in the Supreme Soviet.

Two individuals are singled out for personal attack – V. Ardzinba is labelled as an "extremist" and the ethnographer Shalva Inal-Ipa is depicted as a charlatan masquerading as an academic, a common charge in attempts to belittle Abkhazian scholars.[44] A passage from Inal-Ipa's 1976 book is cited: "I recorded in June 1952 in the village of Eshera these words of a 70 year old . . . The whole Caucasian coast of the Black Sea used to be called Kalxa. The population of Kalxa spoke Abkhaz. Its frontiers stretched far from south to north, and it was ruled by Abkhazian kings, who had a strong army and 350 forts.". This is adduced as the sort of evidence Abkhazians are said to rely on to prove their historical rights over the land. It is a pity that the authors' eyes did not pass over to the top of the following page, where they would have read: "In a word, if in new and old statements of this kind we find a definite exaggeration of the role of the Abkhazian element, *it is equally mistaken*, it seems to me, completely to ignore it in the ethno-cultural history of the enigma that is Colchis".[45]

---

42. With the recent and sudden creation of universities in Kutaisi and Batumi there is even less justification than in 1989 for the existence of a branch of Tbilisi University in Sukhum.

43. *"The Georgians": a minority rights group Soviet update* (1991).

44. The Abkhazians are not alone in finding the sense of national superiority among the Kartvelians objectionable (not to say threatening), even if casual visitors regularly regard what they see as mere "Latin-type bravado" as welcome relief after the drabness of central Russia. Reporting the results of a survey conducted in late 1989 Mickiewicz (1990: 146) gave the following interesting percentages of those responding "yes" to the question "Should someone who takes the position that nationalities are advocating ethnic superiority be allowed to appear on television?": Central Asians 13%, Ukrainians 20%, Belorussians 20%, Russians 21%, Balts 25%, "Georgians" 52%!

45. This accusation flows indisputably from the pen of Pandzhik'idze, for he included it in his article *"aucilebelia ch'eshmarit'ebam gaimarjos"* ["It is essential that truth triumph"] in *Literary Georgia* of 26 May 1989.

Future prospects

It must by now be patently obvious how intricately interwoven the territorial issue is with the difficulties characterizing Abkhaz/Kartvelian inter-
ethnic relations in general. The Abkhazians see the struggle as one for the
survival of their culture and language, or simply the preservation of their
separate identity. The Kartvelians, if nothing else, desperately do not want
to lose territory that could provide an independent Georgia with much-
needed foreign currency from the tourist trade, given the rich potential of
such exotic resorts as Gagra, Pitsunda and Sukhum itself.

Is there any chance of the Abkhazians throwing in their lot with Kartvelian demands for an independent Georgia? It must be quite clear from the
above that this is surely inconceivable. Those who, in spite of all that has
been said above concerning past events, would urge such a course on the
Abkhazian leadership have to consider the difficulty presented by the tenure of the Georgian presidency by Gamsakhurdia. It is true that in an interview with Anatol Lieven of *The Times*, published in *The Georgian Messenger*
in January 1991, when asked about his attitude to Abkhazia's autonomous
status, he replied: "The Abkhaz deserve autonomy, but not in this exaggerated form". But the Abkhazians are well aware that in December 1990,
within less than a week of assuring the South Ossetians that their autonomy was safe in his hands, he actually abolished the South Ossetian
Autonomous Region. Mention of reducing Abkhazian autonomy raises
the spectre of the realization of a proposal from *Chronicle 4* of early 1989,[46]
which was supported by, among others, Gamsakhurdia's Georgian Helsinki Group, whereby all the regions of Abkhazia where there is a Kartvelian majority (namely Gali, Gulripsh, Gagra, Sukhum, and part of
Ochamchira) should come under the direct control of Tbilisi, leaving
Gudauta and the remaining portion of Ochamchira to be downgraded to
national Abkhazian regions. This same proposal was made by Antelava in
his 1990 pamphlet (p. 27).

In addition, certain opposition parties within Georgia, who are members of the alternative parliament, the National Congress, such as the
National Democratic Party of Gia Ch'ant'uria, have begun to circulate documents in the West complaining about Gamsakhurdia's incipient dictatorship, characterized by imprisonment of political opponents, closure of
papers that do not support the president, denial to the opposition of any
access to surviving outlets in the media, creation of the cult of personality

---

46. This is the same document in which the period 1936–54 is presented as an exemplar of
how to deal with Abkhazian "separatists" and prevent their imposition of force on other
races living in the area. Commenting on Ardzinba's complaint about this insulting
remark in his Moscow speech of 1989, Miminoshvili and Pandzhik'idze claimed not to
know which unofficial organization was responsible for this statement (p. 97).

– or, in the laconic description of Ch'ant'uria's wife, Irina Sarishvili, speaking on a BBC World Service report on Georgia by Robert Parsons in May 1991, "neo-Bolshevism". If compromise with such an individual and in such a repressive atmosphere is unthinkable, would continued association with Georgia under some new regime be more feasible? No matter how different purely intra-Kartvelian politics might or might not be under the guidance of some of the parties from the National Congress, can one detect any hint of a more positive attitude to the minorities from those who were voted into the congress in the unofficial elections that preceded the official election of Gamsakhurdia's Round Table block? Sarishvili in her May 1991 interview blamed Gamsakhurdia alone for raising fears among the South Ossetians. But if one looks back to 1989, when the then unofficial parties all enjoyed the same access to the media and freedom to circulate their universally unimpressive political ideas, there was nothing to choose between them in their statements about (specifically) the Abkhazians. All shared the view that the ethnic disturbances had been artificially fomented by the Kremlin – in fact, this still seems to be the unanimous conviction among the Kartvelians. In his article *"Budem lechit bolezni"* ("We shall be treating our diseases")[47] Ch'ant'uria wrote: "It was in the 18th century that the forebears of today's 'Abkhazians' – Adyghe [Circassian] tribes – came down into the territory of Abkhazia". Further, "the Apswa speak a language of Adyghean provenance, which serves as one more proof of the fact that this people do not belong to the indigenous population of the Black Sea coast". In other words, shades of Ingoroq'va precede the final call to fraternal solidarity in the fight for independence. Similar statements from other leaders of the opposition could easily be produced. And so, while some in the West may see the hope for a future democratic Georgia in the National Congress or some of its individual members, the Abkhazians would not necessarily detect any substantive difference between the relevant parties as far as their own problems are concerned, especially in the climate of suspicion and, sadly, hatred that has been produced not by statements emanating from Moscow but by those from Tbilisi over the past few years.

What of the future for Abkhazia outside Georgia? Since its first meeting in Abkhazia in August 1989, Abkhazians have taken an active part in the Assembly of Mountain Peoples of the Caucasus; the first issue of its paper *Kavkaz* appeared on 1 October 1990. It is probably true to say that all the myriad peoples of the north Caucasus side with the Abkhazians in their striving for a secure future, and it should not be forgotten that a caucus of north Caucasians could produce a strong pressure group within Yeltsin's Russian federation. But whether it is as a separate republic or as part of some reconstituted Mountain Caucasian Republic that the Abkhazians

---

47. Published in *Strana i Mir* "Country and World" (5. 1989: 56–60).

eventually seek to enter a new USSR, there will surely remain one large thorn in their side – the 45.7 per cent Kartvelian (essentially Mingrelian) portion of the population.

It is true that in the All Union referendum of 17 March 1991, boycotted by Kartvelians throughout Georgia in general, 52.3 per cent of Abkhazia's electorate did vote with 98.6 per cent of these saying "yes" to remaining within a union of sovereign republics.[48] Regardless of how the dominating presence of Kartvelians in Abkhazia was achieved, if almost half of the population cleaves to fellow Kartvelian rule from Tbilisi, is there any future for such a deeply divided republic, when democratically elected representation from below will become the norm rather than arbitrary appointment from the top, as in recent decades?

Contrary to the claims of the Kartvelian nationalists, there have been no calls among Abkhazians for the expulsion from (as opposed to the halting of the continued flow into) Abkhazia of Kartvelians. However, if an offer were to come from Tbilisi whereby they would give Abkhazia free rein to go its own way as long as the Gali district were surrendered, the Abkhazian leadership might accept this, since in terms of ethnicity the battle for Samurzaqano is recognized to be already lost. Agreement might then follow on arrangements for helping any other Mingrelians north of the Ghalidzga to resettle in Georgia proper. This would create more space for the return to their ancestral lands of any so-minded Abkhazian descendants of those who suffered the nineteenth century diaspora.[49] But, as noted above, such an offer is unlikely to materialize, for the issue is all or nothing. Is there, then, any way in which the Kartvelians in Abkhazia might be convinced that they would be given a better deal inside an Abkhazian republic than by an independent Georgia in which personal rivalries and internecine conflicts can be confidently predicted to continue unabated? In the clashes of 1989 it was a miraculous relief that the Kartvelian residents of Abkhazia did not, by and large, allow themselves to be roused to arms in the way that characterized their brethren in Georgia proper. And those rare Mingrelian voices that have been heard calling for recognition of their non-Georgian identity have come from Mingrelians inside Abkhazia.[50] Since the Georgians and leading Mingrelians, such as President Gamsakhurdia himself,[51] have always fiercely denied the need for any special provision to be made for ensuring the future of this language,[52] what would be the reaction of Abkhazia's Mingrelians if they were offered, in addition to continuing education in Georgian (should they truly desire this), the chance of having a literary language designed for them, along with all that this would entail (e.g. some level of tuition of and in Mingre-

---

48. Newspaper *Abxazija* (26 March 1991).
49. There are similar aspirations to encourage a "return home" movement among the Circassians.

lian, publishing, radio and television broadcasting)? Abkhazians have never regarded the Mingrelians as Georgians, and so why should they not give substance to their beliefs? No-one should seek artificially to divide peoples who otherwise have no problem living together, but the Abkhazians clearly do have a problem about living with the Georgians. In the words of Donald Rayfield,[53] one consequence of the pan-Georgianism that has existed since around 1930 "has been to change the self-awareness of many Mingrelians who were living in mixed Abkhaz/Mingrelian settlements and impose on them the Georgian/Abkhaz split". If the vested interests of the Abkhazians would be served by reversing this manufactured self-interest, one way of attaining this goal could be attitudinally to divorce their Mingrelians from the bulk of the Kartvelians (Mingrelians as well as Georgians proper) across the Ingur, for as long as (Abkhazia's) Mingrelians see themselves as "Georgians", they will never happily leave Georgia to join the Russian federation or a Slavic-dominated USSR (now CIS). Granting official recognition to Mingrelian identity would after all probably prove to be in the best long-term interests of the Mingrelians themselves – Tbilisi has never shown any concern for the preservation of the Mingrelian (and Svan) languages. Is it too naïve to suppose that Abkhazia's Mingrelians could be the first to realize this and to begin actually collaborating with their fellow residents of Abkhazia, instead of trying to thwart their struggle for what they see as their very survival? Such co-operation might then establish peace in at least one corner of the presently much troubled Transcaucasus.

---

50. One can mention at least three from 1989–90: T. Bok'uchava-Gagulia (*Literary Georgia* 28 April 1989), Vano Dgebuadze (*Bzyp* 16 September 1989), and Nugzar Dzhodzhua (*Bzyp* 4 July 1989 and *Unity* July 1990). The onslaught they suffered as a consequence saw the first lambasted for being no real "Georgian" (which, of course, she is not!) if she cannot speak Georgian (*Literary Georgia* 19 May 1989), the second was alleged to have falsified his war record (ibid.: 3 November 1989), and the last lost his job, and his mother was forced to disown him in the press. (The attentions he received from the local KGB in their attempts to "dissuade" him from standing in the elections to the Abkhazian Congress of Deputies in the autumn of 1991 deserve to be made known to Western observers of events in Abkhazia).

51. See his article entitled "The question of Mingrelia" (*Literary Georgia* 3 November 1989).

52. The same applies to Svan. The whole issue of preserving endangered languages in the Caucasus is discussed in Hewitt (forthcoming a); the original talk on which this article was based dealt with both Abkhaz and Mingrelian, whereas the published version will deal with Abkhaz alone.

53. In his seminar paper "Georgia Today", delivered on 8 March 1990 at London University's School of Oriental and African Studies.

The conflict escalates

In mid-August 1991, the signing of Gorbachev's new Union treaty was scheduled to take place, which was to ratify the agreement for a new association between most of the peoples who had formerly made up the USSR, though Gamsakhurdia maintained throughout the discussion period that Georgia would not be signing any document that preserved his republic's subservient status *vis-à-vis* Moscow. The intention was that, in the first round, the agreement would be signed by the various republican authorities and that some weeks later the various autonomies could add their signatures, thereby gaining equal status with the former republics; Ardzinba expected to sign the document some time in September and thus achieve for Abkhazia the desire for the restitution of Abkhazia's full republican status *outside* Georgia. Gamsakhurdia's government of course kept up its pressure against "Abkhazian separatism". In early August 1991 a public meeting of Kartvelians in Sukhum was addressed by Georgia's Minister of Education, Temur Koridze, and the Minister of the Interior, Svan Dilar Xabuliani. Koridze displayed his commitment to rational argument by promising that, if Abkhazia signed the treaty, "rivers of blood would flow". Xabuliani's contribution was to reveal his government's understanding of a neutral law enforcement agency by promising his fellow Kartvelians that in any local struggle the police force would be "on your side". This meeting was secretly filmed and later broadcast on Abkhazian television. But all the carefully laid plans for the new Union treaty became irrelevant in the wake of the Soviet coup, which was precipitated by the imminent signing of this treaty, and the more or less immediate disintegration of the Union.

However, after the failure of the coup, the serious internal dissension that had already appeared within the Gamsakhurdia regime began to widen even more. Unable to resolve their differences with Gamsakhurdia by constitutional means, Tengiz Sigua resigned from the premiership and, together with Defence Minister Tengiz K'it'ovani, sided with oppositionists, and at the beginning of September the first clashes took place on the streets of Tbilisi.

While the Kartvelians were otherwise preoccupied, the Abkhazians pursued discussions with their fellow north Caucasians. In November 1991 the Third Session of the Mountain Peoples of the Caucasus took place in Sukhum. On 2 November, participants ratified a document entitled Treaty for a Confederative Union of the Mountain Peoples of the Caucasus, the first article of which proclaimed the new confederation to be "the legitimate successor of the independent North Caucasian Republic (Mountain Republic), created on 11 May 1918". The full list of participating peoples reads: Abazinians, Abkhazians, Avars, Adyghes, Darginians, Kabardians, Laks, North Ossetians, South Ossetians, Cherkess, Chechens, Auxov-Chechens and the Shapsughs.

Intra-Kartvelian politics descended into open warfare in the very centre of Tbilisi over the Christmas and New Year period 1991–2. Gamsakhurdia's regime collapsed, with Gamsakhurdia fleeing ultimately to Grozny in Chechenia as guest of President Djokhar Dudayev. The Military Council that took over power when Gamsakhurdia fled soon arranged for the return to his homeland of former Soviet Foreign Minister, Eduard Shevardnadze, who had been Georgia's Communist Party Secretary from 1972 until his elevation by Gorbachev onto the international stage in 1985. He was quickly made head of a State Council, which ran Georgia until the elections on 11 October 1992. Although this interim State Council had no constitutional legitimacy, having seized power in a bloody coup that toppled a democratically elected president, Western countries, which had previously hesitated to recognize Georgia under the unpredictable Gamsakhurdia, immediately began (with Great Britain taking an unwholesome lead) not only to recognize Georgia but to establish diplomatic relations with it. Just one of the regrettable consequences of this rash decision, based on nothing more than a shallow desire to do a quick favour for someone who was perceived to be a "friend of the West", was that the position of Abkhazia became fixed in international law as an integral part of Georgia; thus, yet another sacrifice on the depressing altar known as the territorial integrity of states was in line for the sacrificial dagger . . .

The Abkhazian parliament continued trying to function as the legislative assembly of a *de facto* independent republic with the right to choose its own local allies. It consisted of 28 Abkhazians, 26 Kartvelians, plus 11 representatives of the other local nationalities; this constitutional arrangement, known as consociationalism, with its requirement of a two-thirds majority on all votes of significance, is designed to preserve a *status quo* and was introduced during the Gamsakhurdia regime after Tbilisi had rejected the Abkhazians' request for a bicameral parliament. Pro-Abkhazian and pro-Tbilisi cliques developed, and during one of the frequent absences of the latter, a resolution was carried on 23 July 1992 temporarily reinstating Abkhazia's constitution of 1925, in which its status as a full republic with treaty ties to Georgia was enshrined. This was deemed necessary as the Tbilisi authorities had already annulled all legislation introduced since Soviet power came to Georgia in 1921, which meant that Abkhazia was left with no formal status whatsoever, and the return to the 1926 constitution was meant only to be a temporary measure until a new constitutional arrangement could be made. A draft of a federal treaty between Sukhum and Tbilisi had already been prepared and published by the Abkhazians in June 1992; negotiations on this were taking place in Sukhum between Abkhazian and Georgian officials on 13 August. Early the next day, Georgian troops crossed into Abkhazia, thereby initiating the war that continued until 30 September 1993.

The Tbilisi regime had been faced with massive unrest in Gamsakhurdia's native province of Mingrelia ever since his overthrow, and the behaviour of the so-called *Mkhedrioni* (Knights), an ill disciplined militia set up and led by Dzhaba Ioseliani, who at the time was Shevardnadze's deputy in the State Council, towards the citizenry of Mingrelia could not have been better orchestrated had it actually been the intention of Tbilisi to cause Mingrelia to secede from Georgia. Shevardnadze had been in the thick of a hostile welcome in Mingrelia when the news came of the Abkhazian parliament's decision of 23 July. He returned to Tbilisi at once. By the middle of August, two Georgian ministers (A. K'avsadze and R. Gventsadze) had been kidnapped by Zviadists, and this provided Shevardnadze with what he saw as an ideal pretext to attack Abkhazia, for it was alleged that the ministers were being detained on Abkhazian soil with Abkhazian approval – a specious charge, but naïvely accepted by Western commentators ignorant of the fact that Gamsakhurdia was just as much an anathema to the Abkhazians as Shevardnadze, and that Abkhazians wanted nothing to do with internal Kartvelian affairs. Personally, I am convinced that the attack on Abkhazia was quite cynically planned by Shevardnadze, who, certain that his Western friends would not raise even a squeak of protest (as indeed they did not), no doubt hoped, first, that it would unite both his and Gamsakhurdia's supporters around the patriotic campaign to preserve Georgia's territorial integrity in the face of its greatest threat and, secondly, that it would lead to a Kartvelian victory in a matter of days.

If my assessment of events in August 1992 is correct, then Shevardnadze was proved wrong on both counts. Although his ragbag of an army quickly established control over Sukhum and the coastal road south to Mingrelia, forcing the Abkhazian Government into exile in Gudauta, Zviadists did not give up their opposition to the State Council, and the Abkhazians were able to hold out for a length of time sufficient to allow volunteers to come to their aid from the north Caucasian members of the Confederation of Mountain Peoples (particularly Circassians and Chechens), despite Russian attempts to stop them crossing into Abkhazia, a move that raises questions about the extent to which Yeltsin knew in advance of, and indeed supported, the Georgians' resort to arms.

Within a day or so of the invasion, Georgian Defence Minister K'it'ovani publicly acknowledged that the troops had gone in to stop Abkhazian "separatism" and declared that his men would need at least three days to "satisfy themselves" (in terms of their quest for spoils of war). Non-Kartvelian residents (Abkhazians, Armenians, Russians, Greeks, Jews) of those areas of Abkhazia in the invaders' hands were subjected to a campaign of robbery, rape, torture and slaughter; siege was laid to the mining town of T'q'varchal, inland from Ochamchira, and this was not broken until over 400 days later. Almost a hundred pages of details of these abuses of human rights were submitted to Amnesty International in the summer of 1993; up to the autumn of 1993, details of not a single case of abuse by the Abkhazian side against Kartvelians had been lodged with either Amnesty or the British government.

Towards the end of August 1992, the young man who had been put in charge of the Georgian troops operative in Abkhazia, 26 year old Gia Q'arq'arashvili, issued a chilling threat while being interviewed in Russian for a television broadcast, namely that he would sacrifice 100,000 Georgians to wipe out all 93,000 Abkhazians inside Abkhazia, so long as Georgia's borders remained inviolate.

When it became clear that there would be no easy Georgian victory, peace talks were arranged in Moscow by Yeltsin. As part of the 3 September 1992 accords, the Georgian troops (other than those required to control the railway and other essential objects[54]) and the north Caucasian volunteers were to withdraw, and the legitimate authorities were to be allowed to return to Sukhum to resume the proper governance of Abkhazia. The Georgian troops were not withdrawn, nor were the authorities permitted to return from Gudauta. As a consequence of these transgressions of the Moscow agreement, the Georgians holding Gagra were attacked and ejected not only from this important town but from all the territory between it and the border with Russia to the north. Georgian propaganda immediately sprang into action and announced that the peaceful Kartvelian residents of Gagra had been herded into the local stadium and massacred. When the first mission of the Unrepresented Nations and Peoples' Organization (UNPO, based in The Hague) visited Abkhazia in November 1992, they investigated this claim and found no evidence to support it (vid. UNPO's Report in *Central Asian Survey*, 12.3. 1993: 325–45). Needless to say, Shevardnadze's Western friends, from the UN downwards, universally castigated the Abkhazians for breaking the Moscow agreement – a UN mission that visited the area shortly before UNPO actually spoke in the annex to its report (11 November, No. S/24794) of the risk of the Abkhazians capturing Sukhum (a peculiar interpretation of what in fact would have been merely the Abkhazians re-establishing control over their own capital), adding the absurd prediction that this "could trigger major military action, which could engulf the area in a major conflict that could involve neighbouring countries".

A Russian helicopter on a humanitarian mission to evacuate non-combatants from T'q'varchal was deliberately blasted from the skies by Ioseliani's men in December 1992, with the loss of over 50 women and children who were on board. As far as this author is aware, not one word of protest was raised in the West about this act, justified by Shevardnadze on the grounds that weapons *might* have been on board. Apart from purely

---

54. Georgian Defence Minister, K'it'ovani, promptly stated that for these purposes he needed thousands more troops than had constituted the invasion force in the first place!

human suffering, all the cultural monuments of the Abkhazians were deliberately targeted and destroyed, such as the university, museum, public library, state archive, and the research institute (along with its collection of research materials and scholarly books).

Most of 1993 saw a military stand-off, with the two forces facing each other over the River Gumista, to the north of Sukhum. The April edition of *Le Monde Diplomatique* published an article on the war which included a worrying quote from Giorgi Khaindrava, Minister for Abkhazia in Tbilisi, for it demonstrated that the threat from Q'arq'arashvili (who had resigned as military commander in Abkhazia after the loss of Gagra on the pretext of having suffered a nervous breakdown, only to emerge a few weeks later as new Minister of Defence in place of K'it'ovani) of the previous August had been no accidental slip of the tongue. He clinically observed that all the Georgians needed to do to wipe out the Abkhazians was to kill their genetic pool of 15,000 young men, stressing "we are perfectly capable of this . . .".

The Abkhazians continued to consolidate their strength and positions over the early summer as Shevardnadze's troubles continued unabated in Mingrelia, and towards the end of July 1993 it looked as though just one more push was needed for them to retake their capital. However, hoping to avoid further needless casualties and as the result of strong pressure from Moscow, they agreed in Sochi to a new Russian mediated agreement, which came into effect on 28 July 1993. The UN, in another display of the seriousness it attaches to conflict prevention and the safeguarding of minority rights, despatched the mere handful of the observers that had been promised to monitor this ceasefire. As with the Moscow agreement of 3 September 1992, the understanding called for the withdrawal of Georgian troops and weaponry *within 10–15 days* and subsequent restitution of the legitimate government of Abkhazia. However, *six weeks* later on 9 September, President Ardzinba wrote as follows to UN Secretary General Boutros Boutros-Ghali:

> Despite repeated changes in the schedule, the Georgian side has not withdrawn its armed forces and weaponry from Abkhazia up till now. Moreover, the actions undertaken by the Georgian side show that the latter is transferring the weaponry that was not duly registered and withdrawn to local military formations, presenting the fact as the capture of the weaponry by ex-president Gamsakhurdia's supporters. The Georgian party is blocking the reinstatement of the legitimate bodies of power in Sukhum.

A similar statement warning of the dangers of the Georgian non-compliance was issued in Gudauta on 11 September. On the following day the executive committee of the Congress of Kabardian People issued a statement in Nalchik calling on Georgia to fulfil the conditions of the Sochi agreement and urged the north Caucasian volunteers to be ready to return to Abkhazia if Georgia continued to fail to comply with its undertakings. On 16 September those who had been penned up in T'q'varchal for over 400 days (latterly despite the Sochi agreement) decided to make a move to break the siege. When news of the fighting reached the Abkhazians on the heights above Sukhum, they managed to retrieve the weaponry they had handed over to neutral forces, and wide-scale fighting resumed.

It was stated time and again by the largely pro-Georgian Western media that the Georgians had withdrawn the bulk of their weaponry and that the Abkhazians treacherously took advantage of this military weakness to launch their final push for Sukhum. None of those who unthinkingly adopted this stance have attempted to explain why in that case it should have taken no fewer than 14 days of sustained and intensive hostilities before Sukhum finally fell and the bulk of the invaders were expelled from Abkhazian territory.

As soon as the fighting restarted, Shevardnadze decided on yet another of his splendidly theatrical gestures – only a few days earlier in a rage he had walked out of the Tbilisi parliament saying that he had resigned over failing to get his way in connection with events in Mingrelia, only to return to office later in the day – and took off for Sukhum declaring to the world that he would fight with his bare hands alongside his defenceless troops and share their fate to the bitter end. His pointless gesture failed again to achieve its no doubt intended goal, for no Western forces came to his assistance. During the course of the final bloody battle, Russian Defence Minister, Pavel Grachev, offered to send substantial Russian troops to police both the northern and southern borders of Abkhazia. The Abkhazians accepted this, but it was rejected by the hold up Shevardnadze on the grounds that this would be further Russian occupation of his country. Twenty-four hours later he had changed his mind, but Grachev's patience had worn thin, and he responded to Shevardnadze's telegram with the (undeniably correct) statement that the Abkhazian affair was entirely the fault of the Georgians, and that it was too late for the intervention of his men. It was clear that it would be just a matter of days before Sukhum fell to the Abkhazian alliance, and on 20 September 1992 the Abkhazians offered a ceasefire and safe conduct out of Abkhazia for the Georgian forces. The offer was rejected, leading to further unnecessary bloodshed. The Abkhazians prepared a leaflet for general distribution throughout Abkhazia, reminding the population of their moral duty not to harm troops laying down their weapons and not to seek retribution for the sufferings of the previous 14 months.

The presence of Shevardnadze in the thick of the fighting attracted the attention of the world's media, who, as had become their custom, largely reported events as refracted through the muddy filter of Georgian propaganda – the BBC World Service seemed particularly incapable of distinguishing fact from fiction, with the result that virtually all of the BBC's reports from the region (which meant Tbilisi and not Abkhazia) proved to be far removed from reality. On Tuesday 27 September, the Foreign Ministry of Abkhazia issued a statement to the effect that Shevardnadze would be permitted to leave Abkhazia by the commandment of the armed forces of Abkhazia. This fax was immediately forwarded upon receipt in England to the BBC World Service, whose *Newshour* programme nevertheless preferred to broadcast the much more sensational, though factually groundless, report from Alexis Rowell in Tbilisi that the threat to the life of Shevardnadze, who by this time was in hiding somewhere to the south of Sukhum, could be all too easily imagined. There can be no argument about this, as I was the one who forwarded the Abkhazian fax to Bush House and complained later the same day about their total neglect of it.

The world's press were quick to comment on the recapture of Abkhazia by the Abkhazian alliance, airily ascribing it to an assumed involvement of rogue Russian troops on the Abkhazian side. Although it cannot be denied that some individual Russian soldiers based in Abkhazia may have taken the opportunity to get their own back on the Georgians, whose anti-Russian sentiments were hardly a well kept secret across the former Soviet Union, the Western media (as well as foreign ministries) totally underestimated from the start the extent to which the principled Abkhazian stance was supported not only by north Caucasian volunteers but also by most of the non-Kartvelian peoples of Abkhazia itself, who together made up the majority of Abkhazia's population, for all without exception were targets of rabid Georgian chauvinism. It was really only as late as 13 November 1993, with the publication in *The Times Saturday Magazine* of an article by Anatol Lieven ("Cavalier attitudes"), that a more soberingly accurate assessment of Georgian attitudes appeared in the British press.

With the expulsion of most of the Georgian troops from the south of the territory on 30 September 1993, many Kartvelians decided that it might be prudent not to be around when the victorious forces appeared in their villages, and many thousands upped and fled either towards Mingrelia or, more perilously, up the Kodor Valley towards the already snow-covered mountains of Svanetia. Wildly exaggerated reports even suggested that as many as 200,000 might have left – before the war the total number of Kartvelians in Abkhazia had been (only) 240,000. Although it sadly has to be accepted that there will probably have been cases of vengeance taking – the blood-feud has never really died out in the Caucasus – it is impossible to believe the charges from Tbilisi and its core of docile Western journalists, virtually all of whom had totally ignored all the cases of Georgian abuses committed during their 14-month occupation, that Abkhazians and their allies were actively pursuing a policy of ethnic cleansing. The preliminary findings of UNPO's second mission to Abkhazia (30 November to 10 December 1993) released in Moscow on 10 December confirm that there is no evidence supporting the Georgian accusations of an Abkhazian genocide of Kartvelians.

In a by now typical knee-jerk reaction, the UN Security Council in Resolution 876 of 19 October condemned the Abkhazians for breaking the cease-fire and for alleged violations of international humanitarian law. The European Parliament on 22 November 1993 made its own unimpressive contribution by expressing its concern at Abkhazian aggression towards the Georgian [sic] city of Sukhum and by denouncing the Abkhazians, in the English version of the resolution at least, as a "terrorist–separatist movement". Nevertheless, UN Ambassador Brunner brought the two sides (plus the Russians) together in Geneva at the end of November. Both sides agreed to solve their difficulties by peaceful means. This series of sponsored talks to find a final political solution continued in Geneva on 11 January 1994.[55]

Since the retaking of Abkhazia by the Abkhazian alliance, the territory has been largely peaceful, though pockets of resistance have had to be mopped up in some of the villages in the upper reaches of the Kodor valley. Shevardnadze's swift victory (thanks to overt Russian assistance following his humiliating application for Georgia to join the CIS, a policy for which he seems to have little support among his fellow countrymen) over a momentarily revitalized revolt in Mingrelia following Gamsakhurdia's return from exile, meant that his forces under Ioseliani were able to mass again on the Mingrelian side of the River Ingur. But no serious crossing has taken place, perhaps thanks to a stern warning from Moscow that none such would be tolerated – interestingly, Ioseliani himself led the Georgian delegation to Geneva at the end of November 1993. The Abkhazians have been trying to begin the huge challenge of rebuilding their ruined country, which has not been facilitated by sanctions imposed by Moscow for "infringing" the Sochi Agreement, although these seem to have been lifted finally towards the end of 1993.

In the main, the most pressing question still remains exactly what it was before the war began in August 1992, namely what can be the future for Abkhazian language and culture on the Abkhazians' ancestral homeland inside a paranoically hostile Georgia? If the Western world views its commitments to minority rights at all seriously, it must become more closely involved in this question and ensure that if the "West's friend" can hang on to power in Tbilisi, that "friend" is constrained to behave decently in Abkhazia. Had Shevardnadze's Western backers taken these responsibilities seriously in mid-1992, all the senseless slaughter in Abkhazia might

---

55. These periodic negotiations are still in progress at the time of going to press (summer 1995), with the UN and the so-called Friends of Georgia putting heavy pressure on the Abkhazian delegation to accept autonomy within a federal Georgia. This would involve the demilitarization of the region – a great gamble, surely, in view of past history?

possibly have been avoided. The fact that these responsibilities were not taken seriously in 1992 cannot but make one feel pessimistic about the future in 1994. But then a huge question mark also hangs over the future role of Russia in Abkhazian affairs. Sacrificing Abkhazia to Georgian nationalism as a sop to keep Georgia inside the CIS would provoke an immensely dangerous reaction across the whole north Caucasus. On the other hand, will large numbers of Russian peace-keepers along the Ingur be tolerated by Tbilisi, not to mention the West, which in the wake of Zhirinovsky's showing in the 1993 elections is already expressing alarm at the extent to which Russian troops may become involved in the former republics, known as Russia's "Near Abroad"?

References

Amichba, G. A. 1986. *Soobshchenija srednevekovyx gruzinskix pismennyx istochnikov ob Abxazii* [*Reports on Abkhazia from medieval Georgian written sources*]. Suk-hum: Alashara.

— 1988. *Abxazija i abxazy srednevekovyx gruzinskix povestvovatelnyx istochnikov* [*Abkhazia and Abkhazians in medieval Georgian narrative sources*]. Tbilisi: Mecniereba.

Anchabadze, Z. V. 1959. *Iz istorii srednevekovoj Abxazii (VI–XVIIVV)* [*From the history of medieval Abkhazia (VI–XVIICC)*]. Sukhum: State Press.

— 1964. *Istorija i kultura drevnej Abxazii* [*History and culture of ancient Abkhazia*]. Moscow: Nauka.

Antelava, I. P. 1990. K nekotorym voprosam «abxazskoj problemy» [*On some questions of «the Abkhazian problem»*]. In *Gruzija – «malaja imperija»?!* [*Georgia – "a little empire"?!*]. Tbilisi: Sarangi.

Bell, J. S. 1840. *Journal of a residence in Circassia during the years 1837, 1838, 1839* [2 vols]. London.

Christol, A. 1987. Scythica. *Revue des Études Géorgiennes et Caucasiennes* 3, 215–25.

Dumézil, G. 1965. *Documents anatoliens sur les langues et les traditions du caucase: III, nouvelles études oubykh*. Paris: Institut d'Ethnologie.

Dzhanashia, S. 1959. tubal-tabali, tibareni, iberi [Tubal-Tabalian, Tibarenian, Iberian], (written in 1937) In *shromebi III* [Works III], 1–80. Tbilisi: Mecniereba.

— 1988. shavizghvispiretis saist'orio geograpia [The historical geography of the Black Sea coast]. In *shromebi VI* [*Works VI*], 250–322. Tbilisi: Mecniereba (written in the 1930s).

Dzidzarija, G. A. 1982. *Maxadzhirstvo i problemy istorii Abxazii XIX stoletija* [*Exile and the problems of the history of 19th century Abkhazia*]. Sukhum: Alashara.

Gulia, D. 1986 (1925). Istorija Abxazii [History of Abkhazia]. In *Sobranie sochinenij 6* [*Collected Works 6*], 25–279. Sukhum: Alashara.

Gunba, M. M. 1989. *Abxazija v pervom tysjacheletii n. è.* [*Abkhazia in the first millennium AD*]. Sukhum: Alashara.

Hewitt, B. G. 1989. Aspects of language planning in Georgia (Georgian and Abkhaz). In *Language planning in the Soviet Union*, M. Kirkwood (ed.), 123–44. London: Macmillan/SSEES.

— 1992a. The valid and non-valid application of etymology to history. In *SOAS Working Papers in Linguistics 2*. [Also published in a slightly modified form as "The valid and non-valid application of philology to history". In *Revue des Etudes Géorgiennes et Caucasiennes 6–7*, 1990–1991, 247–63 (1993)].

— 1992b. Languages in contact in NW Georgia: fact or fiction? In *Caucasian perspectives*, B. G. Hewitt (ed.), 244–58.

Hewitt, B. G. (forthcoming a). Language and nationalism in Georgia, and the West's response. In *Papers from the 75th anniversary conference of SSEES, vol. I*.

Inal-Ipa, Sh. 1976. *Voprosy etno-kulturnoj istorii Abxazov* [Questions of the ethno-cultural history of the Abkhazians]. Sukhum: Alashara.

K'ech'aghmadze, N. (ed.) 1961. *ariane: mogzauroba shavi zghvis garshemo* [Arrian: Voyage around the Black Sea]. Tbilisi.

Kuipers, A. H. 1960. *Phoneme and morpheme in Kabardian*. 'S-Gravenhage: Mouton.

Lakoba, S. 1990. *Ocherki politicheskoj istorii Abxazii* [*Essays on the political history of Abkhazia*]. Sukhum: Alashara.

Lamberti, A. 1938. *samegrelos aghc'era* [*Description of Mingrelia*], (ed. L. Asatiani). Tbilisi.

Lezhava, G. P. 1989. *Izmenenie klassovo-nacionalnoj struktury naselenija Abxazii (konec XIXv. – 70gg. XXv.)* [*Alteration in the class-national structure of the population of Abkhazia (end of the XIX century – 70s of the XX century)*]. Sukhum: Alashara.

Melikishvili, G. 1970. *k'olxeti jv. c. VI–IV sauk'uneebshi* [Colchis in the 6th–4th centuries BC]. In *sakartvelos ist'oriis nark'vevebi I* [*Essays on the history of Georgia I*], 400–421. Tbilisi: Sabch'ota Sakartvelo.

Menteshashvili, A. & A. Surguladze 1989. Tol'ko fakty i documenty [Only facts and documents]. *Literaturnaja Gruzija* 11 [*Literary Georgia* 11], 143–66.

Mickiewicz, E. 1990. Ethnicity and support: findings from a Soviet–American public opinion poll. *Journal of Soviet Nationalities* 1(1), 140–47.

Puturidze, G. (ed.) 1971. *evlia chelebis «mogzaurobis c'igni»* [*Evliya Çelebi's "travel book"*]. Tbilisi: Mecniereba.

Q'auxch'ishvili, S. 1936. *georgik'a III*. Tbilisi.

— 1965. *georgika II*. Tbilisi: Mecniereba.

Rayfield, D. 1992. Poruganie jazyka i jazykom: sovremennaja gruzinskaja polemika [Abuse of and by language: modern Georgian polemic]. In *Caucasian perspectives*, B. G. Hewitt (ed.), 265–77.

Saxok'ia, T. 1985. *mogzaurobani* [*Travels*]. Batumi: Sabch'ota Ach'ara.

Slider, D. 1985. Crisis and response in Soviet nationality policy: the case of Abkhazia. *Central Asian Survey* 4(4), 51–68.

Tardy, L. 1978. The Caucasian peoples and their neighbours in 1404. *Acta Orientalia Academiae Scientiarum Hung. Tomus* XXXII(1), 83–111.

Appendix

Copy of the leaflet distributed to Abkhazian and allied fighters in the last week of the battle for Sukhum:

ВОИН АБХАЗИИ! БРАТ!

Страшная трагедия разразилась на твоей Родине.
Но твой Народ справится со всеми испытаниями!
Сохрани в себе веру и милосердие!

Помни, твои действия определяют лицо Абхазии
глазах людей и отношение к ней во всем мире.

Будь милосерден, не вымещай свою горечь
гражданском населении и на тех, кто сдается в плен

Соблюдай правила ведения войны, котор
приняты во всем мире, и те вековые традиц
помощи и милосердия, которыми славится тв
Кавказ!

Щади сдающихся в плен вражеских солд
разоружай их и передавай своим командирам.

Оберегай гражданское население. Защищ
женщин, стариков и детей любой национальности.

Помогай всем раненым и пострадавшим. Помог
работе медсестер и врачей.

Будущее Абхазии зависит от тебя!
Храни Господь тебя и твой Народ!

Международная организация "Ненасилие".

Index

Russian conquest of (1805/1813) 96, 97, 121–4
Safavid khanate of 94, 114–15, 117
within state structure of Azerbaijan 8, 115, 116–19, 124–5
and USSR
autonomous province in Azerbaijan 38, 99–100, 102, 124–5
General Guberniate (1919–20) 124
People's Government (1918–19) 98–100
conflict 62–7, 108–12
appeals against Azerbaijani rule 103–4
Armenian invasion of (1992) 15–16, 109
declaration of independence (1992) 7, 108
demands for transfer to Armenia (1988–9) 105–7
Zheleznovodsk agreement (1991) 108
agriculture of 90–1
Armenian identity of people 6–7, 15–16, 25, 96, 103
disputed 125–8
Dashnak party 109, 128
Iranian policy towards 5, 82, 83, 84, 85
meaning of name 92
Russian Federation policy in 48, 53
Turkic culture of 129
see also Armenia; Azerbaijan; Nagorno–Karabakh Autonomous Province
Karachai people, mass deportation (1943) 39
Karachai–Cherkess autonomous province 17, 29, 39
see also Circassian peoples
Karakoyunlu, Turcoman dynasty 92–3
Kars Treaty (1921) 132
Kartli province, eastern Georgia 136, 154
Kartvelian
defined 9–10, 191
language family 191, 198–9
see also Georgia
Kartvelian peoples, in Abkhazia 197–8
Kavburo (Soviet Caucasian bureau) 101, 124, 125
Kelbajar, Nagorno–Karabakh, Armenians capture 65, 110
Kemalist Turks 100, 101
Khachen (Artsakh)
Karabakh melikdom 93, 102
part of Arran lands 116–17

Khadjiev, Solombek, Russian minister in Chechnya 11, 13
Khamane'i, Ayatollah 86
Khankend (Stepanakert), Karabakh 93, 102, 103
Khanzatian, Sero, on Armenian Karabakh 104
Khazar khanate 115–16
Khetagurov, Ossetian national poet 155
Khiabani, Sheikh Mohammad, Azerbaijan nationalist 77
Khojali, Nagorno–Karabakh 63, 109
Khomeini, Ayatollah 81
Khrushchev, Nikita 39, 103
Khugaev, Gerasim, Ossetian leader 179, 185
Kiev Rus', origins of Russian state in 42
Kirov, S., Soviet First Secretary 125
Kitovani, Tengiz, Georgian politician 9, 142–3, 215, 217, 218n
Kochiev, Stanislav, South Ossetian spokesman 175
K'ost'ava, Merab, Georgia dissident 205n
Kubin, khanate of (1740s) 114, 115, 120
Kuchuk Kainarji, Treaty of (1774) 154
Kurdish people
rivalry with Azerbaijanis 79, 80
Sunni muslims 79
and Turkish policy 54, 55–6
Kurdistan, nationalist movement in 81
Kurdistan Workers' Party (PKK) 55–6, 67
Kutaisi region, Georgia 136, 150

Lachin (Laçin) Strip, Armenia–Karabakh corridor 7, 16, 102
occupied (1992) 64, 109
Lakoba, Nestor, Abkhazian Bolshevik 208, 209
language
Armenian dialects 91, 92
Caucasian Albanian 92
Kartvelian
Georgian 162, 165, 186, 191, 198–9
Laz 191
Mingrelian 191, 198–9, 200–1, 203, 213–14
Svan 191, 214n
northwest Caucasian
Abkhaz/Abaza 191, 199, 201, 203–4
Circassian 191
Ubykh 191, 196
Ossetian 152, 161, 164
Russian 203

nationalism and 24–5, 28, 32–3
Russian Federation's role in 32–3, 43, 48, 223
under Czarist Russia 36
within RSFSR (1921) 38
see also Chechnya; Confederation of Mountain Peoples; North Ossetia; Transcaucasia

Ochamchira, Abkhazia 199–200, 206, 211
oil companies, Azerbaijan and 111, 112
oil pipeline, proposed Azerbaijan–Turkey 5, 56, 65, 66 and n, 85n
oil production, importance of 50, 53, 66n
Ordzhonikidze, G. K. 30, 101, 125, 131, 203
Organisation on Cooperation and Security in Europe (OCSE) 20, 70
Ossetian peoples
early history
settlement patterns 152–3
Tualläg subgroup 153, 154, 161
under Czarist Russia 155
demands for reunification 141–2, 158, 177, 186–9
language 152, 161, 164
population distribution 160–1
under Soviet Russia 158, 159–60
unity of 141–2
see also North Ossetia; South Ossetia
Ottoman Empire
and Abkhazians 194, 195, 199–200
Armenia and 36, 37, 95–6, 119–20
control of Ajaria 137
incursions into Transcaucasia 95–6, 98, 119–20
see also Turkey
Özal, Turgut, President of Turkey 63, 66

pan-Turkism
against Armenia 98, 102, 111
decline of 61
Panah, lord of Karabakh (1760) 96, 121
Paytakaran, province of Armenia 89, 91
perestroika
economic failures of 40
effect of nationalism on 4, 35, 39, 104
Persia see Iran
Persian Empire, partition of Armenia (AD 384) 91
Peter the Great, of Russia 95
place names
Soviet changes in Karabakh 102
see also language

Pliny Secundus 193
Plowden, Colonel J. C. 100
population homogenization 27
USSR policy of 25, 28
see also deportations; ethnic cleansing; migration
Potemkin, G. A. 121–2

Qajar dynasty of Persia, in Transcaucasia 73–4, 120
Q'arq'arashvili, Gia, Georgian defence minister 218, 219
Qatran of Tabriz, poet 116

Rafsanjani, Ali Akbar, Iranian President 81–2, 84, 86
refugees
Azeris in Iran 67, 85
from Chechnya 11
from South Ossetia 175, 176, 177, 184, 186
religion
factor in conflicts 16, 17
and Russian imperialism 36–7
see also Christianity; Islam
Roman Empire, and Armenia 115
Romania 18, 58, 59
rouble zone, problems of 50
Russia (pre-1917)
annexation of Abkhazia 136, 194–5, 208–9
annexation of Georgia (1801–10) 36, 37, 136, 155, 194
annexation of North Ossetia 154
and Armenia 36, 37, 96, 97
Azerbaijan ceded to 36, 74
conquest of Karabakh 96, 97, 121–4
empire and concept of statehood 4, 37 and n, 41–3
and Nakhichevan 74, 122–3, 130–1
penetration of Transcaucasia 35–7, 73, 74–6
see also Russian Federation (post-Soviet); USSR
Russian Federation (post-Soviet)
and Armenian–Azerbaijani conflict 12, 53, 64, 68–9
army role in Transcaucasian conflicts 51–3, 147, 220, 221, 223
and BSEC project 59, 60
economic interdependence of new republics 17–18, 49–50
and Georgian–Abkhazian conflict 52–3,